Bloom's Classic Critical Views

ROBERT BROWNING

Bloom's Classic Critical Views

ROBERT BROWNING

Edited and with an Introduction by
Harold Bloom
Sterling Professor of the Humanities
Yale University

**BLOOM'S
LITERARY CRITICISM**
An imprint of Infobase Publishing

Bloom's Classic Critical Views: Robert Browning

Copyright © 2009 Infobase Publishing

Introduction © 2009 by Harold Bloom

Bloom's Literary Criticism
An imprint of Infobase Publishing
132 West 31st Street
New York NY 10001

Library of Congress Cataloging-in-Publication Data
Robert Browning / edited and with an introduction by Harold Bloom ; volume editor, Paul Fox.
    p. cm. — (Bloom's classic critical views)
 Includes bibliographical references and index.
 ISBN 978-1-60413-429-2 (hardcover)
 1. Browning, Robert, 1812–1889—Criticism and interpretation. I. Bloom, Harold. II. Fox, Paul, Ph. D. III. Title. IV. Series.

 PR4238.R585 2009
 821'.8—dc22

2009001602

Contributing editor: Paul Fox

Series design by Erika K. Arroyo

Cover design by Takeshi Takahashi

Printed in the United States of America

IBT EJB 10 9 8 7 6 5 4 3 2 1

This book is printed on acid-free paper.

Contents

Series Introduction

Bloom's Classic Critical Views is a new series presenting a selection of the most important older literary criticism on the greatest authors commonly read in high school and college classes today. Unlike the Bloom's Modern Critical Views series, which for more than 20 years has provided the best contemporary criticism on great authors, Bloom's Classic Critical Views attempts to present the authors in the context of their time and to provide criticism that has proved over the years to be the most valuable to readers and writers. Selections range from contemporary reviews in popular magazines, which demonstrate how a work was received in its own era, to profound essays by some of the strongest critics in the British and American tradition, including Henry James, G.K. Chesterton, Matthew Arnold, and many more.

Some of the critical essays and extracts presented here have appeared previously in other titles edited by Harold Bloom, such as the New Moulton's Library of Literary Criticism. Other selections appear here for the first time in any book by this publisher. All were selected under Harold Bloom's guidance.

In addition, each volume in this series contains a series of essays by a contemporary expert, who comments on the most important critical selections, putting them in context and suggesting how they might be used by a student writer to influence his or her own writing. This series is intended above all for students, to help them think more deeply and write more powerfully about great writers and their works.

Introduction by Harold Bloom

The poet Robert Browning still seems to me the major poet of the English language since the British High Romantics (Blake, Wordsworth, Byron, Shelley, Keats) and the Americans Walt Whitman and Emily Dickinson. The greatest poets of the twentieth century who wrote in English were Thomas Hardy, William Butler Yeats, Wallace Stevens, and Hart Crane, all of them essential, but none quite as original, disturbing, and profoundly exploratory of art's limits as Browning.

I write this brief introduction in March 2009, almost one hundred twenty years after Browning's death in Venice on December 12, 1889, at the age of seventy-seven. Myself now seventy-eight, I reflect that the poet has been out of fashion throughout my life, though intensely admired and imitated by poets as diverse as Ezra Pound, Randall Jarrell, Robert Lowell, and my friend and contemporary Richard Howard. They revived the dramatic monologue, invented and perfected by Browning and his rival, Alfred Lord Tennyson. T.S. Eliot also composed remarkable dramatic monologues, while maintaining silence on Browning.

Browning is unread and untaught primarily because he is a very difficult poet, and the education necessary for appreciating difficulty has been dwindling steadily from about 1968 to the present moment. Difficulty in imaginative literature can be of many kinds. Though Browning is a learned poet, cultivated in all the arts, including music and painting, his authentic difficulty emanates from his powers of mind. We still understand very little about *thinking in poetry*, even when we reread William Shakespeare, supreme among all writers of every era, every language, every genre. Shakespeare, whose gifts are preternatural, is simply the most intelligent author I have ever read, including Plato, Dante, Kant, Hegel, Nietzsche, Freud, and Wittgenstein. Browning does not match Shakespeare as a thinker, but no one else does. Among Shakespeare's cognitive powers of invention is the amazing ability to create human beings: Falstaff, Hamlet, Iago, Lear, Cleopatra, and so many more. Only Chaucer among the poets, and a handful of novelists—Dickens, Tolstoy, Balzac, Joyce, Proust—rival Robert Browning in the Shakespearean art of inventing human beings.

Browning's dramatic monologues have their foundation in Shakespeare's soliloquies and add to the world's vivid characters a company of vivid adventurers in consciousness: Johannes Agricola, the tomb-ordering bishop, Fra Lippo Lippi, Andrea del Sarto, Childe Roland, Cleon, Abt Vogler, Caliban, and the pope of *The Ring and the Book*. This is a curious company, whose appeal is to everything most shadowed in us. Their own self-contradictions, like our own, make for difficulties, but even their form and genre are a problem. Browning's strongest poems are neither dramatic nor monologues but something else: lyric, subjective, and also antiphons in which many voices speak, several of them Browning's own. A psychological atomist, like Montaigne and Shelley, Browning melts down older versions of personality in ways akin to or prophetic of Balzac, Proust, Kafka, D.H. Lawrence, Yeats, and Borges. He holds his own firm place in that exalted and visionary company.

BIOGRAPHY

ROBERT BROWNING
(1812–1889)

Robert Browning was born in London on May 7, 1812. The son of a clerk for the Bank of England, he was largely educated at home. In 1828, he enrolled at London University but withdrew during his second term. Browning's first published poem, *Pauline: A Fragment of a Confession,* appeared anonymously in 1833, attracting little attention. During 1834, he traveled in Russia, and in 1835, he published *Paracelsus,* a dramatic poem in blank verse, which was well received. The success of this poem led to several important friendships, notably with the critic John Forster and the actor William Charles Macready. In 1837, Browning's play *Strafford* was produced at Covent Garden, with Macready playing the principal part.

In 1838, Browning made his first trip to Italy; his impressions there inspired his narrative poem *Sordello* (1840). The critical reception of this poem was extremely hostile and marked the beginning of a decline in his reputation, from which he did not recover for many years. Between 1841 and 1846, Browning published, under the general title *Bells and Pomegranates,* a series of plays and verse collections, consisting of *Pippa Passes* (1841), *King Victor and King Charles* (1842), *Dramatic Lyrics* (1842), *The Return of the Druses* (1843), *A Blot in the 'Scutcheon* (1844), *Colombe's Birthday* (1844), *Dramatic Romances and Lyrics* (1845), and, in one volume, *Luna* and *A Soul's Tragedy* (1846).

In September 1846, Browning married Elizabeth Barrett, with whom he had been corresponding since January 1845, when he first read and admired her poetry. In November 1846, the Brownings moved to Italy, where they remained, principally in Florence and Rome, until Elizabeth's death in 1861. They had one child, Robert Wiedemann Barrett Browning ("Pen," 1849–1913). In 1850, Browning published his poem *Christmas-Eve and Easter Day,* followed in 1855 by the verse collection *Men and Women.* After returning to England in 1861, he published *Dramatis Personae* (1864), a verse collection, and *The Ring and the Book* (1868–69), a long poem that brought about the restoration of his reputation. During the remaining twenty years of his life, which he spent partly in London and partly in the countryside or abroad,

Browning published numerous poems and verse collections, including *Balaustion's Adventure* (1871), *Prince Hohenstiel-Schwangau* (1871), *Fifine at the Fair* (1872), *Red Cotton Night-Cap Country* (1873), *Aristophanes' Apology* (1875), *The Inn Album* (1875), *Pacchiarotto with Other Poems* (1876), *La Saisiaz* and *The Two Poets of Croisic* (1878), *Dramatic Idyls* (1879), *Dramatic Idyls: Second Series* (1880), *Jocoseria* (1883), *Ferishtah's Fancies* (1884), and *Parleyings with Certain People of Importance in Their Day* (1887). Browning's last volume of poems, *Asolando,* was published on December 12, 1889, the day of his death.

PERSONAL

The following extracts detail a number of reminiscences, impressions, and descriptions of Browning's character and personality. They are drawn from almost a seventy-year period, from Browning's younger years as a poet before he had achieved the sort of success he would gain in later life, to retrospectives of his career written a little more than a decade after his death. Collectively the various excerpts and extracts convey a sense of the almost unanimous and singular warmth with which the poet was regarded throughout and after his life. The only possible exception to this common response in the following passages is the critical study by James Fotheringham, a eulogy of an altogether different sort from the other selections in this section. Even so, Fotheringham in his own way touches on the geniality of the poet at the same time he praises Browning's strength of character and his poetic intellect.

The extracts come not only from across the years, presenting Browning at different stages of his career, but also from a wide variety of individuals: a painter, several authors of various levels of fame, an actor and theater manager, a number of journalists, the most famous academic of the period, a lawyer and magazine editor, a jurist and historian, and sundry travelers, both Americans and Englishmen. While some tend to concentrate on Browning's intellect, none can range far from the poet's impressive and genial nature, his sympathy to and for others, and his vigorous and energetic disposition. In the end, it tends to be the later reminiscences from older men, themselves closer to the conclusion of their lives, which seem to suggest a deeper appreciation of the corollary equating Browning's personable temperament and his poetry. His art was always close to life, an expression of his experience with the range of characters in humanity and its many, varied voices. If the poet's own life struck those who met him as being that of a startlingly energetic and gregarious man, one comfortable with anyone he met, then the relationship between that life and his art should not come as a surprise to any reader who can appreciate the sensitive portrayal of character and the vivid language with which Browning presents those personages in his poetry. The man lived life fully and planned to continue to do so despite the waning of his youth, as the passage from Benjamin Jowett's *Life and Letters* shows. Browning's vivacity and joy in the simple life and in simply living never lessened. To paraphrase Frederic Harrison's extract written after the poet's death, also included in this section, Browning had known everyone, been everywhere, and seen everything: It should be no wonder then that his verse embodies such an abundant wealth of life and experience.

WILLIAM CHARLES MACREADY (1835)

William Charles Macready was one of the foremost British actors of the nineteenth century and did much to encourage the creation of a modern English drama. He became manager of the Covent Garden theater in 1837, two years after this diary entry, introducing Browning's newly published play *Strafford* to the public.

It is clear from this extract that Macready was already an admirer of Browning when he produced his play. The actor's words show both an appreciation for the man and an impression of his personality. Browning is described as a gregarious and warm individual, plainspoken and without airs; he is in his appearance and conversation precisely what a young poet is expected by Macready to be. It is not only Macready who is impressed and charmed by Browning: Those gathered with Macready are said to have been equally captivated by the young poet.

Mr. Browning was very popular with the whole party; his simple and enthusiastic manner engaged attention and won opinions from all present; he looks and speaks more like a youthful poet than any man I ever saw.

—William Charles Macready, *Diary*, December 31, 1835

GEORGE STILLMAN HILLARD (1853)

George Stillman Hillard was a Harvard graduate who went on to become a lawyer and an author. In his travelogue about Italy from which the following extract is taken, we are offered a picture of Browning in middle age, an established poet among the literati but still waiting to achieve the success of fellow English artists such as Lord Alfred Tennyson. This success would finally come only after Browning left Italy after the death of his wife, Elizabeth Barrett Browning, in 1861.

Stillman Hillard is clearly a great admirer of Browning and, as in the previous extract, seems taken not only with the poet's speech but also with his personable manner. Once more, Browning's simple character and his good humor are noted; but now in middle age, the poet is also appreciated for a charismatic strength and power in his conversation and appearance. His personal energy is repeatedly mentioned in the extract: his vigor, freshness, passion, and playfulness. His speech is described as being like that in Chaucer's verse (Chaucer was an English poet who was considered to have rivaled Shakespeare in his ability to speak to all people in their own language): Each poet is capable of moving fluently between graceful rhetorical flourishes and the earthy idiom of everyday speech. Stillman Hillard states that one might describe Browning's conversation as being, like his poetry, made transparent (for Browning's poetic style was considered by a number of critics and readers to render his poetry obscure). The still youthful energy and the charisma of the middle-aged Browning become the two predominant traits to which Stillman Hillard repeatedly returns in this portrayal of the poet.

Browning's conversation is like the poetry of Chaucer, or like his own, simplified and made transparent. His countenance is so full of vigor, freshness, and refined power, that it seems impossible to think that he can ever grow old. His poetry is subtle, passionate and profound; but he himself is simple, natural, and playful. He has the repose of a man who has lived much in the open air; with no nervous uneasiness and no unhealthy self-consciousness.

—George Stillman Hillard, *Six Months in Italy*, 1853, p. 114

NATHANIEL HAWTHORNE (1856)

Nathaniel Hawthorne was one of the foremost American novelists and short story writers of the nineteenth century. He met Browning during his residency in England as the U.S. consul in Liverpool. In the following reminiscence, Hawthorne, as other extracts in this volume echo, is impressed by Browning's youth, geniality, and simple manner. Hawthorne seems both surprised and intrigued by Browning's appreciation for one of his novels, a text that others have overlooked when speaking of their admiration for his writing. Browning comes across once more as a humble and simple man, moved by the praise of Hawthorne for his work; indeed, the final sentence of the extract suggests that Hawthorne is concerned that he has not matched the happy reaction displayed by Browning at his praise. It would seem that Browning's natural generosity and warmth of character remarked on by so many is capable of making others reflect on their own personalities and behavior. It is almost as if Hawthorne feels his response must live up to Browning's own.

. . . Mr. Browning introduced himself to me,—a younger man than I expected to see, handsome, with brown hair. He is very simple and agreeable in manner, gently impulsive, talking as if his heart were uppermost. He spoke of his pleasure in meeting me, and his appreciation of my books; and—which has not often happened to me—mentioned that *The Blithedale Romance* was the one he admired most. I wonder why. I hope I showed as much pleasure at his praise as he did at mine; for I was glad to see how pleasantly it moved him.

—Nathaniel Hawthorne,
The English Note-Books, July 13, 1856

BENJAMIN JOWETT (1865)

Benjamin Jowett was the master (president) of Balliol College, Oxford, later the university's vice chancellor, and one of England's foremost nineteenth-century classical scholars. His translations, essays, and commentaries on the philosopher Plato and other ancient Greek writers are still admired today.

In this extract, Jowett relates his impressions after his first meeting with Browning when the poet visits and stays with him for a few days. Once more, Browning's open and warm nature is noted, but, as might be expected of an Oxford academic, the poet's intelligence is also mentioned approvingly. Jowett's impression of poets does not seem to be a particularly favorable one in general (perhaps he feels that none of them can possibly match the common sense and sensibilities of the Greeks), but Browning seems to be an exception: Jowett states that he did not think that any contemporary poet could lack the petty jealousies and arrogance he believes common to the breed. Browning, we are told, considers himself an ordinary down-to-earth individual but one in whom Jowett finds an energy and drive that he finds most impressive.

I thought I was getting too old to make new friends. But I believe that I have made one—Mr. Browning, the poet, who has been staying with me during the last few days. It is impossible to speak without enthusiasm of his open, generous nature and his great ability and knowledge. I had no idea that there was a perfectly sensible poet in the world, entirely free from vanity, jealousy, or any other littleness, and thinking no more of himself than if he were an ordinary man. His great energy is very remarkable, and his determination to make the most of the remainder of life.

—Benjamin Jowett, letter of June 12, 1865, cited
in Evelyn Abbott, Lewis Campbell, *The Life and
Letters of Benjamin Jowett,* 1897, vol. 1, pp. 400–401

ALFRED, LORD TENNYSON (1885)

Lord Alfred Tennyson was England's poet laureate from 1850 to his death in 1892, succeeding William Wordsworth in that position. As the following dedication shows, Tennyson was appreciative, as so many others had been, of Browning's character as a man but also his ability as a poet. He believes Browning has the capacity to forgive the flaws in the collection of poetry dedicated to him by Tennyson, along with the ability to appreciate its best points. Such a hope reflects both on the kindness and intellect of Tennyson's dedicatee. Written after Browning had achieved the success he had been denied for several years, the dedication to *Tiresias and Other Poems* recognizes Browning's genius, now established, and is high praise coming from the poet whom many considered to be England's greatest.

TO MY GOOD FRIEND
ROBERT BROWNING,
WHOSE GENIUS AND GENIALITY
WILL BEST APPRECIATE WHAT MAY BE BEST,
AND MAKE MOST ALLOWANCE FOR WHAT MAY BE WORST,
THIS VOLUME IS AFFECTIONATELY DEDICATED.

> —Alfred, Lord Tennyson, dedication to
> *Tiresias and Other Poems,* 1885

THOMAS ADOLPHUS TROLLOPE (1888)

Thomas Adolphus Trollope was a journalist and travel writer of some sixty volumes. The elder brother of the well-known English novelist Anthony Trollope, Thomas was also an author in his own right. The three-volume publication of his memoirs, *What I Remember,* provides valuable material for any student of the period. In the following extract, Trollope recalls meeting Browning during the poet's years living in Florence.

Trollope remarks that it would have been impossible for any Englishman in the city of Florence at that time not to have been impressed by the figure of Browning on the expatriate social scene. It is clear by the end of the 1880s that Browning is firmly established in the foremost rank of poets, for Trollope states that it is needless to speak of his poetry: everyone is already familiar with it. Equally, he claims not to want to presume to outline the character of Browning in his memoirs. Nevertheless, in this extract he makes some interesting points doing exactly that when he suggests that Browning was not a ready friend to fools. Among the English social set in Florence, Trollope tells us that there was little intellectual conversation but a number of people who believed themselves capable of it. Browning is remembered by Trollope as silencing with a simple, half-hidden smile those with pretensions to intellectual discourse and self-aggrandizement. The facial expression had the capacity to make those who had uttered something foolish almost immediately aware of their mistakes. Trollope also suggests that within this social group Browning was a man of few words, ready to offer an opinion in a dispute, but always politely, sensitively, and without undue criticism of others.

Of course, in the recollections of an Englishman living during those years in Florence, Robert Browning must necessarily stand out in high relief, and in the foremost line. But very obviously this is neither the time nor the place, nor is my dose of presumption sufficient for any attempt at a delineation of the man. To speak of the poet, since I write for Englishmen, would be very superfluous. It may be readily imagined that the "tag-rag and bob-tail" of the men who mainly constituted that very pleasant but not very intellectual society, were not likely to be such as Mr. Browning would readily make intimates of. And I think I see in memory's magic glass that the men used to be rather afraid of him. Not that I ever saw him rough or uncourteous with the most exasperating fool that ever rubbed a man's nervous system the wrong way; but there was a quiet, lurking smile which, supported by very few words, used to seem to have the singular property of making the utterers of platitudes and the mistakers of *non-sequiturs* for *sequiturs*, uncomfortably aware of the nature of their words within a very few minutes after they had uttered them. I may say, however, that I believe that in any dispute on any sort of subject between any two men in the place, if it had been proposed to submit the matter in dispute for adjudication to Mr. Browning, the proposal would have been jumped at with a greater readiness of *consensus* than in the case of any other man there.

—Thomas Adolphus Trollope, *What I Remember*, 1888

George William Curtis
"Editor's Easy Chair" (1890)

George William Curtis was an American writer, journal editor, and orator and here gives us another memory of the poet, from a distance of almost half a century, and a year after Browning's death. Curtis would contribute several articles on Browning to the column titled the "Editor's Easy Chair" published in *Harper's* magazine. The poet is here remembered as being unremarkable in his appearance but of an open, genial temperament. His manner of talking and his energy are the aspects of the poet that Curtis recalls most vividly, the observation of Browning seemingly unable to sit still when an idea had grasped him being a telling detail in the portrayal.

One point to consider in examining Curtis's words is that memoirs are often as much imbued with the moment in which they are written as they are an accurate description of the time they recall. Curtis is writing in 1890, the period when Oscar Wilde was the most famous and public poet in London and arguably the most recognizable even in the United States after his tour there. Wilde was not only considered by many, if not most, as eccentric, he was a flamboyant figure whose conversation was often admired and appreciated more than his writing. His manner of dress and behavior were imitated by many of the younger writers of the day. The fact that Curtis notes that Browning lacked all eccentricity in his physical appearance, in his dress, and in his sense of deportment is telling, speaking as much to the English poet of the 1890s as of Browning in the middle years of the century. Despite this fact, Browning appears as he had previously in other extracts written when he was a younger man. Curtis's memories seem to be accurate if inflected slightly by the time period in which he wrote.

⸻ ⸻ ⸻

The poet was then about thirty-five. His figure was not large, but compact, erect, and active; the face smooth, the hair dark; the aspect that of active intelligence, and of a man of the world. He was in no way eccentric, either in manner or appearance. He talked freely, with great vivacity, and delightfully, rising and walking about the room as his talk sparkled on.

—George William Curtis, "Editor's Easy Chair,"
Harper's New Monthly Magazine, March 1890, p. 637

JAMES FOTHERINGHAM (1898)

James Fotheringham's critical analysis of Browning, written and published in the closing years of the nineteenth century, might stand for a portrait of the ideal poet to many. Fotheringham remarks on Browning's idealism and optimism, his down-to-earth nature and common touch, his manliness and control, his core of passion and his practical intellect; but personal details are lacking. The qualities that typify a "true and sure discerner" of what to many is "remote" and "shadowy," or the "world unseen," seem to be, for Fotheringham, embodied by the poet. Browning personifies the poetic type in this extract, and the passage becomes in many ways a eulogistic portrait of this ideal. As such, and unlike many of the earlier extracts that present a man very much among men, Fotheringham's depiction of Browning almost a decade after his death is almost an abstraction, certainly in contrast to the vital energies he is so often said to have displayed in life.

Despite the eulogistic abstraction of Fotheringham's portrait, noteworthy biographical points are made: mention of the grief and emotional turmoil felt by Browning at the deaths of his mother and wife, his love of music, and his apparent appreciation for London as being the fittest place to observe the common life of others. Each detail plays a part for Fotheringham in capturing the character and poetic life of his subject.

He spent, we have seen, most of his years in London; and this seems fit. There, where man and his problems and ways touched and interested him. He was a man with men, mixing with the life of his fellows; friendly and manly, taking his part in conversation frankly, and in fit circles an able and interesting talker. In a certain way he was a man of the world, measuring men and their affairs at their due value in the world, yet independent and unworldly at the heart of him. Observant, practical, common-sensible, but with a core of passion and ideality. His nature was, in fact, richly passioned, on a ground of strong intellect, with manly control and even reserve of emotion. But in his love for his mother and for his wife, and in the disturbance of feeling roused by the deaths of these, or by whatever touched the memory of the latter, we see the depth and force, we feel the fire and tenderness of his mind. His strong sensibility to music is another test of his emotional quality. He had, owing to this, a marked tenacity and constancy of affection. He had a keen memory for suffering and a certain shrinking from it. He was thus an optimist by temper and habit, forced by bias and energy of the brain, and by dramatic observation and sympathy, to weigh his optimism, yet inclined to make the best of things. He was not on the surface sympathetic, and never sentimental. His centre was not in the emotions any more than it was in the sphere of facts. With the core of passion went a power of "abstraction," a life of thought and imagination. He was, we may say, very real and down upon the earth, but aware, too, and all the time, of the "world unseen," that world of principles, laws, ideals, souls, which seems shadowy and remote to many, but is life of life to the true and sure discerner.

—James Fotheringham, *Studies of the Mind and Art of Robert Browning*, 1898, pp. 42–43

FREDERIC HARRISON
"PERSONAL REMINISCENCES" (1901)

Frederic Harrison was a British lawyer, a literary critic, and a well- and widely published historian. The following extract written more than a decade after Browning's death contrasts strongly with the preceding passage's description of the poet. Whereas Fotheringham writes an idealistic, almost abstract list of qualities that he finds embodied in Browning, Harrison's depiction of the poet is personal, heartfelt, and displays the character of his subject in a larger-than-life fashion (or might be said to do so if the poet's life did not already conform to such a description).

Harrison is thoroughly familiar with his subject, and the warmth with which he writes is evident. He describes Browning as both a genius and the most unpretentious of men; comfortable in any setting, his verve in conversation never dominating the simplest of gatherings; displaying the most sound moral judgments (and this from one of Britain's foremost jurists), but original, personable to a fault, and a true cosmopolite. Throughout the extract, Harrison presents to the reader a portrait of the truly generous spirit of the man and, once again as in some of the previous extracts, notes the absence of any mannerism or eccentricity in Browning's character.

Robert Browning, for all his original genius and fine culture in literature, painting, and music, had less of the eccentric in him than almost any famous man of his time. A man of the world to his finger tips, who knew every one, went everywhere, and had seen everything, he might pass as a social lion, but not as a poet, or a genius. His animal spirits, his bonhommie, his curious versatility and experience, made him the autocrat of the London dinner table, of which he was never the tyrant— or the bore. Dear old Browning! how we all loved him; how we listened to his anecdotes; how we enjoyed his improvised "epitaphs in country churchyards," till we broke into shouts of laughter as we detected the amusing forgery. At home in the smoking room of a club, in a lady's literary tea-party, in a drawing-room concert, or in a river picnic, he might have passed for a retired diplomat, but for his buoyancy of mind and brilliancy of talk. His heart was as warm, his moral judgment as sound as his genius was original.

—Frederic Harrison, "Personal Reminiscences,"
George Washington and Other American
Addresses, 1901, p. 207

WILLIAM JAMES STILLMAN (1901)

William James Stillman was an American painter, photographer, and journalist. He traveled to Europe in the middle years of the nineteenth century to study art, returning to his homeland as a fervent supporter of the English pre-Raphaelite style in contemporary painting. This extract is taken from his autobiography published in the year of his death.

Stillman describes his first meeting with Browning taking place in Cortina, a town in northern Italy. Stillman is honest in stating that he is not charmed by others' intellects and is inclined not to consider it in reckoning their personal attraction: In his experience, the more intellectual an individual, the less personable his or her nature. Not so with Browning. Stillman, after his initial meeting, saw the poet again many times, and his growing acquaintance with the Englishman increased his appreciation for the man's mind and personality. It seems that he expected the remote academic type who might find it difficult to converse with others but instead found a healthy, energetic man who was as sensitive to people as he was to the topic of conversation at hand. Stillman says that there was nothing of aggression in Browning's character, only the inward strength of a man at ease with his own person and opinions and with the world at large.

Stillman's expectations for the temperament and personality of Browning based on his poetry are also openly expressed in this extract. He suspected that Browning was deliberately and affectedly obscure in his writing but found when he met the man that the complexity of feeling and sense expressed in his work was actually an honest reflection of the poet's own individuality and unique sense of the world. There was nothing affected about Browning's character; indeed, Stillman relates that his opinion could not have been further from the sincerity and truthfulness he discovered in the poet himself.

The final analogy made by Stillman is a telling one, comparing the direct nature of Browning's intellect in his art, an intellect that lesser minds found difficult to follow, with the leaps that a mathematician might make in the solution of an equation. What he had initially thought could well be an unsympathetic treatment of the reader in Browning's poetry, Stillman now admits to be an unconscious mark of the poet's mental agility.

———❧——— ———❧——— ———❧———

At Cortina I met and first knew Browning, who, with his sister Sariana, our old and dear friend, came to stay at the inn where we were. I am not much inclined to reckon intellectual greatness as a personal charm, for experience has shown me that the relation is very remote; but Browning always impressed me—and then and after I saw a good deal of him—as one of the healthiest and most robust minds I have ever known, sound to the core, and with an almost unlimited intellectual vitality and an individuality which nothing could infringe on, but which a singular sensitiveness towards others prevented from ever wounding even the most morbid sensibility; a strong man armed in the completest defensive armor, but with no aggressive quality. His was a nature of utter sincerity, and what had seemed to me, reading his poetry before knowing him, to be more or less an affectation of obscurity, a cultivation of the cryptic sense, I found to be the pure expression of his individuality. He made short cuts to the heart of his theme, perhaps more unconscious than uncaring that his line of approach could not be followed by his general readers, as a mathematician leaves a large hiatus in his demonstration, seeing the result the less experienced must work out step by step.

—William James Stillman, *The Autobiography of a Journalist*, 1901, vol. 2, p. 627

GENERAL

The extracts included in this section represent critical writings from almost three-quarters of a century, from the years of Browning's initial publications to a decade after his death. The criticism of the poet includes everything from the eulogistic to the near damning, but each extract affords the reader an insight into the contemporary views of Browning's verse both in itself and in relationship to his fellow poets' collections (notably Lord Alfred Tennyson's). There are attitudes that are repeatedly voiced both by Browning's defenders and also by those who take a grimmer critical view of his abilities: the poet's undeniable capacity to understand the human condition; the structural innovations in his versification; the possible short-fall between his startling, poetic imagination and his artistic craftsmanship; his place within the canon of English poetry; the faddishness of his verse in the later years of his life. Each extract expands on or rejects, but consistently replies to, these critical concerns, affording the reader a view of the changing attitudes to Browning's works throughout the Victorian era.

Of particular interest are those extracts written upon the poet's death in 1889 and the continuing critical disagreement about his verse that played out during the succeeding ten years. Tennyson is used repeatedly as a poet against whom Browning is contrasted or measured, but Shakespeare and Chaucer are also markers deployed a number of times to place and contextualize Browning's talents. The ongoing, critical support for traditional poetic structures, "poetic" language, and metrical convention is clear; but equally there are those critics who can now be considered as correctly situating Browning as a forerunner of the early-twentieth-century modernists' experimentation in verse. At the time, however, literary opinion could not have foreseen Browning's relationship with the future of the poetic canon. Even so, the reader should be able to trace the growing critical understanding of and appreciation for the importance of what Browning was accomplishing over the course of his creative life.

Elizabeth Barrett Browning (1844)

Elizabeth Barrett was an established poet in her own right when she eloped with Robert Browning in 1846. It was after reading her poem *Lady Geraldine's Courtship*, from which the following lines are extracted, that Browning wrote his first love letter to his poetic wife-to-be.

In these lines Elizabeth refers to verses from Browning's collections *Bells and Pomegranates* (eight volumes) published between 1841 and 1846. The extract reveals Elizabeth's appreciation for the depth of humanity Browning's poetry reveals, like a heart full of life and subtle in its portrayals. The suggestion that, in reading *Bells and Pomegranates,* one must "cut deep down the middle" perhaps is an intimation that Browning's poetry cannot be appreciated fully by a simple, surface reading but only in uncovering the core beneath, the living heart of the matter wherein its true vitality lies.

. . . from Browning some "Pomegranate," which, if cut deep
     down the middle,
Shows a heart within blood-tinctured, of a veined humanity.

—Elizabeth Barrett Browning, *Lady
Geraldine's Courtship,* 1844, stanza 41

Walter Savage Landor
"To Robert Browning" (1845)

Walter Savage Landor was an English writer in various genres but one who never acquired the level of acclaim that his contemporaries often received. He was, however, appreciated by the Brownings: Elizabeth acclaimed his poem *Pentameron*, and Robert dedicated a copy of his work to Landor. In his later life, Browning would furnish Landor, near destitute in Italy after a series of misfortunes, with a residence first in Siena and later in Florence, also obtaining an allowance for the unfortunate writer and his family. Landor would die in Florence a few years later and was buried in the English cemetery there near the tomb of his friend Elizabeth Barrett Browning.

The following extract expresses the admiration the older Landor feels for Browning and his poetry. He measures the younger poet just below Shakespeare, about whom he cannot claim to speak, the Bard being the world's poet. But about Browning he can permit himself to say little more, for only the great English poet Chaucer suffices for Landor as a point of comparison. As he does with Chaucer, Landor describes Browning as being imbued with the language and experiences of life, as having an eye for the details to which most common men and lesser poets are blind, and as having the capacity to express in his verse the speech of the full range of human types. He also mentions the attractions of the southern climate of Italy, the region to which Browning would elope with Elizabeth Barrett the year after this extract was written. The equal attractions of Browning's poetry are also clearly expressed by Landor: Robert is described as being comparable to a siren, the mythical creature whose songs were irresistible to sailors.

There is delight in singing, though none hear Beside the singer; and there is delight In praising, though the praiser sit alone And see the prais'd far off him, far above. Shakspeare is not *our* poet, but the world's, Therefore on him no speech; and short for thee, Browning! Since Chaucer was alive and hale, No man hath walk'd along our roads with step So active, so inquiring eye, or tongue So varied in discourse. But warmer climes Give brighter plumage, stronger wing; the breeze Of Alpine heights thou playest with, borne on Beyond Sorrento and Amalfi, where The Siren waits thee, singing song for song.

—Walter Savage Landor,
"To Robert Browning," 1845

Margaret Fuller "Browning's Poems" (1846)

Margaret Fuller was an American journalist, critic, and early activist for women's rights. She was sent to Italy as the foreign correspondent of the *New York Tribune* in 1846, the same year that Browning and Elizabeth Barrett eloped, married, and settled in Florence.

In the following extract, Fuller follows a not uncommon critical line, finding a great deal that was obscured from common understanding in Browning's poetry. She suggests that before 1846 Browning could not control his own talents, that his verse's secondary ideas had been excessive and had tended to draw from the strengths of his major poetic theme. She sees in his minor works a greater claim for greatness, where a concentration on the task at hand rather than to secondary ideas occluding and obscuring his theme, no matter how well conceived these secondary ideas might be, affords Browning a condensation of his talents.

She believes that he will develop the poetic capacity to prune his work of these accumulated ideas as his experience grows, until all that remains is the power of his central intent.

His writings have, till lately, been clouded by obscurities, his riches having seemed to accumulate beyond his mastery of them. So beautiful are the picture gleams, so full of meaning the little thoughts that are always twisting their parasites over his main purpose, that we hardly can bear to wish them away, even when we know their excess to be a defect. They seem, each and all, too good to be lopped away, and we cannot wonder the mind from which they grew was at a loss which to reject. Yet, a higher mastery in the poetic art must give him skill and resolution to reject them. Then, all true life being condensed into the main growth, instead of being so much scattered in tendrils, off-shoots and flower-bunches, the effect would be more grand and simple; nor should we be any loser as to the spirit; it would all be there, only more concentrated as to the form, more full, if less subtle, in its emanations. The tendency to variety and delicacy, rather than to a grasp of the subject and concentration of interest, are not so obvious in Browning's minor works as in *Paracelsus*, and in his tragedy of *Strafford*.

—Margaret Fuller, "Browning's Poems," 1846,
from *Art, Literature, and the Drama*, 1860, p. 209

GEORGE ELIOT (1856)

George Eliot (Mary Ann Evans) was one of nineteenth-century England's most successful and acclaimed authors. Apart from novels, she wrote for the leading radical journal, *The Westminster Review*, from which the following extract is taken. She became the publication's editor in 1858.

Here, Eliot begins by suggesting that much contemporary poetry requires little active, intellectual engagement by a reader, its conventional language and rhythms described as being pleasurable but anodyne. She proceeds to state that attitudes to Browning's poetry share little in common with such a description of modern readers' responses to contemporary verse. The reader must actively engage the language and thought behind Browning's dramatic presentations of character, must assess what is left unsaid by the protagonist in verse, and is challenged repeatedly by the unexpected rhythms, constructions, and language of each poem. Eliot claims that the rewards of grappling with Browning's poetry are great: While his verse is not perfect, Browning's appreciation and understanding of human life and intent, of character and motivation, make him a startlingly original poet. His vision and insight are acute, his presentation of each impressive. Browning is described by Eliot as being distinct from the conventional romantic poet whose poetry is rife with emotion and the "dreamy." Rather, he is an energetic and vigorous portrayer of life as it is lived. He does not shirk from speaking of what he sees. Eliot suggests that Browning's gifts are all the more remarkable because they marry this energy with subtle insights, the outward, lived life with the hidden workings of psychological and emotional motivations. Quoting "How It Strikes a Contemporary" from Browning's collection *Men and Women*, Eliot states that in his description of the character of the poet we can see Browning's own person: he senses, feels, and sees all without staring, can foretell the behavior of individuals before they themselves have contemplated an action. It is perhaps this uncanny ability to dramatically portray the inner workings of human minds and hearts that Eliot admires most in Browning's poetry and person. She would not be the last critic to hold such a view.

⌐∿∿⌐ ⌐∿∿⌐ ⌐∿∿⌐

To read poems is often a substitute for thought: fine-sounding conventional phrases and the sing-song of verse demand no co-operation in the reader; they glide over his mind with the agreeable unmeaningness of 'the compliments of the season', or a speaker's exordium on 'feelings too deep for expression'. But let him expect no such drowsy passivity in reading Browning. Here he will find no conventionality, no melodious commonplace, but freshness, originality, sometimes eccentricity of expression; no didactic laying-out of a subject, but dramatic indication, which requires the reader to trace by his own mental activity the underground stream of thought that jets out in elliptical and pithy verse. To read Browning he must exert himself, but he will exert himself to some purpose. If he finds the meaning difficult of access, it is always worth his effort—if he has to dive deep, 'he rises with his pearl'. Indeed, in Browning's best poems he makes us feel that what we took for obscurity in him was superficiality in ourselves. We are far from meaning that all his obscurity is like the obscurity of the stars, dependent simply on the feebleness of men's vision. On the contrary, our admiration for his genius only makes us feel the more acutely that its inspirations are too often straitened by the garb of whimsical mannerism with which he clothes them. This mannerism is even irritating sometimes, and should at least be kept under restraint in *printed* poems, where the writer is not merely indulging his own vein, but is avowedly appealing to the mind of his reader.

Turning from the ordinary literature of the day to such a writer as Browning, is like turning from Flotow's music, made up of well-pieced shreds and patches, to the distinct individuality of Chopin's Studies or Schubert's Songs. Here, at least, is a man who has something of his own to tell us, and who can tell it impressively, if not with faultless art. There is nothing sickly or dreamy in him: he has a clear eye, a vigorous grasp, and courage to utter what he sees and handles. His robust energy is informed by a subtle, penetrating spirit, and this blending of opposite qualities gives his mind a rough piquancy that reminds one of a russet apple. His keen glance pierces into all the secrets of human character, but, being as thoroughly alive to the outward as to the inward, he reveals those secrets, not by a process of dissection, but by dramatic painting. We fancy his own description of a poet applies to himself: He stood and watched the cobbler at his trade, The man who slices lemons into drink, The coffee-roaster's brazier, and the boys That volunteer to help him at the winch. He glanced o'er books on stalls with half an eye, And fly-leaf ballads on the vendor's string, And broad-edge hold-print posters by the wall *He took such cognizance of men and things, If any beat a horse, you felt he saw; If any cursed a woman, he took note; Yet stared at nobody,—they stared at him, And found, less to their pleasure than surprise, He seemed to know them and expect as much.* Browning has no soothing strains, no chants, no lullabys; he rarely gives voice to our melancholy, still less to our gaiety; he sets our thoughts at work rather than our emotions. But though eminently a thinker, he is as far as possible from prosaic; his mode of presentation is always concrete, artistic, and, where it is most felicitous, dramatic.

—George Eliot, *Westminster Review,*
January 1856, pp. 290–291

JOHN RUSKIN (1856)

John Ruskin was an author, journalist, social commentator, artist, and England's foremost art critic. In the following extract, he discusses the subject of the medieval period as portrayed by Browning in his poetry, admiring the poet's sensitivity to the character of the people and the time. Ruskin states that Browning is more succinct than any other poet or prose writer known to him in his summation of the Renaissance spirit, catalyzing in thirty lines what Ruskin himself took thirty pages to describe in his well-known work *The Stones of Venice*. He mentions, as have other writers of extracts in this volume, that many give up on Browning's work precisely because of its concentrated quality, finding his verse both intellectually and metaphorically insoluble. Rather, Ruskin suggests, Browning's poetry affords readers the type of mental and spiritual exercise that can only yield a greater health and vitality in their lives, and it is for this quality that his art should be considered to be of the highest benefit.

—————

. . . Robert Browning is unerring in every sentence he writes of the Middle Ages; always vital, right, and profound; so that in the matter of art, . . . there is hardly a principle connected with the mediaeval temper, that he has not struck upon in those seemingly careless and too rugged rhymes of his. There is a curious instance, by the way, in a short poem ("The Bishop Orders His Tomb in St. Praxed's Church") referring to this very subject of tomb and image sculpture; and illustrating just one of those phases of local human character which, though belonging to Shakespere's own age, he never noticed, because it was specially Italian and un-English. . . .

I know no other piece of modern English, prose or poetry, in which there is so much told, as in these lines, of the Renaissance spirit,—its worldliness, inconsistency, pride, hypocrisy, ignorance of itself, love of art, of luxury, and of good Latin. It is nearly all that I said of the central Renaissance in thirty pages of the *Stones of Venice* put into as many lines, Browning's being also the antecedent work. The worst of it is that this kind of concentrated writing needs so much *solution* before the reader can fairly get the good of it, that people's patience fails them, and they give the thing up as insoluble; though, truly, it ought to be to the current of common thought like Saladin's talisman, dipped in clear water, not soluble altogether, but making the element medicinal.

—John Ruskin, *Modern Painters,*
1856, part 5, chapter 20

JAMES THOMSON
"THE POEMS OF WILLIAM BLAKE" (1864)

James Thomson was a Scottish writer, best known for his pessimistic poem *The City of Dreadful Night*. He published under the pseudonym Bysshe Vanolis, and the letters B.V. are usually deployed to distinguish him from an earlier Scottish poet of the same name. In this extract from his study of the English poet William Blake's verse, he praises Browning as having an intellect of the highest order. Like the previous Margaret Fuller extract, Thomson suggests that occasionally readers' difficulties in

understanding Browning's verse are directly due to the vigorous nature
of the poet's intellect: He sometimes leaves ideas and characters in his
work incomplete, as he is constantly being swept along toward a new
subject. Browning's genius is credited in some of his poems as bypassing
the occasional obscurity of his language, and Thomson remarks on the
poet's immediate possession of the "light" of genius to the detriment of
Lord Alfred Tennyson who, Thomson claims, rather reflects that same
light. He is left wondering how it is that so many people yet fail to see
Browning's outstanding abilities both in relation to Tennyson's achievements and also in and of themselves.

Robert Browning, a really great thinker, a true and splendid genius, though
his vigorous and restless talents often overpower and run away with his genius
so that some of his creations are left but half redeemed from chaos, has this
simplicity in abundant measure. In the best poems of his last two works,
Men and Women and *Dramatis Persona?*, its light burns so clear and steadfast
through the hurrying clouds of his language (Tennyson's style is the polished
reflector of a lamp) that one can only wonder that people in general have not
yet recognised it. I cannot recommend a finer study of a man possessed by the
spirit of which I am writing than the sketch of Lazarus in Browning's "Epistle
of Karshish, an Arab Physician."

—James Thomson, also known as "B.V.,"
"The Poems of William Blake," 1864, from
Biographical and Critical Studies, 1896, pp. 266–267

EDWARD FITZGERALD (1869)

Edward FitzGerald was an English poet most famous as the first translator
of the collection of Persian verse *The Rubaiyat of Omar Khayyam.* He was a
friend of Lord Alfred Tennyson and in this letter expresses his inability to
read Browning's latest composition, finding it well below the standard of
a number of other poets' work, including that of Tennyson. He does not
believe that Browning's verse will survive appreciated into the future but
expects his friend Tennyson to tell him he is being unfair to the poet and
his poetry. This extract from a letter is notable for two reasons: First, it
shows a talented poet in his own right reading Browning and finding his
verse obscure; secondly, it is a private correspondence between two old
friends and, as such, is an unguarded and particularly open expression of
frustration with Browning's writing. If a man such as Edward FitzGerald

can neither understand nor appreciate Browning, then what must regular, middle-class readers have made of the poet's verse?

————— ————— —————

I have been thinking of you so much for the last two or three days, while the first volume of Browning's *Poem* has been on my table, and I have been trying in vain to read it, and yet the *Athenaeum* tells me it is wonderfully fine. And so sometimes I am drawn to write to you (with only one eye, the other scorched by reading with a paraffin lamp these several winters), and, whether you care for my letter or not, you won't care to answer; and yet I want to know what you yourself think of this poem; you, who are the one man able to judge of it, and magnanimous enough to think me capable of seeing what is fine in it. I never could read Browning. If Browning only gave a few pence for the book he drew from, what will posterity give for his version of it, if posterity ever find it on a stall? If Shakespeare, Milton, Dryden, Pope and Tennyson survive, what *could* their readers make out of this Browning a hundred years hence? Anything so utterly unlike the *Ring* too which he considers he has wrought out of the old gold—*this* shapeless thing. "You are unjust, Fitz"— that is what you will say or think, I fancy.

—Edward FitzGerald, letter to Alfred,
Lord Tennyson, April 1869

EDWARD CLARENCE STEDMAN (1875)

Edward Stedman's critical reading of Browning's work is a fine example of a specific reaction many had to the poet and his writing. It is, despite its criticism, a reasonably evenhanded interpretation of Browning's strengths and weaknesses (although Stedman does not presume that he is correct in his criticisms, only in the manner in which he expresses himself); Stedman does not appear to have any personal grudge against Browning.

Stedman begins by lauding the originality of Browning and his art but immediately tempers this praise by saying that if he is the most original of contemporary poets, his poetry is also the least calibrated: It can both descend to the everyday and prosaic and can also rise to the giddy heights that the poet laureate, Tennyson, has reached in his own verse (once more we see the comparison between Browning and Lord Alfred Tennyson).

Stedman's fundamental criticism of Browning's verse is a structural one: He claims that the poet does not realize the formal laws of the art, nor does he submit his imagination to the benefits of accepted poetic forms. The extract states that a poet's adherence to formal restrictions allows his ideas to achieve a more excellent conception. As a consequence, Browning is an "eclectic," his poetry a "mixture," an "arabesque" in which he revels. Stedman considers the poetry strange and confused; if original, it is for all the wrong reasons.

It is not only the structural cohesion of Browning's poetry that Stedman dislikes but also the confusion of sentiment that he feels Browning's verse often expresses. This criticism has been seen before to varying degrees in Margaret Fuller's and James Thomson's extracts. Stedman advances the critique, however, claiming that on one hand Browning presents in his poetry an intimate understanding of other people's hearts, but equally and too often makes his characters speak his own thoughts in their particular voices. This is considered by Stedman to be a flaw in poetic conception, for how many individuals are capable of the type of high-flown, metaphysical conceits and musings that the poet can ponder?

Stedman recognizes that Browning has an exquisite and subtle "moral sentiment" in his poetry and also many admirers: He is followed by a host of young poets who are attempting to imitate his work; a "school" of Browning had developed from his early poetry and style with its adherents and naysayers, Stedman obviously being of the latter camp. He offers the critical suggestion that, by the 1870s, younger poets were no longer attempting to imitate Browning's more recent style. It seems that Browning has become unique to the point of summoning only defensive appreciators rather than active imitators. The defenders of Browning fall into two camps: those who, as Stedman has claimed Browning himself does, simply disregard the poetic conventions of form, feeling, and theme, and those who are aware of Browning's failings but who, because they also appreciate the poet's greatness, defend him from any and all attacks.

Stedman concludes by discussing Browning's poetry in relation to Richard Wagner's music. Wagner was one of the best-known composers of the latter half of the nineteenth century, appreciated by many as writing the "music of the future" and turning structural and conceptual convention on its head. Is Browning's verse the poetic equivalent of the compositions of Wagner? Stedman states that, if this is the case, then the whole idea of poetry must be redefined. He recognizes that Browning has significant creative ability and respect for his office as a poet but that he suffers from the criticism often made of those who simply affect genius and who, in actuality, despise art and its conventions. This distinction is important: Stedman is not saying that Browning is of the latter type, only that he is often criticized in the same manner in which that class of dilettante has been. Nevertheless, Stedman maintains that Browning either has only contempt for beauty (presumably in the formal sense expressed throughout the extract), or he has the inability to express it in his verse. The greatest poets are described as uniting art (form and style) with spiritual power (the "passion" mentioned earlier in the extract). Stedman does not consider that Browning has achieved this unity in his own writing, and, indeed, he has maintained that either Browning has simply no intention of attempting it or is, in actuality, incapable of doing so.

I have called him the most original and the most unequal of living poets; he continually descends to a prosaic level, but at times is elevated to the Laureate's highest flights. Without realizing the proper functions of art, he nevertheless sympathizes with the joyous liberty of its devotees; his life may be conventional, but he never forgets the Latin Quarter, and often celebrates that freedom in love and song which is the soul of Beranger's

Dans un grenier qu'on est bien a vingt ans.

Then, too, what working man of letters does not thank him when he says,—

But you are of the trade, my Puccio!
You have the fellow-craftsman's sympathy.
There's none knows like a fellow of the craft
The all unestimated sum of pains
That go to a success the world can see.

He is an eclectic, and will not be restricted in his themes; on the other hand, he gives us too gross a mixture of poetry, fact, and metaphysics, appearing to have no sense of composite harmony, but to revel in arabesque strangeness and confusion. He has a barbaric sense of color and lack of form. Striving against the trammels of verse, he really is far less a master of expression than others who make less resistance. We read in *Pippa Passes*: "If there should arise a new painter, will it not be in some such way by a poet, now, or a musician (spirits who have conceived and perfected an Ideal through some other channel), transferring it to this, and escaping our conventional roads by pure ignorance of them?" This is the Pre-Raphaelite idea, and, so far, good; but Browning's fault is that, if he has "conceived," he certainly has made no effort to "perfect" an Ideal.

And here I wish to say,—and this is something which, soon or late, every thoughtful poet must discover,—that the structural exigencies of art, if one adapts his genius to them, have a beneficent reaction upon the artist's original design. By some friendly law they help the work to higher excellence, suggesting unthought-of touches, and refracting, so to speak, the single beam of light in rays of varied and delightful beauty.

The brakes which art applies to the poet's movement not only regulate, but strengthen its progress. Their absence is painfully evinced by the mass of Browning's unread verse. Works like *Sordello* and *Fifine,* however intellectual, seem, like the removal of the Malvern Hills, a melancholy waste of human power. When some romance like the last-named comes from his pen,—an addition in volume, not in quality, to what he has done before,—I feel a sadness like that engendered among hundreds of gloomy folios in some black-letter alcove: books, forever closed, over which the mighty monks of old wore out their lives, debating minute points of casuistic theology, though now the very memory of their discussions has passed away. Would that Browning might take to heart his own words, addressed, in "Transcendentalism," to a brother-poet:—

> Song's our art:
> Whereas you please to speak these naked thoughts Instead of draping
>   them in sights and sounds. —True thoughts, good thoughts,
>   thoughts fit to treasure up!
> But why such long prolusion and display, Such turning and adjustment
>   of the harp?
> But here's your fault; grown men want thought, you think; Thought's
>   what they mean by verse, and seek in verse:
> Boys seek for images and melody, Men must have reason,—so you aim
>   at men. Quite otherwise!

Incidentally we have noted the distinction between the drama of Browning and that of the absolute kind, observing that his characters reflect his own mental traits, and that their action and emotion are of small moment compared with the speculations to which he makes them all give voice. Still, he has dramatic insight, and a minute power of reading other men's hearts. His moral sentiment has a potent and subtle quality:—through his early poems he really founded a school, and had imitators, and, although of his later method there are none, the younger poets whom he has most affected very naturally began work by carrying his philosophy to a startling yet perfectly logical extreme.

Much of his poetry is either very great or very poor. It has been compared to Wagner's music, and entitled the "poetry of the future"; but if this be just, then we must revise our conception of what poetry really is. The doubter incurs the contemptuous enmity of two classes of the dramatist's admirers: first, of the metaphysical, who disregard considerations of passion, melody, and form; secondly, of those who are sensitive to their master's failings, but, in view of his greatness, make it a point of honor to defend them. That greatness lies in his originality; his error, arising from perverseness or congenital defect, is the violation of natural and beautiful laws. This renders his longer poems of less worth than his lyrical studies, while, through avoidance of it, productions, differing as widely as *The Eve of St. Agnes* and *In Memoriam,* will outlive *The Ring and the Book.* In writing of Arnold I cited his own quotation of Goethe's distinction between the dilettanti, who affect genius and despise art, and those who respect their calling though not gifted with high creative power. Browning escapes the limitations of the latter class, but incurs the reproach visited upon the former; and by his contempt of beauty, or inability to surely express it, fails of that union of art and spiritual power which always characterizes a poet entirely great.

—Edmund Clarence Stedman,
Victorian Poets, 1875, pp. 338–341

ALGERNON CHARLES SWINBURNE (1875)

Algernon Charles Swinburne was an English poet who burst on the literary scene in the 1860s and who for several decades was considered England's most controversial writer of verse. He lived into the first decade of the twentieth century, by which point he had become both familiar enough to escape controversy and an admired writer of criticism. As a young man, he was thought by many to be the heir apparent to Tennyson and Browning. He continued to believe this to be the case in later life, despite others having changed their attitude in regard to his achievements. His poetry was famous for its original use of rhyme, meter, and word choice, but he, like Browning although to a lesser degree, was often criticized for the unusual, formal qualities of his verse. Unlike Browning, who was generally regarded to have the highest moral sense in his poetry, Swinburne was attacked for the often radical sexual and irreligious themes he presented in his own verse.

In this extract Swinburne vehemently defends Browning from the charge of writing obscure poetry. He recognizes that such an attack is most likely intended to destroy the career of a poet and finds that in Browning's case it is more misapplied than in any other instance. Swinburne claims that the charge of obscurity arises from a variety of qualities in Browning's poetry that are actually based on the precision, clarity, and rapid motion of the poet's intellect. He uses particularly modern metaphors—the railway and the telegraph—to describe the speed and power of Browning's mind. He describes the type of reader who will appreciate and understand Browning's art as one whose mind is "electric in its motion" and aligned with that same dynamic in the poetry he reads. In the same vein as that of George Eliot in her extract, Swinburne suggests that to read Browning's verse properly requires the application of one's mind when working at its fullest powers. It is only "foggy" and clumsy thinkers who find in Browning's work the obscurity of their own mind reflected back to them.

Students of Browning familiar with reader-response theories might consider Swinburne's suggestion that "to do justice to any book which deserves any other sort of justice than that of the fire or the waste-paper basket, it is necessary to read it in the fit frame of mind." He appears to maintain that readers will find cast back upon themselves those aspects of mind with which they approach the text, or perhaps will discover in a text the very things they have brought to it. Swinburne also suggests in the final line of the extract that it is more difficult for an author to pitch his writing to the muddled thinker than to one whose mind is in tune with the poet's own rhythms and motion of thought. Of course, one might ask why a writer would want to produce anything for those with inadequate reading abilities? Perhaps this is Swinburne's point: Those who attack Browning should be more concerned with the state of their own intellectual capacities than those of a man whose mind far and swiftly outruns their own.

—·/)/)/—   —·/)/)/—   —·/)/)/—

The charge of obscurity is perhaps of all charges the likeliest to impair the fame or to imperil the success of a rising or an established poet. It is as often misapplied by hasty or ignorant criticism as any other on the roll of accusations; and was never misapplied more persistently and perversely than to an eminent writer of our own time. The difficulty found by many in certain of Mr. Browning's works arises from a quality the very reverse of that which produces obscurity properly so called. Obscurity is the natural product of turbid forces and confused ideas; of a feeble and clouded or of a vigorous but unfixed and chaotic intellect.... Now if there is any great quality more perceptible than another in Mr. Browning's intellect it is his decisive and incisive faculty of thought, his sureness and intensity of perception, his rapid and trenchant resolution of aim. To charge him with obscurity is about as accurate as to call Lynceus purblind or complain of the sluggish action of the telegraphic wire. He is something too much the reverse of obscure; he is too brilliant and subtle for the ready reader of a ready writer to follow with any certainty the track of an intelligence which moves with such incessant rapidity, or even to realize with what spider-like swiftness and sagacity his building spirit leaps and lightens to and fro and backward and forward as it lives along the animated line of its labour, springs from thread to thread and darts from centre to circumference of the glittering and quivering web of living thought woven from the inexhaustible stores of his perception and kindled from the inexhaustible fire of his imagination. He never thinks but at full speed; and the rate of his thought is to that of another man's as the speed of a railway to that of a waggon or the speed of a telegraph to that of a railway. It is hopeless to enjoy the charm or to apprehend the gist of his writings except with a mind thoroughly alert, an attention awake at all points, a spirit open and ready to be kindled by the contact of the writer's. To do justice to any book which deserves any other sort of justice than that of the fire or the waste paper basket, it is necessary to read it in the fit frame of mind; and the proper mood in which to study for the first time a book of Mr. Browning's is the freshest, clearest, most active mood of the mind in its brightest and keenest hours of work. Read at such a time, and not "with half-shut eyes falling asleep in a half-dream," it will be found (in Chapman's phrase) "pervial" enough to any but a sluggish or a sandblind eye; but at no time and in no mood will a really obscure writer be found other than obscure. The difference between the two is the difference between smoke and lightning; and it is far more difficult to pitch the tone of your thought in harmony with that of a foggy thinker, than with that of one whose thought is electric in its motion.

—Algernon Charles Swinburne, *George Chapman:*
A Critical Essay, 1875, pp. 15–18

HARRIET MARTINEAU (1877)

Harriet Martineau was an English journalist, philosopher, political economist, abolitionist, and feminist. In this extract taken from her autobiography, Martineau describes first reading Browning and also her impressions of the poet when hearing him talk. She stayed up all night excitedly reading *Paracelsus* but later was disappointed to find she was unable to understand Browning's *Sordello*. She found the latter poem to be utterly unlike Browning's conversation, which she describes as being clear, controlled, and straightforward. Like the writers of other extracts in this volume, Martineau remarks on Browning's humor, geniality, friendliness, moral strength, and intellectual energy. In the concluding line she seems, rather amusingly, to suggest that Browning's wisdom and character were proved by his successfully negotiating a marriage to another poet, Elizabeth Barrett. The claim is that this was a type of undertaking full of potential perils.

It was a wonderful event to me,—my first acquaintance with his poetry.—Mr. Macready put *Paracelsus* into my hand, when I was staying at his house; and I read a canto before going to bed. For the first time in my life, I passed a whole night without sleeping a wink. The unbounded expectation I formed from that poem was sadly disappointed when *Sordello* came out. I was so wholly unable to understand it that I supposed myself ill. But in conversation no speaker could be more absolutely clear and purpose-like. He was full of good sense and fine feeling, amidst occasional irritability; full also of fun and harmless satire; with some little affectations which were as droll as any thing he said. A real genius was Robert Browning, assuredly; and how good a man, how wise and morally strong, is proved by the successful issue of the perilous experiment of the marriage of two poets.

—Harriet Martineau, *Autobiography*, ed. Maria
Weston Chapman, 1877, vol. 1, pp. 314–315

JUSTIN MCCARTHY (1879–80)

Justin McCarthy was an Irish nationalist, a member of the British Parliament, a historian, and a novelist. In the following extract, McCarthy suggests that Browning's concerns in his verse are with human emotions in and reaction to unusual circumstances. He believes Browning to have proved that he has the poetic ability to write gracefully and formally but that often the poet deliberately seems to choose taking pleasure in shocking the reader with his unusual deployment of language. As others have agreed, Browning is here criticized for allowing his fascination with human psychology to absorb almost all of his poetic gifts, and, as a consequence,

McCarthy suggests, it is often difficult for the reader to follow the thought process in Browning's writing. Once more, the critical charge against Browning's work is one of obscurity. McCarthy states that he believes Browning's interest in the psychology of individuals to have led him into a morbid fascination with the more grotesque aspects of life, an interest that has become apparent in the often grotesque structure of his verse.

The question of the confusing nature of Browning's poetry is developed by McCarthy: He replies to those (such as Swinburne in a previous extract in this section) who suggest that readers' own lack of intellect is the cause of their inability to fully understand Browning's art. Rather, McCarthy claims, if one can enjoy an array of the best English poets, and if a poet can sufficiently clarify in his own mind the ideas he wishes to express, then there is no reason that any poetry should be beyond a regular reader's grasp; that is, unless the poet's ideas have not been properly developed and presented. The English language is certainly rich enough for any concept to be clearly translated into verse. If various philosophers can express themselves clearly in English and be understood, then an English poet's ideas should certainly be just as transparently realized and just as easily accessible to a general reader.

Nevertheless, and despite these criticisms, McCarthy states that Browning is a great poet despite his doing practically all he can to stand between himself and popularity. It is in his poetry's depictions of pathos, of melancholic feeling, of passion, humor, and of general human emotion that Browning can be considered to have shown his genius. McCarthy concludes that at least in its expression of the emotional realm, Browning's verse is greatly superior to that of Lord Alfred Tennyson's.

—◦◦◦— —◦◦◦— —◦◦◦—

Mr. Browning ... delights in perplexed problems of character and life—in studying the effects of strange contrasting forces of passion coming into play under peculiar and distracting conditions. All that lies beneath the surface; all that is out of the common track of emotion; all that is possible, that is poetically conceivable, but that the outer air and the daily walks of life never see, this is what specially attracts Mr. Browning. ... No poet ... certainly can be more often wanting in grace of form and delight of soft sound than Mr. Browning. There are many passages and even many poems of Browning which show that the poet could be melodious if he would; but he seems sometimes as if he took a positive delight in perplexing the reader's ear with harsh, untuneful sounds. Mr. Browning commonly allows the study of the purely psychological to absorb too much of his moods and of his genius.

It has a fascination for him which he is seemingly unable to resist. He makes of his poems too often mere searchings into strange deeps of human character and human error. He seldom abandons himself altogether to the inspiration of the poet; he hardly ever deserves the definition of the minstrel given in Goethe's ballad who "sings but as the song-bird sings." Moreover, Mr. Browning has an almost morbid taste for the grotesque; he is not unfrequently a sort of poetic Callot. It has to be added that Mr. Browning is seldom easy to understand, and that there are times when he is only to be understood at the expense of as much thought and study as one might give to a controverted passage in an ancient author. This is a defect of art, and a very serious defect. The more devoted of Mr. Browning's admirers will tell us, no doubt, that the poet is not bound to supply us with brains as well as poetry, and that if we cannot understand what he says it is the fault simply of our stupidity. But an ordinary man who finds that he can understand Shakspeare and Milton, Dryden and Wordsworth, Byron and Keats without any trouble, may surely be excused if he does not set down his difficulty about some of Browning's poems wholly to the account of his own dulness. It may well be doubted whether there is any idea so subtle that if the poet can actually realize it in his own mind clearly for himself, the English language will not be found capable of expressing it with sufficient clearness. The language has been made to do this for the most refined reasonings of philosophical schools, for transcendentalists and utilitarians, for psychologists and metaphysicians. No intelligent person feels any difficulty in understanding what Mill, or Herbert Spencer, or Huxley means; and it can hardly be said that the ideas Mr. Browning desires to convey to his readers are more difficult of exposition than some of those which the authors we name have contrived to set out with a white light of clearness all round them. The plain truth is that Mr. Browning is a great poet, in spite of some of the worst defects that ever stood between a poet and popularity. He is a great poet by virtue of his commanding genius, his fearless imagination, his penetrating pathos. He strikes an iron harp-string. In certain of his moods his poetry is like that of the terrible lyre in the weird old Scottish ballad, the lyre that was made of the murdered maiden's breastbone, and which told its fearful story in tones "that would melt a heart of stone." In strength and depth of passion and pathos, in wild humor, in emotion of every kind, Mr. Browning is much superior to Mr. Tennyson.

—Justin McCarthy, *A History of Our
Own Times*, 1879–80, chapter 29

Unsigned (1886)

This anonymous essay from the popular *London Quarterly Review* suggests that Browning's verse has changed over the years only so far as its stylistic aspects are concerned, not in its poetic intention. The *Review* author asks the obvious question then: What in fact has been Browning's poetic intention all of these years? It is a question that requires and is worthy of a long answer, it seems, but his intention could be summarized as having been to create human life in language. The writer distinguishes between the dramatic nature of Browning's verse and its lack of theatrical aspects; the metaphor the extract uses to explain the distinction is one of catching and holding a wave at the moment it peaks, its power, energy, and dynamic movement temporarily frozen. Such an act, the extract's writer claims, is the motivating intention of Browning's writing: to subsume into a single moment the gamut of human emotion, action, and thought and to suggest this totality in the singular moments of his poems.

A secondary aspect of Browning's work the reviewer thought worthy of attention is the poet's intellect. He agrees with those who have said that Browning is the greatest poetic thinker in English since Shakespeare, claiming for both poets the ability to present to their readers the fullest range of human psychology and philosophy and at the same time maintaining a sympathy for the multitude of human types in their verse. The extract ends with only the slightest of demurrals, allowing the author to place Shakespeare above Browning in the poetic canon: The reviewer feels that there are occasions when the latter's lack of formal and linguistic grace does not suitably correlate with the intention of his poetry. In other words, the review suggests that Browning's artistic craftsmanship does not always live up to his poetic genius. It is a position taken many times in this volume's extracts.

The poetry of Browning, far more than that of Tennyson or Swinburne, is a growth. His career, while seeming at each point of its progress to be defiantly stationary, has been in reality one continuous march; a march in the course of which he has resolutely thrown aside, one by one, everything hampering to a direct passage. The progress, being gradual and continuous, and extending from 1833 to 1884, has naturally led a long way. To read in the *Pauline* of 1833, say, the lines commencing—

Night, and one single ridge of narrow path
Between the sullen river and the woods;

and on laying down the book to turn to the *Ferishtah's Fancies* of 1884, and read—

> 'Look, I strew beans,' resumed Ferishtah, 'beans
> Blackish and whitish,'

is to experience the sensation of one who should step from Italy to Iceland. But, let it be remembered, this is only in matters of style, of technique. In tone and intention there is no body of poetry known to us more consistent in its unity than that of Browning. The thing he wishes to say is the same now as it was long ago; it is only the manner of saying it that has changed.

And what is the thing that he wishes to say? This is a light question to ask, but it needs a long answer. Browning is not one of those who may be dismissed when you have complimented them on their pretty tunes. His aim has never been to please our ears by the tinkle and jingle of rhyme, or even, primarily, by the music of rhythm, but to sing such songs as should not slip easily into our minds, nor easily slip out of them. To be accounted a poet, is to him to be held that which the Greeks meant when they said, not singer, but maker—Ποιμτής. The poetry of most of our modern masters is directed to other ends than that of *making*. They sing with Shelley, meditate with Wordsworth, dream with Keats, declaim with Byron. But the poetry of Browning is neither an attempt to sing, nor to meditate, nor to dream, nor to declaim. It may be all of these, in measure, at times; but in aim it is none of them. It is rather an endeavour to create. It is concerned with live men and women, with their thoughts and loves and hates, with their creeds, their whims, their passions, their hopes, fears, struggles, conquests, defeats; with these as an object, not as a means; in their entirety and nakedness, as they subsist in the soul, not so much in a cunning adjustment of them to the requirements of the modern theatre.

Browning's art is essentially dramatic, but essentially untheatrical. Elsewhere we have tried to show that his informal drama of the soul may be claimed as the nineteenth century equivalent—equivalent, observe, not imitation—of the formal drama of action which flourished gloriously in the right sixteenth-century soil. His drama has all the life of action, but it is not action. It is as if one caught a wave at its poise, and held it for a moment, motionless with all its suspended thrill and fury of movement. In an eloquent pause and silence, when life lived to the fullest culminates in one crisis of joy, pain, passion, or disgust, Browning seizes and possesses his opportunity. Into that one moment he crowds the thought, action and emotion of a lifetime; the poem will be a little drama, perhaps only fifty lines, but yet *multum in parvo*, instinct with vitality and suggestion.

It is this aim of dramatic picturing that Browning has always had before him—an aim, as we have shown, at expressing, with the utmost delicacy of perfection, in a word, with the utmost *truth*, every phase and feature of the human mind. Coexistent with this primary aim, there is another and secondary. Browning is not merely a great dramatist but a great thinker. 'Browning is the greatest thinker in poetry since Shakespeare', we have heard it said; and the remark appears to us no exaggeration. Like Shakespeare, too, he has that universality, that range of philosophic insight, that profound and subtle sympathy with every form of individual belief, which can seem to embrace opposites. Shakespeare, as we know, has been proved everything, from devout Christian to blasphemous Atheist. Papers have been read before the Browning Society in which the modern poet has been credited with almost as many creeds as his predecessor. And in the case of Browning at least, whatever may be the fact as to Shakespeare, this is not to be attributed to any vagueness or indifference on the part of the poet, but wholly to the breadth of his grasp on many-sided truth, and the sureness of his dramatic method. Unlike Shakespeare, however, our ultimate pattern and guide in all things, Browning has not possessed the art of always clothing his thought in the garb of grace which should belong to poetry.

—Unsigned, *The London Quarterly
Review*, January 1886, 1xv, pp. 238–250

EDWARD DOWDEN (1887)

Edward Dowden was an Irish poet and literary critic. In the following extract from his critical essay on Victorian literature published in the journal the *Fortnightly Review*, Dowden contrasts Browning to Matthew Arnold who, along with John Ruskin and Thomas Carlyle, was generally considered to be a "Victorian sage," writing poetry and essays dealing with cultural concerns, the "state of England," and social and aesthetic matters. Arnold, Dowden suggests, suffers greatly from *la maladie du siècle*, or the century's spiritual ailment, his work tending toward the pessimistic and diagnostic. Browning, in contrast, is described as seeing the world as akin to a classical Greek gymnasium, in which the individual hones himself both mentally and physically, preparing himself for the competitions and struggles that life offers. Dowden states that the greatest of sins for Browning would be apathy and lethargy and depicts his poetry metaphorically as being an energy-giving battery for those whose spirits are paralyzed. Thus, Browning's poetry becomes a cure for the type of *maladie du siècle* from which his contemporaries suffer. Dowden understands that those who undergo this reading cure may be initially shocked, but as their strength grows, they will return to it in greater and greater numbers.

Where Arnold is described as turning away from the problems of the world to seek self-sufficient peace and quiet, and Tennyson, the author of *In Memoriam*, retreats defensively from life's pain into his own inner self, Browning struggles joyously through the world understanding that to simply live is in itself beautiful, that all aspects of existence can and must be celebrated. This appreciation is what he has sought to present in his verse bravely, honestly, and beneficially. Dowden defines Browning's asceticism as not the withdrawal from the world practiced on occasion by Arnold and Tennyson but the active and healthy life of the Greek athlete, the foremost characteristic of a man living fully and fully engaged by the world. The extract is evidence that even two years before the poet's death, his poems' most agreed-upon characteristics remain, as they had been since the 1830s, their energy, verve, and fundamental relationship to life.

<hr />

If Mr. Arnold is the poet of our times who as poet could least resist *la maladie du siècle* in its subtler forms, he whose energy of heart and soul most absolutely rejects and repels its influence is Mr. Browning. To him this world appears to be a palæstra in which we are trained and tested for other lives to come; it is a gymnasium for athletes. Action, passion, knowledge, beauty, science, art—these are names of some of the means and instruments of our training and education. The vice of vices, according to his ethical creed, is languor of heart, lethargy or faintness of spirit, with the dimness of vision and feebleness of hand attending such moral enervation. Which of us does not suffer now and again from a touch of spiritual paralysis? Mr. Browning's poetry, to describe it in a word, is a galvanic battery for the use of spiritual paralytics. At first the shock and the tingling frightened patients away; now they crowd to the physician and celebrate the cure. Which of us does not need at times that virtue should pass into him from a stronger human soul? To touch the singing robes of the author of *Rabbi Ben Ezra* and *Prospice* and *The Grammarian's Funeral*, is to feel an influx of new strength. We gain from Mr. Browning, each in his degree, some of that moral ardour and spiritual faith and vigour of human sympathy which make interesting to him all the commonplace, confused, and ugly portions of life, those portions of life which, grating too harshly on Mr. Matthew Arnold's sensitiveness, disturb his self-possession and trouble his lucidity, causing him often, in his verse, to turn away from this vulgar, distracting world to quietism and solitude, or a refined self-culture that lacks the most masculine qualities of discipline. To preserve those spiritual truths which are most precious to him Mr. Browning does not retreat, like the singer of *In Memoriam*, into the citadel of the heart; rather, an armed combatant, he makes a sortie into the world of worldlings and unbelievers, and from among errors and falsehoods and basenesses and crimes, he captures new truths for the soul. It is not in calm meditation or a mystical quiet that the clearest perception of divine things comes to him; it is rather through the struggle of the will, through the strife of passion, and as much through foiled desire and defeated endeavour as through attainment and success. For asceticism, in the sense of that word which signifies a maiming and marring of our complete humanity, Mr. Browning's doctrine of life leaves no place; but if asceticism mean heroic exercise, the *askesis* of the athlete, the whole of human existence, as he conceives, is designed as a school of strenuous and joyous asceticism. 'Our human impulses towards knowledge, towards beauty, towards love,' it has been well said, 'are reverenced by him as the signs and tokens of a world not included in that which meets the senses.' Therefore, he must needs welcome the whole fulness of earthly beauty, as in itself good, but chiefly precious because it is a pledge and promise of beauty not partial and earthly, but in its heavenly plenitude. And how dare he seek to narrow or enfeeble the affections, when in all their errors and their never-satisfied aspirations, he discovers evidence of an infinite love, from which they proceed and towards which they tend? Nor would he stifle any high ambition, for it is a wing to the spirit lifting man towards heights of knowledge or passion or power which rise unseen beyond the things of sense, heights on which man hereafter may attain the true fulfilment of his destiny.

—Edward Dowden, "Victorian Literature,"
Fortnightly Review, June 1887, xlvii, pp. 433–457

EDGAR FAWCETT (1888)

Edgar Fawcett was an American journalist and novelist. The following extract was written for the then popular *Lippincott's Monthly Magazine* a year before the poet's death. Fawcett discusses the "Browning Craze" that he said began to assume its present proportion about ten years earlier. He amusingly suggests that many had heard of the "Craze" while hardly knowing anything of Browning himself and certainly not his

poetry. Fawcett claims that as a young boy he had heard of it and wished
to take part in what he describes as being similar to a club of initiates or a
mystery cult. Fawcett says that part of the pleasure of being a member of
this troupe was patronizing one's fellows when they said they could not
understand Browning's work: The suggestion that the poet had caused
more baldfaced lying among the youth of a generation than any other
writer borders on the comic. Readers should note Fawcett's grievance
with those admirers of Browning who constantly claim the poet to be a
far greater artist than Lord Alfred Tennyson. The suggestion is that the
passing of time will show that this is not the case.

Fawcett examines the faddishness of literary crazes, first the "Browning
Craze" and then those that seek to rank various writers according to the
feeling of the moment. He mentions those who claimed that the uncouth
writer Carlyle was greater than dignified Macaulay and how that fashion
had passed in a few years. He expresses his distress at those who have
placed Browning in higher esteem than Tennyson, stating that the latter
has shown only the most noble faithfulness to his art, whereas Browning
has often "insulted" his poetry as if it had stolen something from him.
We can presume that, like many other critics before him, Fawcett is
suggesting that Browning is not a great *artist*, no matter how much one
might appreciate the ideas and passions expressed in his poetry.

Critical surprise has been more than once expressed, of late, that in an age
so militant against the development of the poetic spirit, a single man should
find himself (and that, too, at an advanced period of his life) surrounded, not
to say besieged, by hosts of ardent admirers. Everybody has now heard of the
'Browning Craze', and it is quite probable that many had heard of it while Mr.
Robert Browning himself was hardly more to them than a meaningless name.
And yet to the majority of literary men and women in England and America
this cult has long been a familiar one. Not until perhaps a decade ago did
it begin to assume its present spacious proportions. I remember meeting
devout Browningites at least twenty years ago, when almost a boy. And as
boys will, when their thoughts turn toward the letters of their time and land,
I soon felt an ambitious craving to graduate into a Browningite myself.

Such a worship then possessed so fascinating an element of rarity! It was
so attractive a role for one to give a compassionate lifting of the brows and
say, 'No, really?' when somebody declared himself quite unable to understand
the obscure author of *Sordello*. You knew perfectly well that any number of
his lines were Hindostanee to you, and yet you made use of your patronizing

pity and your 'No, really?' all the same. There is safety in the assertion that Mr. Browning has driven more pedantic youngsters to unblushing falsehood than any other writer in the language. . . .

One of the most distressing features about Mr. Browning's existent reputation—distressing, I mean, to those who discern and measure its basis of humbug—is the way in which his admirers are never tired of saying that it wholly outshines the renown of Lord Tennyson and that its possessor has touched, thus far in our century, the high-tide mark of English poetry. So, until not very long since, fanatics cried that Carlyle, with his barbarisms, loomed above that most masterly and dignified of writers, Macaulay; but now the brief prejudice of the hour has passed, and the morrows have begun to dole out equity, as they generally do, with no matter how tardy a service. Never was a greater literary injustice perpetrated than the placing of Mr. Browning above Lord Tennyson. The Laureate has indeed served his art with a profound and lovely fidelity, while it is no exaggeration to state of Mr. Browning that he has not seldom insulted his as though it were a pickpocket.

—Edgar Fawcett, "The Browning Craze," *Lippincott's Monthly Magazine* January 1888, xli, pp. 81–96

WILLIAM JOHN ALEXANDER (1889)

This extract from the critic William John Alexander's introduction to Browning's poetry affords a view of the poet's stature in Victorian society in the year of his death. As such, it is a fine vantage point from which to examine earlier extracts and to develop an idea of how popular and critical reaction both changed and remained constant in its appreciations and dislikes over the course of Browning's literary lifetime.

Alexander recognizes that Browning's originality is unquestioned, but whether this is a compliment or a criticism has always been the question. As the other extracts in this volume show, taken as a whole, Browning's poetry had divided opinion throughout his entire career. Alexander claims that no poet has caused such sharp disagreement as to his worth and that Browning has provoked not only the most extreme reactions in his critical reception, he is the most obscure poet of the times, his output prodigious but also extremely varied in its quality.

Alexander suggests that Browning's poetry was the poet's means of developing and expressing his own individuality and that this motive imbues the poetry with originality. He does not write for art's sake, for his readership, or to produce great literature, but to allow his own character space in which to expand and grow. This is the reason, as Alexander states Browning himself admits, that his work is never perfect and has been so uneven through the years. The important qualification made by Alexander about the content of Browning's verse is that because the poet desires to express himself in his work, there are many things that he writes that are incidental or, indeed, detrimental to his art; but they are absolute and necessary components in the development of his own intellect and individuality.

There is no poet of our time more original, be that originality good or bad, than Browning. . . . There is no poetry on which opinions are so much divided, none so at variance with preconceived ideas, none, therefore, which it is so difficult fairly to appreciate. There is no poet of our time so uneven, none so voluminous, none so obscure. There is no poet, then, who so much needs an interpreter. . . .

His poetry, then, is for Browning, but a form of activity, a means of realizing his own individuality. He is not an Eglamour; his poetry is not the end of his existence; he does not submit to his art, nor sacrifice his perfection as a man to the perfection of his work. Like Goethe, he writes not so much to produce a great work,—to please others, as to afford play to his own individuality. Necessarily, then, as he points out in *Sordello*, his work is imperfect. He has himself rather than his reader in view. He is seeking to give complete and accurate expression to what is within him, rather than to give beauty and artistic completeness to his work. Accordingly, the incongruous and non-essential from the artistic point of view, he does not prune away; these are needful for the true and complete expression of his own mind.

—William John Alexander, *An Introduction to the Poetry of Robert Browning*, 1889, pp. 2, 210

ANDREW LANG "INTRODUCTORY: OF MODERN ENGLISH POETRY" (1889)

Andrew Lang was a Scottish novelist and literary critic. In the following extract taken from his study of contemporary English poetry, Lang begins by addressing the relative merits of Browning and Lord Alfred Tennyson. He touches on the "Browning Craze" (mentioned earlier in Fawcett's extract), the motivation behind which he compares to religious fervor. He does not believe that all of Browning's poetry will endure alongside that of Tennyson, the poet laureate, in the future, for many enjoy it simply as a means to prove to others they can appreciate and understand what their fellow readers find obscure. While Lang's point is similar to the American Edgar Fawcett's, as expressed in a previous extract, it is also written with a much less humorous intention in mind. It should be noted, however, that Lang does not say that Tennyson is the better poet, rather he suggests that perhaps future readers will not have the patience to fight to understand much of Browning's work. Tennyson will, as a consequence, become a more popular and consequently more highly regarded poet in the future. He does say that posterity is "impartial," implicitly stating that at present, without the distance of years, Browning's appreciation is artificially inflated by those who enjoy the "enigma" of his verse and take pleasure in deciphering it. The relationship of a poet and his poetry to the time at which it is viewed is thus recognized by Lang as being of the highest significance. Readers may want to consider the logic and strength of the stages of Lang's argument here.

If there are some of Browning's poems that will not be "struggled" over by posterity, Lang recognizes that Browning's dramatic characterizations, the individuals who spring to life in his verse, will unquestionably endure. Browning's obscure style, his often unconventional use of language, will not detract from an appreciation of these vivid personas; no other artist in contemporary letters has achieved a similar feat of characterization, nor does Lang believe that it is possible for another to do so.

There are many who make it a kind of religion to regard Mr. Browning as the greatest of living English poets. In him, too, one is thankful for a veritably great poet; but can we believe that impartial posterity will rate him with the Laureate, or that so large a proportion of his work will endure? The charm of an enigma now attracts students who feel proud of being able to understand what others find obscure. But this attraction must inevitably become a stumbling-block.

Why Mr. Browning is obscure is a long question; probably the answer is that he often cannot help himself. His darkest poems may be made out by a person of average intelligence who will read them as hard as, for example, he would find it necessary to read the *Logic* of Hegel. There is a story of two clever girls who set out to peruse *Sordello*, and corresponded with each other about their progress, 'Somebody is dead in *Sordello*,' one of them wrote to her friend. 'I don't quite know *who* it is, but it must make things a little clearer in the long run.' Alas! a copious use of the guillotine would scarcely clear the stage of *Sordello*. It is hardly to be hoped that *Sordello,* or *Red Cotton Night Cap Country,* or *Fifine,* will continue to be struggled with by posterity. But the mass of *Men and Women,* that unexampled gallery of portraits of the inmost hearts and secret minds of priests, prigs, princes, girls, lovers, poets, painters, must survive immortally, while civilisation and literature last, while men care to know what is in men.

No perversity of humour, no voluntary or involuntary harshness of style, can destroy the merit of these poems, which have nothing like them in the letters of the past, and must remain without successful imitators in the future. They will last all the better for a certain manliness of religious faith—something sturdy and assured—not moved by winds of doctrine, not paltering with doubts, which is certainly one of Mr. Browning's attractions in this fickle and shifting generation. He cannot be forgotten while, as he says,

A sunset touch, A chorus ending of Euripides,

reminds men that they are creatures of immortality, and move 'a thousand hopes and fears.'

—Andrew Lang, "Introductory: Of Modern English
Poetry," *Letters on Literature,* 1889, pp. 8–11

JOHN T. NETTLESHIP "ROBERT BROWNING" (1889)

John Trivett Nettleship was an English painter who wrote the first critical study of Browning's poetry in 1868, a time at which Browning had not yet found favor with the general reading public. As a consequence, Nettleship received Browning's heartfelt gratitude, and the two men became lifelong friends. Nettleship was a prominent member of the Robert Browning Society, and it should come as no surprise that in this extract his opinion of Browning is about as favorable as any could possibly be.

Having written the first critical study of Browning some two decades earlier and writing this extract in the year of Browning's death, Nettleship gives voice to many of the ideas expressed in previous extracts, for it is important to note that Nettleship was fundamental to the development of many of these critical opinions, and he was in many instances the first to express them in his 1868 text. Thus, this extract reveals a critic reviewing, from a distance of more than twenty years, many of his own impressions that have become standard attitudes in regard to Browning.

Nettleship praises every aspect of Browning's poetry: its appreciation of beauty, its use of language and rhythm, its intellectual content, its religious tendencies, philosophy, honesty, and the genius that existed in a poet to maintain at once all these qualities in his verse. Because of the combination of these abilities, Nettleship states that it is pointless to compare Browning to any other poet, whether English or foreign (and perhaps he has those intent on constantly contrasting Browning and Lord Alfred Tennyson in mind). Browning is inimitable and those who try to reproduce his style simple parodists.

While the English public still seems, after almost half a century, to be unsure of its regard for Browning, Nettleship praises the aspect of the poet's verse that is still considered to be of the highest worth today: his dramatic characterization. Life itself was Browning's material, and his insight into human action and psychology are stated by Nettleship to be of the greatest and lasting value in his art.

———————

The truth is that, from a fortunate fusion of several races and characters, we find united in Browning the poet's sensuous love of all earthly beauty, keen ear for rhythm and turn of speech, pregnant eloquence and high range of thought and image, run through by a steel fibre of unflinching probity and courage, high mystic and religious tendencies, philosophic insight, plastic and perceptive gifts, and virile stability. But he is necessarily, by this very fusion, a poet of a unique growth. It is a waste of time to compare or associate him with other poets, English or not—to draw parallels as to style or cast of thought; and, though you may parody, you can never imitate him. It has taken the English people nearly half-a-century to make up their minds about him in any large numbers; and even now a great majority of his admirers seek philosophy where they might easily find live men and women. To Browning, from the minutest detail of gesture or habit to the most thrilling psychological crisis, all humanity has been welcome material; while in actual poetic construction the manner of a phrase or even a grotesque rhyme have, when needful, been as carefully studied in producing and finishing a mental portrait or scene as have his most resonant and majestic passages of poetic eloquence.

—John T. Nettleship, "Robert Browning,"
Academy, December 21, 1889, p. 406

Algernon Charles Swinburne
"A Sequence of Sonnets on the Death
of Robert Browning: I" (1890)

Swinburne's sequence of poems was published a month after Browning's death and is a subtle and insightful appreciation of the poet's verse; but the sequence was also written to remember and praise a man admirable for many qualities beyond his work. Swinburne begins by praising Browning's clarity of vision and states that his death does not and cannot mean the death of his art. In saying that Browning's passing cannot remove the many laurels with which the poet had been crowned, Swinburne simultaneously presents the reader with an image of the enduring power of Browning's poetry, his glory in the world of letters, and also perhaps makes a sly suggestion about the relative worth of Browning to the British laureate, Lord Alfred Tennyson. Browning's thought cannot be conquered by death, nor can his fame. His poetry will always live on, and it is impossible, Swinburne says, for England not to be proud to own and to remember such a great mind and a great poet.

The clearest eyes in all the world they read
With sense more keen and spirit of sight more true
Than burns and thrills in sunrise, when the dew
Flames, and absorbs the glory round it shed,
As they the light of ages quick and dead,
Closed now, forsake us: yet the shaft that slew
Can slay not one of all the works we knew,
Nor death discrown that many-laurelled head.
The works of words whose life seems lightning wrought,
And moulded of unconquerable thought,
And quickened with imperishable flame,
Stand fast and shine and smile, assured that nought
May fade of all their myriad-moulded fame,
Nor England's memory clasp not Browning's name.

—Algernon Charles Swinburne, "A Sequence of
Sonnets on the Death of Robert Browning: I,"
Fortnightly Review, January 1890, p. 1

Aubrey De Vere "Robert Browning" (1890)

Aubrey Thomas De Vere was an Irish poet who in this poetic extract remembers Robert Browning a few months after the poet's death. De Vere describes Browning's language in his verse as "rough," meaning that it lacked the conventional refinements associated with contemporary poetry; but if Browning's deliberate choice of language was untraditional, his themes were "austere," or honest and uncompromising. De Vere's own poetry often dealt with religious subjects and employed an unusual intensity and seriousness in its tone; to describe Browning's poetry as "austere" was high praise from the Irishman. Browning's art was unemotional but depicted a deep sympathy for humankind, even if it presented the reader with as much that was obscure (or a "maze") as was beautiful (a "garden"). De Vere states that Browning's verse did not attempt to depict the usual or commonplace but rather the "byways" of life, the common man in unusual circumstances. In both the manner and content of his art, Browning is described here as having a "key" of his own, a musical term meaning that he sang, or wrote, in his own original way but also suggesting that it was perhaps only the poet himself who could unlock the meanings of his poems.

Gone from us! that strong singer of late days—
Sweet singer should be strong—who, tarrying here,
Chose still rough music for his themes austere,
Hard-headed, aye but tender-hearted lays,
Carefully careless, garden half, half maze.
His thoughts he sang, deep thoughts to thinkers dear,
Now flashing under gleam of smile or tear,
Now veiled in language like a breezy haze
Chance-pierced by sunbeams from the lake it covers.
He sang man's ways—not heights of sage or saint,
Not highways broad, not haunts endeared to lovers;
He sang life's byways, sang its angles quaint,
Its Runic lore inscribed on stave or stone;
Song's short-hand strain,—its key oft his alone.

—Aubrey De Vere, "Robert Browning,"
Macmillan's Magazine, February 1890, p. 258

Annie E. Ireland "Browning's
Types of Womanhood" (1890)

This extract from Annie E. Ireland's article for *The Woman's World* is unusual in this collection in that it does not focus, as other extracts have, on Browning's skill in the general depiction of character but specifically on his ability to portray women in his poetry. Ireland's initial suggestion that Browning was better placed than any other poet in studying woman's character is perhaps more a reference to his close relationship with his wife, Elizabeth Barrett Browning, than to any predilection he might have had for female conversation and company at house or dinner parties.

Ireland claims that Browning's portrayal of women was his foremost talent, and he was able to present the female character to his readers without the usual appeal to sympathy or romantic description so often seen in contemporary Victorian literature and verse. His studies of women brought them out of the background of the world of letters and made them human; before they had been pale, sentimentalized, two-dimensional caricatures. He portrayed them both sympathetically and as flawed in his poetry, relating each character's physical description to her equivalent, moral temperament. In this final idea, readers might consider whether Ireland's own opinions about what women are and should be are questionable.

No poet ever had more perfect opportunity to study woman's character in its sweetest and noblest aspects than Mr. Browning, and nowhere does this great artist show more consummate power, or more delicate intuition, than in his portraiture of women. Independently of all mere conventional claim on our sympathy, relying by no means exclusively upon slender forms, taper fingers, ruby lips, or the like, Mr. Browning's women step out of shadowland into the atmosphere of breathing humanity. They have their adorable perfections and imperfections; they are feminine to the very core. Each word-painting of physical beauty has its spiritual counterpart in characters whose every outward trait bespeaks a corresponding moral quality.

—Annie E. Ireland, "Browning's Types of Womanhood," *The Woman's World*, 1890

John Addington Symonds "A Comparison of Elizabethan with Victorian Poetry" (1890)

John Addington Symonds was one of late Victorian England's foremost literary critics, his most famous work being a seven-volume cultural study of the Renaissance. Symonds himself published some poetry and was widely regarded among his contemporaries as being one of the leading intellects of the period.

This brief extract, from Symond's comparative critical analysis of Elizabethan and Victorian poetry, is a wonderfully succinct portrait of Browning. It describes the poet's energetic engagement with life, his literary and intellectual vigor and suppleness, the uncompromising character and the lack of dissimulation in his verse, but also the dangers he faced in writing this particular type of poetry. Symonds is suggesting that Victorian opinion could be unforgiving, often no more so than in the world of art. The unique style and content of Browning's work left him open to a great variety of critical and public attacks (as readers will have seen in many other extracts in this volume); nevertheless, the poet did not compromise, and this was an artistic and personal stance that Symonds's tone here suggests is a most admirable quality.

Browning is animated by a robust optimism, turning fearless somersaults upon the brink of the abyss.

> —John Addington Symonds, "A Comparison
> of Elizabethan with Victorian Poetry," *Essays
> Speculative and Suggestive*, 1890, vol. 2, p. 246

Barrett Wendell (1891)

Barrett Wendell was an American academic who had graduated from Harvard University, later rising to the position of professor of English at his alma mater. In this extract from one of his well-known textbooks, Wendell examines the charge faced by Browning of being obscure in his verse. Wendell's suggestions amount to a sensitive and thoughtful analysis of the most common charge made against Browning and his poetry and would be valuable to those who wish to contrast Wendell's own position to that of those critics who blame the poet for what is perhaps their own failure. Wendell begins by drawing a distinction between the process of Browning's thought and that of Ralph Waldo Emerson. Emerson had been one of America's most esteemed writers, dying about a decade before Wendell was writing, but here Wendell brings him to task for lacking coherent and structured thoughts. Wendell says that Browning, on the other hand, was aware of what his verse meant, where his thoughts proceeded, and the relationship of each idea to the totality of his composition. Like the authors of previous extracts in this volume, Wendell suggests that to find Browning's poetry obscure is most often the fault of the reader. Those opening a volume of Browning's verse usually come to it with expectations that are dependent on contemporary styles of writing, which tend to be much more long winded than the approach readers will find in a Browning collection. It is Browning's precise and succinct use of language that causes difficulties for those readers unused to the poet's meticulous care. Wendell additionally suggests that many people have been unable to follow even a single passage of Browning's poetry because of his unexpected and original use of syntax.

Emerson's obscurity comes, I think, from want of coherently systematic thought. Browning's, on the other hand, as some recent critic has eagerly maintained, is only an "alleged obscurity." What he meant he always knew. The trouble is that, like Shakspere now and then, he generally meant so much and took so few words to say it in, that the ordinary reader, familiar with the simple diffuseness of contemporary style, does not pause over each word long enough to appreciate its full significance. What reading I have done in Browning inclines me to believe this opinion pretty well based. He had an inexhaustible fancy, too, for arranging his words in such order as no other human being would have thought of. Generally, I fancy, Browning could have told you what he meant by almost any passage, and what relation that passage bore to the composition of which it formed a part; but it is not often that you can open a volume of Browning and explain, without a great deal of study, what the meaning of any whole page is.

—Barrett Wendell, *English Composition,*
1891, p. 208

OSCAR WILDE (1891)

Oscar Wilde was an Irish poet, dramatist, novelist, journalist, and magazine editor. In 1891, he was arguably the most recognizable poet in the world, at the height of both his literary powers and fame. In this extract, taken from his essay *The Critic as Artist*, Wilde shows his trademark, unusual take on things, starting from general commonplaces and arriving at an unexpected conclusion. His tone is gently mocking as it so often was, but his flippancies hide a deeper seriousness, his critical witticisms disguising an incisive and profound intellect.

Wilde begins by making light of the Browning Society, stating that its members have tended to hurt and hinder Browning's critical reputation more than they have helped it. George Saintsbury's extract, included in this section, gives readers a more detailed and less humorous description of the type of activities that Wilde might have had in mind when poking fun at the society's pretensions in his own essay. Wilde states that Browning was categorically great, it is merely the question of the category in which to place him that his essay is examining. Browning's verse is criticized for being formally chaotic, although this is unsurprising, as Wilde was himself a master and aesthetic proponent of the formal aspect of art. The question of Browning's thought is carefully distinguished in the extract: It is not that Browning was enamored of thought itself, rather the manner in which thought moved. Wilde's statement that the method by which a fool arrives at his folly was as important to Browning as the way the wise achieve wisdom is a delightfully original idea.

Wilde hammers Browning's poetry repeatedly for its lack of music, its absence of rhythm, and its lack of formal care for language; but still Wilde calls Browning great. Despite his failures in Wilde's eyes, it is Browning's ability to bring men and women to life in his verse, his touch in depicting dramatic situation, that places him just below Shakespeare for the Irishman; indeed, Wilde suggests that if Browning had been articulate (an example of Wilde's often sharp humor) he would have stood alongside Shakespeare as the finest literary artist ever produced by England. To posterity Browning will not be remembered as a poet but as a prose writer who used poetry as his medium, as perhaps the greatest writer of prose fiction that England has ever produced. Shakespeare is the finer poet, singing "with myriad lips"; but Browning's understanding of dramatic character was perhaps equal to Shakespeare's, allowing him to "stammer through a thousand mouths" (while lacking the Bard's abilities with language and form). For those who find Wilde's humor singular, it should be noted that this simultaneous expression of mockery and praise was not unusual for the wit. He is praising Browning in this essay, it is just not for those reasons that many others have praised him in other extracts in this volume. The assertions he makes in *The Critic as Artist* are not uncommon ones for Wilde when he turns his intellect to the examination of critical commonplaces. It might be of benefit to the reader to examine Wilde's comparison of Browning and Shakespeare in light of Walter Savage Landor's views on the matter. Where Landor is straightforward and full of the highest praise for Browning, Wilde is, in contrast, formulating a complex, nuanced appreciation of the poet that at once suggests several distinct perspectives.

Nowadays we have so few mysteries left to us that we cannot afford to part with one of them. The members of the Browning Society, like the theologians of the Broad Church Party, or the authors of Mr. Walter Scott's Great Writers Series, seem to me to spend their time in trying to explain their divinity away. Where one had hoped that Browning was a mystic they have sought to show that he was simply inarticulate. Where one had fancied that he had something to conceal, they have proved that he had but little to reveal. But I speak merely of his incoherent work. Taken as a whole the man was great. He did not belong to the Olympians, and had all the incompleteness of the Titan. He did not survey, and it was but rarely that he could sing. His work is marred by struggle, violence and effort, and he passed not from emotion to form, but from thought to chaos. Still, he was great. He has been called a thinker, and was certainly a man who was always thinking, and always thinking aloud; but it was not thought that fascinated him, but rather the processes by which thought moves. It was the machine he loved, not what the machine makes. The method by which the fool arrives at his folly was as dear to him as the ultimate wisdom of the wise. So much, indeed, did the subtle mechanism of mind fascinate him that he despised language, or looked upon it as an incomplete instrument of expression. Rhyme, that exquisite echo which in the Muse's hollow hill creates and answers its own voice; rhyme, which in the hands of the real artist becomes not merely a material element of metrical beauty, but a spiritual element of thought and passion also, waking a new mood, it may be, or stirring a fresh train of ideas, or opening by mere sweetness and suggestion of sound some golden door at which the Imagination itself had knocked in vain; rhyme, which can turn man's utterance to the speech of gods; rhyme, the one chord we have added to the Greek lyre, became in Robert Browning's hands a grotesque, misshapen thing, which at times made him masquerade in poetry as a low comedian, and ride Pegasus too often with his tongue in his cheek. There are moments when he wounds us by monstrous music. Nay, if he can only get his music by breaking the strings of his lute, he breaks them, and they snap in discord, and no Athenian tettix, making melody from tremulous wings, lights on the ivory horn to make the movement perfect, or the interval less harsh. Yet, he was great: and though he turned language into ignoble clay, he made from it men and women that live. He is the most Shakespearian creature since Shakespeare. If Shakespeare could sing with myriad lips, Browning could stammer through a thousand mouths. Even now, as I am speaking, and speaking not against him but for him, there glides through the room the pageant of his persons. There, creeps Fra Lippo Lippi with his cheeks still burning from some girl's hot kiss. There, stands dread Saul with the lordly male-sapphires gleaming in his turban. Mildred Tresham is there, and the Spanish monk, yellow with hatred, and Blougram, and Ben Ezra, and the Bishop of St. Praxed's. The spawn of Setebos gibbers in the corner, and Sebald, hearing Pippa pass by, looks on Ottima's haggard face, and loathes her and his own sin, and himself. Pale as the white satin of his doublet, the melancholy king watches with dreamy treacherous eyes too loyal Strafford pass forth to his doom, and Andrea shudders as he hears the cousins whistle in the garden, and bids his perfect wife go down. Yes, Browning was great. And as what will he be remembered? As a poet? Ah, not as a poet! He will be remembered as a writer of fiction, as the most supreme writer of fiction, it may be, that we have ever had. His sense of dramatic situation was unrivalled, and, if he could not answer his own problems, he could at least put problems forth, and what more should an artist do? Considered from the point of view of a creator of character he ranks next to him who made Hamlet. Had he been articulate, he might have sat beside him. The only man who can touch the hem of his garment is George Meredith. Meredith is a prose Browning, and so is Browning. He used poetry as a medium for writing in prose.

—Oscar Wilde, *The Critic as Artist,* 1891

ARTHUR CHRISTOPHER BENSON
"THE POETRY OF EDMUND GOSSE" (1894)

Arthur Christopher Benson was an English author, critic, and academic, the master (president) of Magdalene College, Cambridge. This brief statement is taken from his study of another contemporary Victorian English writer, Edmund Gosse. Benson is describing in metaphor his ideas concerning Browning's poetry, seeing it as sublime as a whole, but having awkward obstructions impeding a reader's pleasurable impressions. The obstructing boulders may be a reference to Browning's use of language or perhaps to his obscure thought process, and while Benson says that they have a particular, rugged quality worthy of appreciation, they are, generally speaking, out of place within the broader scene. In other words, even though Browning's lack of grace in language and his difficult leaps of imagination within his verse can be recognized as having something admirable about them in and of themselves, they are not, Benson claims, fit to be found in such places as the sublime realm of poetry.

Browning's style may be compared to a Swiss pasture, where the green meadows which form the foreground of a sublime landscape are yet cumbered with awkward blocks and boulders—things not without a certain rough dignity of their own, but essentially out of place.

—Arthur Christopher Benson, "The Poetry of
Edmund Gosse," 1894, from *Essays*, 1896, p. 298

George Saintsbury (1896)

George Edward Bateman Saintsbury was an English author and literary critic. This extract is taken from his critical study and history of nineteenth-century literature. The piece is valuable as an objective summary of Browning's critical reception over the years, its suggested reasons for the variance of opinion and the related problems that the poet faced from a variety of critical sources.

Saintsbury declares that Browning's reputation was held back for many years by the reading public as well as by academics who were predisposed against him. Initially, Saintsbury says, these prejudices were ignorant; in Browning's later years, they were often caused by the craze for the poet, the *"cultus"* that grew up around him swearing fervent support for his work. Browning's recognition of the society bearing his name was not something that Saintsbury believes that many other authors would have indulged in themselves, and the society's sense of its own self-importance is evidenced by its production of a Browning dictionary, which suggests that the study of the poet was something of a mystery into which initiation was required. It was not surprising then that the society caused a reaction opposite to the impression it had hoped to achieve. Many turned against Browning and his verse even more intensely as a result.

Saintsbury maintains that it is only the most blinkered critic who cannot see what have always been Browning's poetic shortcomings, especially during that period between 1870 and 1885 when the poet wrote and published an unusually large amount of material, its quality suffering in direct relationship to its quantity. He suggests that Browning may have deliberately attempted to provoke critical opinion in his younger years through formal, metrical, and thematic innovations in his poetry, but that in his later years he had become fixed in those attitudes due to the practice of an unconscious habit. In summary, Saintsbury wishes that Browning had been more careful with his craft and less prolific in his output, saying that much of his later work might be safely discarded as unworthy of the man and his art.

Nevertheless, Saintsbury says that there is indeed much to admire in Browning's verse. If his longer poems have the greatest flaws, they also show his gift for dramatic characterization, for pathos, passion, and psychological insight. Saintsbury suggests that, while Browning may have been virtually hopeless in the formal skills required of dramatic construction, the quality of the drama depicted in his human studies is matchless.

It is as a lyricist and In those shorter poems that Saintsbury says Browning truly reveals his genius, and a genius of the highest order. Even though these shorter lyrics still contain the same defects contained in his longer verse, they do so to a much lesser degree and remain uniformly fine from his younger years to the end of his poetic career. If the English poets Shakespeare, Robert Burns, Percy Bysshe Shelley, and Samuel Taylor Coleridge surpass Browning in their ability as lyricists in the conventionally "poetic" sense, Browning's verse is unequalled by any other poet in the fullness of its life and thought, the human behavior and psychology it portrays.

Critical estimate of Browning's poetry was for years hampered by, and cannot even yet be said to have been quite cleared from, the violent prepossessions of public opinion respecting him. For more than a generation, in the ordinary sense, he was more or less passionately admired by a few devotees, stupidly or blindly ignored by the public in general, and persistently sneered at, lectured, or simply disliked by the majority of academically educated critics. The sharp revulsion of his later years has been noticed; and it amounted almost to this, that while dislike to him in those who had intelligently, if somewhat narrowly, disapproved of his ways was not much affected, a Browning *cultus*, almost as blind as the former pooh-poohing or ignoring, set in, and extended from a considerable circle of ardent worshippers to the public at large. A "Browning Society" was founded in 1881, and received from the poet a kind of countenance which would certainly not have been extended to it by most English men of letters. During his later years handbooks solemnly addressed to neophytes in Browningism, as if the cult were a formal science or art, appeared with some frequency; and there has been even a bulky *Browning Dictionary,* which not only expounds the more recondite (and, it is fair to say, tolerably frequent) allusions of the master, but provides for his disciples something to make up for the ordinary classical and other dictionaries with which, it seemed to be presumed, their previous education would have made them little conversant.

This not very wise adulation in its turn not unnaturally excited a sort of irritation and dislike, to a certain extent renewing the old prejudice in a new form. To those who could discard extraneous considerations and take Browning simply as he was, he must, from a period which only very old men can now remember, have always appeared a very great, though also a very far from perfect poet. His imperfections were always on the surface, though perhaps they were not always confined to it; and only uncritical partisanship could at any time have denied them, while some of them became noticeably worse in the period of rapid composition or publication from 1870 to 1885. A large license of unconventionally, and even of defiance of convention, may be claimed by, and should be allowed to, persons of genius such as Mr. Browning undoubtedly possessed. But it can hardly be denied that he, like his older contemporary Carlyle, whose example may not have been without influence upon him, did set at naught not merely the traditions, but the sound norms and rules of English phrase to a rather unnecessary extent. A beginning of deliberate provocation and challenge, passing into an after-period of more or less involuntary persistence in an exaggeration of the mannerisms at first more or less deliberately adopted, is apt to be shown by persons who set themselves in this way to innovate; and it was shown by Mr. Browning. It is impossible for any intelligent admirer to maintain, except as a paradox, that his strange modulations, his cacophonies of rhythm and rhyme, his occasional adoption of the foreshortened language of the telegraph or the comic stage, and many other peculiarities of his, were not things which a more perfect art would have either absorbed and transformed, or at least have indulged in with far less luxuriance. Nor does it seem much more reasonable for anybody to contend that his fashion of soul-dissection at a hand-gallop, in drama, in monologue, in lay sermon, was not largely, even grossly, abused. Sometimes the thing was not worth doing at all—there are at least half a dozen of the books between *The Ring and the Book* and *Asolando* from the whole of which a judicious lover of poetry would not care to save more than the bulk of the smallest of them should they be menaced with entire destruction. Even in the best of these what is good could generally, if not always, have been put at the length of the shorter *Men and Women* with no loss, nay, with great advantage. The obscurity so much talked of was to some extent from the very first, and to the last continued to be, in varying degrees, an excuse, or at least an occasion, for putting at great length thought that was not always so far from commonplace as it looked into expression which was very often not so much original as unkempt. "Less matter with more art" was the demand which might have been made of Mr. Browning from first to last, and with increasing instance as he became more popular.

But though no competent lover of poetry can ever have denied the truth and cogency of these objections, the admission of them can never, in any competent lover of poetry, have obscured or prevented an admiration of Browning none the less intense because not wholly unreserved. Even his longer poems, in which his faults were most apparent, possessed an individuality of the first order, combined the intellectual with no small part of the sensual attraction of poetry after a fashion not otherwise paralleled in England since Dryden, and provided an extraordinary body of poetical exercise and amusement. The pathos, the power, at times the humour, of the singular soul-studies which he was so fond of projecting with little accessory of background upon his canvas, could not be denied, and have not often been excelled. If he was not exactly what is commonly called orthodox in religion, and if his philosophy was of a distinctly vague order, he was always "on the side of the angels" in theology, in metaphysics, in ethics; and his politics, if exceedingly indistinct and unpractical, were always noble and generous. Further, though he seems to have been utterly destitute of the slightest gift of dramatic construction, he had no mean share of a much rarer gift, that of dramatic character; and in a century of descriptions of nature his, if not most exquisite, have a freedom and truth, a largeness of outline combined with felicity of colour, not elsewhere to be discovered.

But it is as a lyric poet that Browning ranks highest; and in this highest class it is impossible to refuse him all but the highest rank, in some few cases the very highest. He understood love pretty thoroughly; and when a lyric poet understands love thoroughly there is little doubt of his position. But he understood many other things as well, and could give strange and delightful voice to them. Even his lyrics, still more his short non-lyrical poems, admirable as they often are, and closely as they group with the lyrics proper, are not untouched by his inseparable defect. He cannot be prevented from inserting now and then in the midst of exquisite passages more or fewer of his quirks and cranks of thought and phrase, of his vernacularity or his euphuism, of his outrageous rhymes (which, however, are seldom or never absolutely bad), of those fantastic tricks of his in general which remind one of nothing so much as of dashing a bladder with rattling peas in the reader's face just at the height of the passion or the argument.

Yet the beauty, the charm, the variety, the vigour of these short poems are as wonderful as the number of them. He never lost the secret of them to his latest years. The delicious lines "Never the time and the place, And the loved one all together" are late; and there are half a dozen pieces in *Asolando,* latest of all, which exhibit to the full the almost bewildering beauty of combined sound, thought, and sight, the clash of castanets and the thrill of flutes, the glow of flower and sunset, the subtle appeal for sympathy in feeling or assent in judgment. The song snatches in *Pippa Passes,* "Through the Metidja," "The Lost Leader," "In a Gondola," "Earth's Immortalities," "Mesmerism," "Women and Roses," "Love among the Ruins," "A Toccata of Galuppi's," "Prospice," "Rabbi Ben Ezra," "Porphyria's Lover," "After," with scores of others, and the "Last Ride Together," the poet's most perfect thing, at the head of the list, are such poems as a very few—Shakespeare, Shelley, Burns, Coleridge—may surpass now and then in pure lyrical perfection, as Tennyson may excel in dreamy ecstasy, as some seventeenth century songsters may outgo in quaint and perfect fineness of touch, but such as are nowhere to be surpassed or equalled for a certain volume and variety of appeal, for fulness of life and thought, of action and passion.

—George Saintsbury, *A History of Nineteenth Century Literature*, 1896, pp. 272–276

AUGUSTINE BIRRELL
"ROBERT BROWNING" (1897)

Augustine Birrell was an English politician, lawyer, and author. In this extract, Birrell describes Browning's slow progress to fame and recognition and the difficulties the poet had to overcome to achieve this progress. Birrell gives the reader an idea of the critical reception afforded Browning's verse in the closing years of the nineteenth century, almost ten years after the poet's death. Birrell suggests that not enough time has passed since the poet's death to assess the true worth of his verse. He recognizes that, for many, Browning's art was strange and obscure, that the poet had neither the family background nor friends to allow him to advance swiftly and unhindered in the world of letters, that no university encouraged him or eased his way in life. Browning's fame was slowly and difficultly won. Birrell, in the same manner in which other critics have approached and praised Browning's work in this volume, focuses on the color and vitality found in its depictions of life as being its greatest asset.

Robert Browning is far too near us to enable even the most far-seeing to lay out his kingdom by metes and bounds. Besides, who ever dare tether the spirit of poesy? It bloweth where it lists. In old days one was sometimes asked, 'But who reads Browning?' It was always easy to reply, 'More people than are dreamed of in your philosophy.' But that particular foolish question, at all events, is no longer asked. The obscure author of the undoubtedly obscure *Sordello,* who came from nobody knew where, and wrote a poem about nobody knew what; who was vouched for by none of the great schools and universities, of which Englishmen are wont to make much; who courted no critic and sought no man's society; slowly, very slowly, won his audience, made his way, earned his fame without puffs preliminary in the newspapers, or any other of the now well-worn expedients of attracting attention to that lamentable object one's self. . . .

Is it any wonder we love Browning? With him life is full of great things—of love and beauty and joy. His poems, particularly of that period which ends in *The Ring and the Book,* are all aglow with the colour of life, its many-hued interests. Hence, while we are reading him, we find it easy to share his strenuous hope, his firm faith, particularly his undying faith in immortality. It is the poverty of our lives that renders it hard to believe in immortality.

—Augustine Birrell, "Robert Browning," 1897,
from *Essays and Addresses,* 1901, pp. 185–194

Thomas Wentworth Higginson "The Biography of Browning's Fame" (1897)

Thomas Wentworth Higginson was an American minister, author, a prominent abolitionist, and a soldier in the Civil War. In this extract he relates how, as a young man in the 1840s, he read and memorized both

Lord Alfred Tennyson's and Browning's early works. It was the former poet's verse in particular which he found most accessible. Now writing at the end of the century, he finds that while Tennyson's verse still holds its charm for him, it is to Browning that he returns more and more eagerly. The latter poet's work continues to offer up new ideas and becomes of greater value to Higginson as time passes.

⚡⚡⚡

I began to read the two poets (Tennyson and Browning) at about the same period, 1841, when I was not quite eighteen, and long before the collected poems of either had been brought together. I then read them both constantly and knew by heart most of those of Tennyson, in particular, before I was twenty years old. To my amazement I now find that I can read these last but little; the charm of the versification remains, but they seem to yield me nothing new; whereas the earlier poems of Browning, *Paracelsus, Sordello, Bells and Pomegranates*—to which last I was among the original subscribers—appear just as rich a mine as ever; I read them over and over, never quite reaching the end of them. In case I were going to prison and could have but one book, I should think it a calamity to have Tennyson offered me instead of Browning, simply because Browning has proved himself to possess, for me at least, so much more staying power.

—Thomas Wentworth Higginson, "The Biography
of Browning's Fame," The Boston Browning
Society Papers, 1897, p. 5

FRANCIS THOMPSON "ACADEMY PORTRAITS: XXVI. ROBERT BROWNING" (1897)

Francis Thompson was an English poet and author who had been rescued from vagrancy and opium addiction by admirers of his verse. In this extract from Thompson's "Academy Portraits," or character studies, Browning is recognized at the end of the 1890s as being, as he was for much of his life, a poet still often argued over in terms of the quality of his verse. Thompson makes it clear that Browning's status as a poet is indisputable despite what other men in the literary world, such as W.E. Henley and Coventry Patmore, might suggest. As so many before them, these critics believe that Browning's rejection of conventional form and rhythm have destroyed any claim he might have made to being a composer of art. Like Oscar Wilde in a previous extract, the charge that

Browning did not "sing" is made. Thompson agrees that Browning's voice was decidedly "rough."

But Thompson suggests that a distinction should be made between roughness and ruggedness in poetic meter. Unlike Shakespeare, who displayed a rugged grandeur in many passages of his dramas, Browning seems to have enjoyed the harsh roughness displayed in his verse as much for its own sake as any other. But Browning, says Thompson, like John Donne, the seventeenth-century English metaphysical poet whose verse was as rough as any other he can suggest, was able to command attention through this same quality of meter. If there was a "defect" in his poetic style, and there is no question that Thompson considers Browning's style to be defective, the quality of his subject matter more than made up for it.

—ᔕᔕ—   —ᔕᔕ—   —ᔕᔕ—

Browning is the most hotly disputed of all indisputable poets. Such a critic as Mr. Henley will not hear of his being a poet at all; neither would such a critic as Mr. Coventry Patmore. The reason of both was the same: Browning's extreme disregard of recognised poetic form and conventions. He would, even in the midst of his most poetical poems, introduce passages of unquestionable rhymed prose; he could never proceed for long without exhibiting flagrant roughness and unmetricalness in metre. Consequently, such critics said that he lacked the most primary requisite of a singer—he could not sing. In our opinion, there are two distinct things to be separated in metre—ruggedness and roughness. . . . Shakespeare, in his greatest blank verse, that of his latest period, is rugged in the very nature of his harmonics. They roll with the grandeur of mountain boulders, only to be understood by a large and masculine ear. It is not so with Browning. There are in him no harmonies moving on so colossal a scale, that the individual frictions play only the part of the frictions in a male, as compared with a female voice. It is not ruggedness; it is veritable roughness, like the roughness of a harsh male voice. We must allow, therefore, that he lacks something of the quality of a singer. Yet it sometimes happens that a singer with a rough voice commands attention in despite of its roughness. And so, we think, it is with Browning. Donne is another example. Criticism has come round to the recognition of Donne, in spite of the roughest utterance ever employed by a poet of like gifts. Upon this precedent we rest our recognition of Browning as a poet. He went out of his way to be rough, apparently for roughness' sake, and without any large scale of harmonies to justify it. But his intrinsic qualities, far more than in the case of Donne, make him a poet in the teeth of this defect of execution: such is our opinion. Fineness of manner has often carried off smallness of matter. And, though to a rarer extent, we think that fineness of matter may sometimes carry off defect of manner.

> —Francis Thompson, "Academy Portraits: XXVI.
> Robert Browning," *Academy*, May 8, 1897, p. 499

ARTHUR WAUGH (1899)

Arthur Waugh was an English publisher, literary critic, and author of the first biography of Lord Alfred Tennyson in 1892, the year of the laureate's death. In the following extract, Waugh reveals a rather unusual argument against Browning's status as a great poet, stating that his claim to fame has been queried because he did nothing for England and spoke of very little that was of value to his immediate time. If this argument seems peculiar, readers might consider just how valuable Tennyson's work was relative to this time period ("The Charge of the Light Brigade," for example) and should also consider the verse of the poet Rudyard Kipling, nicknamed the "poet of Empire" and one of the most popular writers in England at the end of the nineteenth century. Certain historical events such as the Boer War and the jingoism that marked the last years of the century are no doubt directly relevant to the arguments against Browning's importance that Waugh raises here.

Waugh, then, states that Browning's poetry was not the most relevant to his times and suggests that one reason he was not more popular was because he did not write for the marketplace, did not compose "ballads" or popular songs (Kipling's collection of poetry *Barrack-Room Ballads* had been published a few years earlier in 1892). Waugh maintains that Browning was not a poet just for England but for the world as a whole and that his portrayals of humanity are relevant far beyond the shores of his native land.

Waugh feels that it is impossible to speculate about how popular Browning will become in the future, remarking on how long it took him to achieve any name for himself in his own lifetime, and suggests that his own generation's grandchildren might well hold Browning in higher esteem. Like many other critics' extracts contained in this volume, Waugh believes that Browning was second only to Shakespeare: in this instance in his capacity to depict that to which humanity aspires.

The extract concludes with a fine, if romantic, depiction of Browning's memorial in the Poets' Corner of Westminster Abbey in London (readers might compare Henry James's description also included in this volume). Waugh makes clear his position about the poet's genius as a writer when he states that the deceased author has been grouped with his peers, or equals, in the abbey. The final lines of verse are taken from Browning's poem "The Grammarian's Funeral" and are used by Waugh to show that the poet's place in the literary pantheon is no doubt one much higher than his contemporaries can suspect at that time.

It has been objected against Browning's claim to greatness that he did but little to reflect the aims and aspirations of his own countrymen, that he was very little moved by the stream of events, and that his historical value is affected by his lack of immediate value to his time. It is true, indeed, that Browning was at no time a "topical" poet; and much of his long unpopularity was, no doubt, due to his disinclination to come down into the market-place, with his singing robes about him, and make great ballads of the day to the chorus of the crowd. But there is a higher part even than that of a national poet; and Browning is, in a very real sense, the poet, not of England alone, but of the world. His attitude to men and life was never distraught by petty interests of blood or party: the one claim upon him was the claim of humanity. He was a man, and nothing that pertained to man was foreign to himself. What will be his final place in the long array of English poetry it is still impossible to say. It took long for him to come into his own, and even then many outside developments helped him. We think ourselves to-day far wiser than our grandparents: we fancy, perhaps, that, if *Pauline* had come to one of us fresh from the press, we should have hailed it forthwith as a work of coming genius. All this may be, and yet the last word will always remain to be said. Time brings in, not only revenges, but redresses; and it is probable that Robert Browning is not even yet appreciated as he will be by our children's children. But even now we know him for much that he is,—the subtlest, strongest master of human aspiration, save only Shakespeare, that has ever dignified the English language with poetry; a man who felt for men with all the intensity of a great, unselfish heart; a genius crowned with one guerdon which genius cannot always boast,—a pure and noble life. Standing in the twilight shades of the whispering Abbey, in that sacred corner full of haunting melodies and immortal yearnings, we may gladly feel that, however long and weary was the neglect of him, he is now, at last, gathered to his peers.

Lofty designs must close in like effects: Loftily lying,
Leave him,—still loftier than the world suspects, Living and dying.

—Arthur Waugh, *Robert Browning,*
1899, pp. 150–152

WORKS

The following section begins with critical examinations of specific publications by Browning before moving on to more general studies of the
poet's work and thought. As in previous sections of this volume, there is
a startlingly extreme variety of critical stances in regard to Browning's
poetry and drama, and these positions do not greatly alter in the course
of the poet's career, nor after his death when retrospectives of his entire
catalog began to be published. Readers will benefit from seeing the perspective of criticism on the poet and his verse, his craft and thought, over
a period of approximately seventy years. What is perhaps most surprising
is how little entrenched positions alter over this period; certain events,
such as the formation of the Browning Society and the poet's interment
in Poets' Corner in Westminster Abbey, cause some critical fluster, but,
generally speaking, the arguments in favor of, and against, Browning's
poetry remain familiar. There are distinctive voices in this section, however, most notably those of George Santayana and G.K. Chesterton at its
conclusion: Contrasting these two critical extracts should prove of great
value to readers. Those interested in the development of a young poet's
career will find the initial extracts by critics and friends eager to boost
Browning's reputation of particular interest. No critic takes an ambiva-
lent stance on Browning's work, and each has something to say about
the man and his verse. Many might have seen this as praise enough, for it
might well be true that, to paraphrase Oscar Wilde, the only thing worse
than being written about is not being written about. Browning certainly
would have a great deal written about him and his poetry over a poetic
career of more than half a century.

PARACELSUS

W.J. Fox (1835)

The critic W.J. Fox had championed Browning's first publication, *Pauline*, in the *Monthly Repository* in 1833 and in this extract continues his praise for Browning's second published work, *Paracelsus*. He applauds the labor and skill that have gone into the construction of the poem and, while recognizing that there are flaws in it, states that they are fundamental to the enduring qualities of the verse, not based on some haphazard, short-lived whimsy on the poet's part designed solely for the entertainment and delight of his readership.

This poem is what few modern publications either are, or affect to be; it is a work. It is the result of thought, skill, and toil. Defects and irregularities there may be, but they are those of a building which the architect has erected for posterity, and not the capricious anomalies of the wattled pleasure house, which has served its turn when the summer-day's amusement is over, and may be blown about by the next breeze, or washed away by the next torrent, to be replaced by another as fantastic and as transient.

—W.J. Fox, *Monthly Repository*, November 1835, p. 716

LEIGH HUNT (1835)

Leigh Hunt was an English critic, essayist, journal editor, and poet. In the following extract, Hunt praises the genius behind *Paracelsus* but questions the suggestion made in the poem's preface that Browning had been writing and editing the verse for six months after its initial idea came to him. Hunt maintains that the genius behind the work would surely have made the poem finer than it appeared upon publication had the six months really been a beneficial part of the creative process.

Hunt was a product of English romanticism, and the reader might note that the predominant attitude struck in this extract is one of unquestioning support for the ideal of the poet as "genius." To the romantics, the poet was often simply an inspired amanuensis, and, as such, Hunt's criticism, important if mild, that Browning had taken six months to write a poem that in the end was of the same quality it had been at its conception, should be understood as typical of his generation. The extract praises Browning but contains in its approbation an implicit criticism.

Some questions may be raised as to points in the execution of Mr Browning's poem, but there can be none as to the high poetic power displayed in it. There are, as it appears to us, some marks of haste in the composition, and we should have been better pleased with the absence both of the statement in the preface, that the poem had not been imagined six months before its publication, and of any ground for making such a statement; for we cannot doubt that the same genius which, in the space of time mentioned, produced the work as it now appears, would not have spent six months longer in brooding over its conceptions and their first rapid embodiment, without making the finished whole something still finer than it is.

—Leigh Hunt, *London Journal*,
November 21, 1835, p. 405

JOHN FORSTER "EVIDENCES OF A NEW GENIUS FOR DRAMATIC POETRY" (1836)

Browning considered that John Forster's reviews of *Paracelsus* played a large part in altering the initial, critical disquiet with the poem. The two men had met, and Forster was favorably enough impressed with the poet to write the following review in praise of his work. Considering that Browning was a young, unheralded poet of twenty-four, Forster's statement that he should be classed immediately with Shelley, Wordsworth, and Coleridge, the most applauded and popular poets of the period, is high praise indeed. It is clear from the extract that Browning has not met with the success Forster suggests will ultimately come to him, but the critic claims that genius is always eventually recognized. The poem is described as "scantily-noticed" and Forster attempts as best he can to encourage an alteration of that fact. He seems almost to try to encourage Browning, who no doubt felt somewhat despondent with his poem's critical reception, as much as he does to encourage the general reader to open, consider, appreciate, and thereby benefit from *Paracelsus*.

(Paracelsus) opens a deeper vein of thought, of feeling, and of passion, than any poet has attempted for years. Without the slightest hesitation we name Mr. Robert Browning at once with Shelley, Coleridge, Wordsworth. He has entitled himself to a place among the acknowledged poets of the age. This opinion will possibly startle many persons; but it is most sincere. It is no practice of ours to think nothing of an author because all the world have not pronounced

in his favour, any more than we would care to offer him our sympathy and concern on the score of the world's indifference. A man of genius, we have already intimated, needs neither the one nor the other. He who is conscious of great powers can satisfy himself by their unwearied exercise alone. His day will come. He need never be afraid that truth and nature will wear out, or that Time will not eventually claim for its own all that is the handywork of Nature. Mr. Browning is a man of genius, he has in himself all the elements of a great poet, philosophical as well as dramatic,—

The youngest he
That sits in shadow of Apollo's tree

—but he sits there, and with as much right to his place as the greatest of the men that are around him have to theirs. For the reception that his book has met with he was doubtless already well prepared,—as well for the wondering ignorance that has scouted it, as for the condescending patronage which has sought to bring it forward, as one brings forward a bashful child to make a doubtful display of its wit and learning. "We hope the best; put a good face on the matter; but are sadly afraid the thing cannot answer." We tell Mr. Browning, on the other hand, what we do not think *he* needs to be told, that the thing WILL answer. He has written a book that will live—he has scattered the seeds of much thought among his countrymen—he has communicated an impulse and increased activity to reason and inquiry, as well as a pure and high delight to every cultivated mind;—and this in the little and scantily-noticed volume of *Paracelsus!*

—John Forster, "Evidences of a New Genius
for Dramatic Poetry," *New Monthly Magazine,*
March 1836, pp. 289–290

R.H. HORNE "ROBERT BROWNING
AND J.W. MARSTON" (1844)

Richard Hengist Horne (born Richard Henry Horne) was an English poet, dramatist, critic, and editor. In the following extract, Horne makes a comparison between Browning's creative attempts in *Paracelsus* and the content of the poem itself. The poem is a study of the temptations of genius and a story of ambition and failure. The Promethean character (Prometheus being the Greek mythological figure who stole fire from the gods and brought it to humans, only to be horrifically punished) is critically classed with Faust (the character portrayed by a number of writers, notably Christopher Marlowe and Johann Wolfgang von Goethe, who makes a deal with the devil for personal ambition's sake). Horne states that such characters whose ambitions lie beyond human capacity must always, naturally, fail, and his suggestion is that Browning's creativity and attempt in writing his work can never match the lofty ambition of the ideal conceived by the poet. Horne says that original it might be, positive aspects it might have, but the poem is evidence of a premature ambition, for Browning's youthful, poetic powers are not yet sufficient to the portrayal of such themes. Readers seeking a brilliant rebuttal to Horne's position need look no further than G.K. Chesterton's essay at this volume's conclusion. The argument contained therein speaks to Horne's stance on human incapacity and inadequacy.

Paracelsus is evidently the work of a young poet of premature powers—of one who sought to project his imagination beyond the bounds of his future, as well as present, experience, and whose intellect had resolved to master all the results thus obtained. We say the powers were premature, simply because such a design could only be conceived by the most vigorous energies of a spirit just issuing forth with "blazing wings," too full of strength and too far of sight to believe in the ordinary laws and boundaries of mortality. It is the effort of a mind that wilfully forgets, and resolves to set aside its corporeal conditions. Even its possible failure is airily alluded to at the outset, and treated in the same way, not merely as no sort of reason for hesitating to make the attempt to gain "forbidden knowledge," but as a result which is solely referable to the Cause of its own aspirations and impulses. . . .

A Promethean character pervades the poem throughout; in the main design, as well as the varied aspirations and struggles to attain knowledge, and power, and happiness for mankind. But at the same time there is an intense craving after the forbidden secrets of creation, and eternity, and power, which place *Paracelsus* in the same class as *Faust,* and in close affinity with all those works, the object of which is an attempt to penetrate the mysteries of existence—the infinity within us and without us. Need it be said, that the result is in all the same?—and the baffled magic—the sublime occult—the impassioned poetry—all display the same ashes which were once wings. The form, the mode, the impetus and course of thought and emotion, admit, however, of certain varieties, and *Paracelsus* is an original work. Its aim is of the highest kind; in full accord and harmony with the spirit of the age; and we admit that it has been accomplished, in so far as such a design can well be: for since the object of all such abstractions as *Paracelsus* must necessarily fail, individually and practically, the true end obtained is that of refining and elevating others, by the contemplation of such efforts, and giving a sort of polarity to the vague impulses of mankind towards the lofty and the beneficent. It also endeavours to sound the depths of existence for hidden treasures of being.

—R.H. Horne, "Robert Browning and J.W. Marston,"
A New Spirit of the Age, 1844, pp. 280–282

THOMAS LOVELL BEDDOES (1844)

Thomas Lovell Beddoes was an English poet and dramatist. This short extract from a letter describing Beddoes's journey through Basel suggests the tremendous difference between the real, historical character of Paracelsus and the Faustian figure from Browning's poetic description of the man. Beddoes's claim is in stark contrast to that made by Harriet Waters Preston in her extract immediately following this one.

My journey brought me thro' Basel, where Paracelsus (not Mr. Browning's) (the historical P. was a complete charlatan, seldom sober, clever and cunning, living on the appetite of his contemporaneous public for the philosopher's stone and the universal medicine; castrated as a child by the jaws of a pig, all his life a vagabond, who at last died drunk in his single shirt at Salzburg:) where P. burnt Galen's works openly as professor of the university, beginning the medical reform so, as Luther did that in religion by his public conflagration of the bull launched against him.

—Thomas Lovell Beddoes, letter to
Thomas Forbes Kendall, November 13, 1844

HARRIET WATERS PRESTON "ROBERT AND ELIZABETH BROWNING" (1899)

Harriet Waters Preston's short extract from the American literary and cultural journal the *Atlantic* praises Browning's *Paracelsus* for its content, language, and the subtle imagination and thought it displayed. But it is the recognition of his poetic gift by Browning himself that Waters Preston states is the most important aspect of the work, for the poet had with his poem realized an appreciation of human character as one, organically related whole. Waters Preston recognizes Browning's ability to magically restore the forgotten historical figure of Paracelsus to life; unlike the previous extracted letter by Lovell Beddoes, she claims that Browning has presented a historically accurate portrayal of Paracelsus, proved by subsequent research. An interesting biographical point is also made in Waters Preston's extract: With the publication of this poem Browning made the acquaintance of various famous, contemporary authors, most notably William Wordsworth and Thomas Carlyle.

—⁓⁓⁓—   —⁓⁓⁓—   —⁓⁓⁓—

... Paracelsus lives, and will continue to live, not so much through the subtlety of its metaphysical speculations, and through certain scattered passages of the narrative, which are instinct with the highest kind of imaginative beauty, nor even through the rich and haunting music of the superb song, "Over the sea our galleys went;" but because in it the youth of twenty-three discovered his own distinctive and surpassing gift,—the divination of individual human character as an organic whole. Nobody had known for several hundred years, nor cared particularly to know, what manner of man Paracelsus was. The callow youth at Camberwell resuscitated and evoked him out of the past; not without patient research, to be sure, yet still by a species of magic. The dry and laborious investigations of later students have all gone to confirm the main truth to historic fact of what then seemed the creation of an audacious fancy.

Paracelsus, in the nature of things, could never have won more than a success of esteem; but incidentally it brought its author the acquaintance of Wordsworth, Carlyle, Talfourd, Horne, and Landor, and fairly launched him among men of letters.

—Harriet Waters Preston, "Robert and
Elizabeth Browning," Atlantic, June 1899, p. 814

STRAFFORD

WILLIAM CHARLES MACREADY (1837)

William Charles Macready, the actor, critic, theater manager, and friend of Browning who presented Strafford onstage for its short run, here praises reading the drama. In reality, he was not particularly enamored of Browning's play as it appeared on his stage, although that was no doubt as much for commercial reasons as for any other. Here he shows that his attitude to the quality of the art itself was not a concern. He accurately touches on Browning's intention in writing the drama (and also its shortcomings in many critics' minds): It is not dramatic action itself, nor emotional drama as it affects character, that is important to Browning; rather it is how character itself is a type of internal dynamic action. The "drama" of *Strafford* was virtually all psychological and self-reflective. *Strafford* would importantly develop for Browning the poetic possibilities of dramatic monologue as evidenced in his later work, and in this extract the reader can see the incipient, critical realization that Browning's artistic trajectory would reveal many things quite new and original.

——————

Read *Strafford* in the evening, which I fear is too historical; it is the policy of the man, and its consequence upon him, not the heart, temper, feelings, that work on this policy, which Browning has portrayed—and how admirably.

—William Charles Macready, *Diary*,
March 19, 1837

Herman Merivale "Browning's *Strafford; A Tragedy*" (1837)

Herman Merivale was an English academic, civil servant, and critic. In the following extract, Merivale sees in *Strafford* an excess of affectation and bad taste in the language of Browning. The general tone of the article is avuncular (and/or patronizing), Merivale suggesting that Browning, a young man, has a great many talents as an artist that should not be squandered in pursuing the type of (or rather the lack of) art shown in *Strafford*. Merivale makes it clear, therefore, that his purpose in criticizing the play is not malicious, and he praises certain aspects and qualities of Browning's drama; but it is, he says, Browning's lack of taste in dramatic matters that have allowed him to write such a play.

Readers might compare the impetus behind Merivale's criticism with the point made in the following extract by Charlotte Porter concerning preconceived critical notions about what precisely constitutes drama.

——————

In the general phraseology of the play,—even in the manner in which the rough old Puritans address each other,—there is a sort of affected, fondling tone, which perfectly disconcerts us. As for poor Lady Carlisle, seeing that she is desperately in love with Strafford from the beginning of the play, we can perhaps excuse his calling her 'girl', and 'Lucy', in every line; but really we do not think there was any thing in the character of the lady to justify him in supposing that Denzil Hollis would have taken the liberty of addressing her as 'girl' too.

All these, we must once more repeat it, are, chiefly, defects of taste. They are peculiarities belonging to that which (by the leave of Mr Landor) we must still take the liberty of calling, for want of a better name, the 'Cockney school' of dramatic authorship. And we have not been thus severe in our observations on the bad taste and affectation with which this play abounds, from any malice of criticism. But the author is a young man, and this essay exhibits powers which we can ill afford to see thrown away in the pursuit of false reputation. Had it been otherwise, we should not have taken the trouble to examine his claims to the distinction which he has earned. His defects are fostered by a corrupt taste in theatrical matters; and those defects in turn, meeting with applause instead of correction, tend to increase and perpetuate the evil. For the rest, his success is a proof that his work affords striking situations and dramatic interest. He has developed his matter with breadth and simplicity of purpose, instead of breaking it up into highly-wrought details and insulated scenes; and this is the first great requisite in order to produce effect on miscellaneous readers and spectators. Even his style, of which we have thought it our duty to present a few singular specimens, is, on other occasions, wanting neither in power nor richness. When he lays aside affectation, and condescends to employ continuous dramatic dialogue, there is an energy about him not unworthy of the scenes and epochs which he has chosen to represent.

—Herman Merivale, "Browning's *Strafford*;
A Tragedy," *Edinburgh Review*, July 1837,
pp. 147–148

CHARLOTTE PORTER "DRAMATIC MOTIVE IN BROWNING'S *STRAFFORD*" (1893)

Charlotte Porter's review of dramatic motive as it was portrayed in *Strafford* was written almost sixty years after the play's short run onstage. Porter reviews the play's place in European dramatic history, stating that the problems inherent to the theme of Browning's drama made it difficult for critics to place it within the history of staged performance. The subject of *Strafford* had been immediately seen as a difficult one for these reasons, but Porter, looking back from the distance of more than half a century, places the play within a more modern context, referring to the relationship of the individual to impersonal forces and the conundrums of modern existence. Porter, again with the benefit of critical hindsight, recognizes that for many of Browning's detractors, their preconceived opinions of what constituted drama required them to reject Browning's play; rather, Porter states, the possibilities and potentialities that were afforded to dramatic art with *Strafford* will ultimately prove to have been of significant importance in the development of stagecraft.

Is there a more potential moment in the life of England than that which poises, in even scales, the struggle between the king's prerogative and the people's will? Is there another man than Strafford who so perfectly incarnates the fated issue of that portentous clash of the old with the new? It is this moment that Browning selects for the opening of his first stage-play; it is this man he makes its protagonist.

The subject he chose has been called difficult. Its great difficulty consists, I think, in the peculiarly modern quality of its motive, and in the fact that an original path for it had to be struck out. Fate steers the action of the Greek tragedies through the personal adventures of the heroes of famous houses. Revenge, reconciliation, pride, ambition, passion, dominate the later European drama, or that punctilio of "honour" which Spanish playwrights introduced and which has been cunningly appropriated by France no less in the romantic drama of Victor Hugo than in the classic drama of Corneille. What road in common have such plays of family or personal interest with the play whose attempt must be to show personal interests and abilities in the vague grasp of an impersonal and unrecognised—until then an almost unexistent—power? . . .

Strafford rests under this adverse cloud of pre-conceived opinion as to the capabilities of art. Yet, in the light which Browning's genius has shed upon these "possibilities of future evil," I believe a new fact in the development of dramatic craft may be descried which promises to show that they are not necessarily undramatic.

—Charlotte Porter, "Dramatic Motive in
Browning's *Strafford*" (1893), *The Boston
Browning Society Papers*, 1897, pp. 190–191

SORDELLO

RICHARD HENGIST HORNE
"ROBERT BROWNING'S POEMS" (1842)

The following extract from R.H. Horne's study of Browning's poems for *The Church of England Quarterly* details the critic's attitude toward Browning's *Sordello*. Horne replies to various critical attacks on the poem that had claimed the verse was inarticulate and incomprehensible, stating that the work has passages of the highest quality and that literary attitudes have been extreme to a reprehensible degree. He recognizes, however, the difficulties in the poem calling it a modern hieroglyph but one, he believes, that should be studied, treasured, and used as the basis for students' poetic instruction. Horne finds the poem echoes other poets' styles without compromising its own originality. If Browning is ever capable of focusing the chaotic quality of his allusions and themes, Horne suggests, the poet will be recognized as the visionary discoverer of a poetic promised land, an artistic Columbus.

Horne's suggestions concerning the difficulties faced by readers of *Sordello* are equally true about Browning's other poetic works in terms of their often chaotic forms and movement of thought. As many other critics have suggested, Browning's verse is not for the fainthearted but certain to benefit those who persevere in reading and studying it. The poet of verse such as that found in *Sordello* can only be considered a genius as far as Horne and others are concerned. There were always dissenters, and many of the extracts contained in this volume are evidence that reviews of Browning's work had often to concentrate as much on defending it and attacking other critical views as they did finding that which was praiseworthy about the work being scrutinized. This extract is a fine example of not only literary attitudes toward Browning's poem but to his poetry as a whole, attitudes that would persist throughout, and after, his lifetime.

⚬⚬⚬ ⚬⚬⚬ ⚬⚬⚬

Containing, as it does, so many passages of the finest poetry, no manner of doubt can exist but that *Sordello* has been hitherto treated with great injustice. It has been condemned in terms that would lead any one to suppose there was nothing intelligible throughout the whole poem. We have shown its defects in detail, and we have also shown that it has some of the highest beauties. The style, the manner, the broken measure, the recondite form; these have constituted still greater difficulties than even the recondite matter of which it treats--though the latter only were quite enough to 'settle' or 'unsettle' an ordinary reader.

The poem of *Sordello* is a beautiful globe, which, rolling on its way to its fit place among the sister spheres, met with some accident which gave it such a jar that a multitude of things half slipt into each other's places. It is a modern hieroglyphic, and should be carved on stone for the use of schools and colleges. Professors of poetry should decypher and comment upon a few lines every morning before breakfast, and young students should be *ground* upon it. It is a fine mental exercise, whatever may be said or thought to the contrary. The flowing familiar style sometimes reminds us of Shelley's *Julian and Maddalo* with a touch of Keat's *Endymion*, broken up into numerous pit-falls, whether mines of thought or quirks of fancy; but there are also other occasions when it becomes spiral, and of sustained inspiration, not unlike certain parts of the *Prometheus Unbound* put into rhyme; yet is it no imitation of any other poet. Certain portions also remind us of the suggestive, voluble, disconnected, philosophical jargon of Shakespeare's fools, and with all the meaning which they often have for those who can find it. The poem is thick-sown throughout with suggestions and glances of history, biography, of dark plots, tapestried chambers, eyes behind the arras, clapping doors, dreadful galleries, and deeds in the dark, over which there suddenly bursts a light from on high, and looking up you find a starry shower, as from some remote rocket, descending in silent brilliancy upon the dazzled page. Each book is full of gems set in puzzles. It is like what the most romantic admirers of Goethe insist upon 'making out' that he intended in his simplest fables. It is the poetical portion of three epics, shaken together in a sack and emptied over the hand of the intoxicated reader. It is a perfect storehouse of Italian scenery and exotic fruits, plants, and flowers; so much so, that by the force of contrast it brings to mind the half-dozen flowers and pastoral common-places of nearly all our other modern English poets, till the recollection of the sing-song repetitions makes one almost shout with laughter. It is pure Italian in all its materials. There is not one drop of British ink in the whole composition. Nay, there is no ink in it, for it is all written in Tuscan grape juice, embrowned by the sun. It abounds in things addressed to a second sight, and we are often required to *see double* in order to apprehend its meaning. The poet may be considered the Columbus of an impossible discovery, as a worthy divine pleasantly observed to us. It is a promised land, spotted all over with disappointments, and yet most truly a land of promise, if ever so rich and rare a chaos can be developed into form and order by revision, and its southern fulness of tumultuous heart and scattered vineyards be ever reduced to given proportion, and wrought into a shape that will fit the average mental vision and harmonize with the more equable pulsations of mankind.

> —Richard Hengist Horne, from his unsigned review,
> "Robert Browning's Poems," *The Church of*
> *England Quarterly*, October 1842, pp. 464–483

EDWARD DOWDEN "MR. BROWNING'S *SORDELLO*" (1867)

Edward Dowden, the Irish poet and critic, begins this essay about Browning's *Sordello* for *Fraser's Magazine* by referencing the question that had been asked: "Who was actually able to understand the verse?" Dowden was writing some twenty-five years after the work's publication, but critical opinion still remained divided over the poem. Dowden mentions that Browning himself was not immune to the criticism, the poet saying that he could not change any part of the work without fatally damaging the whole. The Irishman is of the opinion that enough has been said about the difficulty in syntax and structure of Browning's writing, stating that it is the unrelenting demand placed upon the intellect of the reader that many critics have misconstrued as a problem with the writing itself.

Dowden's interpretation of the character of humanity found in *Sordello* and *Paracelsus* (which is described as the former poem's companion piece) is insightful: Browning sees people as imperfect creatures, spiritually restricted, but with indefinite room for growth in their characters and souls; humans are simply preparing themselves on earth for another, higher, more gloriously spiritual life (Chesterton will make a similar point in the last extract in this volume). In this extract, Dowden excellently details Browning's poetic analysis of his belief, describing the poet's views on the pitfalls, inadequacies, and errors that constantly plague our earthly lives. Each of Browning's poems through the years has added to his perspectives on these problems, and Dowden examines how every aspect of the poet's thought is underpinned with his convictions about humanity's situation: his views on art, religion, nature, love, beauty, and knowledge. Each of these specific incarnations of Browning's "faith" is examined in turn by Dowden, making this extract a particularly valuable, interpretative resource for those readers unfamiliar with Browning's poetry and his philosophical bent.

Here is a singular fact: Mr. Browning is declared by his contemporaries to be a distinguished poet, a true artist, a profound and original thinker; and when we ask, 'What of his most laborious undertaking?' the answer is (the answer of his ablest critic), 'We do not at all doubt that Mr. Browning understands his own drift clearly enough,' but 'probably no man or woman except the author ever yet understood it;' and 'We suspect that if it be true, as his dedication appears to indicate, that there is really one mortal who to his own satisfaction has understood Mr. Browning in *Sordello,* it would be found on cross-examination of that one, that (like Hegel's sole philosophical confidant) even he has misunderstood him. So wrote an admirable critic in the *National Review.* And what says Mr. Browning himself? That the poem is one which the many may not like, but which the few must; that he imagined it with so clear a power of vision, and so faithfully declared what he saw, that no material change can be made in it without injury; and that though the faults of expression are numerous, they are such as 'with care for a man or book' may be surmounted.[1] The truth on the critic's side—not a very productive truth—has perhaps received adequate consideration in the last twenty-seven years; we may now perhaps with a good conscience try to see the truth on the author's side, which may happen to be more productive.

One word on the obscurity of *Sordello.* It arises not so much from peculiarities of style, and the involved structure of occasional sentences (too much has been said on this; as a rule the style of *Sordello* is vigorously straightforward), as from the unrelaxing demand which is made throughout upon the intellectual and imaginative energy and alertness of the reader. This constant demand exhausts the power of attention in a short time, and the mind is unable to sustain its watchfulness and sureness of action, so that if we read much at a sitting we often find the first few pages clear and admirable, while the last three or four over which the eye passes before we close the book leave us bewildered and jaded; and we say, '*Sordello* is so dreadfully obscure.' The truth is, Mr. Browning has given too much in his couple of hundred pages; there is not a line of the poem which is not as full of matter as a line can be; so that if the ten syllables sometimes seem to start and give way under the strain, we need not wonder. We come to no places in *Sordello* where we can rest and dream or look up at the sky. Ideas, emotions, images, analyses, descriptions, still come crowding on. There is too much of everything; we cannot see the wood for the trees. Towards the end of the third book Mr. Browning interrupts the story that he may 'pause and breathe.' That is an apt expression; but Mr. Browning seems unable to slacken the motion of his mind, and during this breathing-space heart and brain, perceptive and reflective powers, are almost more busily at work than ever.

Before proceeding to trace in detail the story of *Sordello,* including what the author has called 'the incidents in the development of a soul,' it will be right to indicate the place of *Sordello* amongst the poems of Mr. Browning, and to make clear its purport as a whole. *Sordello* is a companion poem of *Paracelsus* (five years after the publication of which it appeared), and no one can possess himself of the ideas of Mr. Browning without a study of the two. 'Je sens en moi l'infini,' exclaimed Napoleon one day, with his hand upon his breast. 'Je sens en moi l'infini' is the germ-idea of these poems. An account of Mr. Browning as a thinker would be an insufficient account of his genius, for he is also an artist. But more than almost any other poet he is an intellectual artist, and especially in *Paracelsus* and *Sordello* he worked— worked too much, perhaps—under the guidance of ideas, abstract views of character, or the translation into intellectual theorems of the instincts of the heart (an 'analyst' Mr. Browning calls himself in *Sordello),* too little perhaps through a pure sympathy with life in some of its individual, concrete forms. If any artist may be said to embody in his work a clearly defined system of thought, this may be said of Mr. Browning; a system, however, which is not manufactured by logic, but the vital growth of his whole nature in an intellectual direction. Man here on earth, according to the central and controlling thought of Mr. Browning, man here in a state of preparation for other lives, and surrounded by wondrous spiritual influences, is too great for the sphere that contains him, while at the same time he can exist only by submitting for the present to the conditions it imposes; never without fatal loss becoming content with such submission, or regarding those conditions as final. Our nature here is unfinished, imperfect; but its glory, its peculiarity—that which makes us men, not God and not brutes—lies in this very character of imperfection, giving scope as it does for indefinite growth and progress. This progress is at the present time commonly thought of as progress of the race; Mr. Browning does not forget this (witness the concluding pages of *Paracelsus),* but he dwells chiefly upon the progress of the individual. Now a man may commit either of two irretrievable errors: he may renounce (through temptations of sense and other causes, but most frequently through supineness of heart, or brain, or hand, or else through prudential motives) his future, his spiritual, his infinite life and its concerns. That is one error. Or he may try to force those concerns, and corresponding states of thought, feeling, and endeavour into the present material life, the life of limitation and of inadequate and imperfect resources. That is the other. He may deny his higher nature, which is ever yearning upward to God through all high forms of human thought, emotion, and action (Mr. Browning loves to insist on this point); he may weary of failure, which is his glory (as generating a higher tendency), and fall back upon a limited and improgressive perfection; or else he may spurn at the conditions of existence, and endeavour to realise in this life what is work for eternity. To deny heaven and the infinite life—that is one extreme; to deny earth and the finite life—that is the other. If we are content with the limited and perishable joys, and gifts and faculties of the world, we see not God and never shall see him. If, on the contrary, we aim at accomplishing under all the restrictions of this life the work of eternity—if we desire absolute knowledge or none at all, infinite love or no love, a boundless exercise of our will, the manifestation of our total power, or no exercise of our will— then we shall either destroy ourselves, dash ourselves to pieces against the walls of time and space, or else, seeing that our objects are unattainable, sink into a state of hopeless enervation. But between these two extremes lies a middle course, and in it will be found the true life of man. He must not rest content with earth and the gifts of earth; he must not aim at 'thrusting in time eternity's concern;' but he must perpetually grasp at things which are just within, or almost without his reach, and, having attained them, find that they are unsatisfying; so that by an endless series of aspirations and endeavours, which generate new aspirations and new endeavours, he may be sent on to God and Christ and heaven.

These ideas lead us to the central point, from which we can perceive the peculiarity and origin of Mr. Browning's feeling with regard to nature, art, religion, love, beauty, knowledge. Around them we observe, as we read through his works, one poem after another falling into position, each bringing in addition something of its own.

Is it of external nature that Mr. Browning speaks? The preciousness of external nature lies in its being but the manifest power and love of God to which our heart springs as fire. In that *Easter Dream* of the last judgment what is the doom of God upon the condemned soul? It is to take all that the soul desires; and since the soul of the lost man loved the world, the world with its beauty, and wonder, and delight, but never yearned upward to God, who dwelt in them, the decree is pronounced:

> Thou art shut
> Out of the heaven of spirit; glut
> Thy sense upon the world.

And no condemnation could have been more awful; for nature has betrayed and ruined us if we rest in it,—betrayed and ruined us unless it sends us onward unsatisfied to God.

And what are Mr. Browning's chief doctrines on the subject of art? No one has so profoundly exposed the worldliness of the connoisseur or virtuoso, who, feeling none of the unsatisfied aspirations of the artist, rests in the visible products of art, and looks for nothing beyond them. 'The Bishop Orders His Tomb at St. Praxed's,' will recur to the mind of the reader. The true glory of art is that in its creation there arise desires and aspirations which can never be satisfied on earth; but which generate new aspirations and new desires, by which the spirit mounts to God himself. The artist who can realise his ideal has missed the true gain of art. In *Pippa Passes* the regeneration of Jules the sculptor's art turns on his foreseeing in the very perfection he had attained to an ultimate failure. And Andrea del Sarto being weighed is found wanting, precisely because he is 'the faultless painter:'

A man's reach should exceed his grasp, Or what's a heaven for? All is silver-grey, Placid and perfect with my art—the worse! But Andrea with a copy of one of Raphael's paintings before him can imagine his contemporary

Reaching, that heaven might so replenish him, Above and through his art—for it gives way; That arm is wrongly put—and these again— A fault to pardon in the drawing's lines. The true artist is ever sent through and beyond his art to God. Tears start into the eyes of Abt Vogler, who has been extemporising on his musical instrument, because now in the silence he feels the beauty of that palace of music which he reared, and which is gone never to be recalled. There is in the silence a sense of loss, vacancy, and failure. But the failure generates a higher aspiration, and the musician reaches upward to God:

Therefore to whom turn I but to Thee, the ineffable Name?
Builder and maker, thou, of houses not made with hands.
What, have fear of change from thee who art ever the same?
Doubt that thy power can fill the heart that thy power expands?

Honour to the early Christian painters who rejected a limited perfection such as that of Greek art, the subject of which was finite, and which taught men to submit, and who dared to be faulty; faulty, because the subject of their art was full of infinite hopes and fears, and because they would lead men to aspire.[2] Is it love of which Mr. Browning speaks? No passion so much as love can

Make time break,
And let us pent-up creatures through
Into eternity our due.[3]

But the means which love can command on earth are always incommensurate to its nature and its desires. Yet in apparent failure there may be gain, not loss. Let the reader turn to those companion poems—poems of subtle meaning—*Love in a Life,* and, *Life in a Love.* In each poem love is represented as pursuing its object without ever attaining it. This is a real failure, says Mr. Browning, when love is dependent on a life, and controlled by a life's limitations. But in its own nature, love is infinite; and if we could but *live in love,* life would partake of the infinity and eternity of the passion or essence with which it would be consubstantial; the object of desire could never be attained, but it would be for ever pursued, and apparent failure would but urge on to the real success, to everlasting aspiration and endeavour. Once more: does Mr. Browning speak of knowledge? Its gleams were meant to 'sting with hunger for full light.' Its goal is God himself. Its most precious part is that which is least positive; those momentary intuitions of things which eye hath not seen, nor ear heard—'fallings from us, vanishings.'[4] Even the revelation of God in Christianity left room for doubts and guesses; because growth is the law of man's nature, and perfect knowledge would have stayed his growth;[5] while, at the same time, its assurances of a boundless life beyond the grave saved Christianity from the failure of heathenism, which could not extinguish man's longings for a higher than material or worldly perfection, but was unable to utilise them, or suggest how they could be changed from restlessness and self-conflict to a sustaining hope.[6] The reader may complete the impression now produced by a thoughtful reading of a poem in which these ideas of Mr. Browning find perhaps their noblest expression,—'Rabbi Ben Ezra.'

So far Mr. Browning's system of thought has been illustrated chiefly by his shorter poems. But to the same central ideas belong *Paracelsus* (published 1835), *Sordello* (1840), and *Easter Day* (1850). In each we read 'a soul's tragedy.' Paracelsus aspires to absolute knowledge, and to power based on such knowledge, the attainment of which is forbidden by the conditions of our existence. In the same poem, a second phase of the same error—that of refusing for the present to submit to the terms of life—is represented in Aprile, who would 'love infinitely and be loved;' the boundlessness of his desires produces a disdain of such attainments and accomplishments as are possible on this earth; his ideal being beyond possibility of realisation, he rejects all the means of life since they are proved inadequate to his aspirations, and rejects the results of life because they are limited and imperfect; he cannot stoop from his sublime isolation in a world of dreams to task himself for the good of his fellows, and he sinks into a state of hopeless enervation. Paracelsus is the victim of the temptations of an aspiring *intellect*; Aprile, of the temptations of a yearning, passionate *heart*. Mr. Browning decided to complete our view of this side of the subject by showing the failure of an attempt to manifest the infinite scope, and realise the infinite energy of *will*, the inability of a great nature to deploy all its magnificent resources, and by compelling men in some way or other to acknowledge that nature as their master, to gain a full sense of its existence. With this purpose he wrote *Sordello*.

Notes

1. 'My own faults of expression were many; but with care for a man or book such would be surmounted, and without it what avails the faultlessness of either? I blame nobody, least of all myself, who did my best then and since; for I lately gave time and pains to turn my work into what the many might, instead of what the few must like; but after all I imagined another thing at first, and therefore leave it as I find it.'—*Dedication of Sordello to J. Milsand of Dijon.* M. Milsand's article on Mr. Browning's poetry which appeared many years ago in the *Revue des Deux Mondes*, may still be read with advantage.

2. *Old Pictures in Florence.*

3. *Dis Aliter Visum, or Le Byron de nos jours.*

4. *Easter Day*, xxvii., xxviii.

5. A *Death in the Desert.*

6. *Cleon.*

—Edward Dowden, "Mr. Browning's
Sordello," Fraser's Magazine, October 1867,
pp. 518–522

PIPPA PASSES

Unsigned (1841)

The anonymous reviewer for the journal *The Athenæum* examines Browning's poem *Pippa Passes*, from the collection *Bells and Pomegranates*, finding in it a great deal with which he takes critical issue. He states that many readers have long been forgiving of Browning, trying time and again to navigate the difficulties inherent to his work, but that their patience must run out with the publication of *Pippa Passes*. The writer sarcastically says that the poem might have been better served if its meaning had been delivered in English, describing the work as affected, obscure, and arrogantly formatted for the everyday reader, as if such an individual could find the time or intellectual wherewithal to attempt such poetry. The caustic tone is almost unrelenting throughout the review, the author describing the poem as "still-born" and probably the "last of its race." The poem's central idea is recognized as being beautiful, but the reviewer swiftly passes over this praise to describe the idea as having been mummified by the excessive wrapping of Browning's style, language, and unnecessary obscurities. The writer ultimately claims that Browning does justice neither to himself nor to the beauty of the idea contained in his poem.

Readers might compare this extract to that of Edward Dowden in the selection preceding it. The single point of comparison is that of the nobility in Browning's poetic view of humanity; every additional opinion remarked on in one review is in stark contrast to the other. While Dowden wrote his essay a quarter of a century after this unsigned review, the problems noted here are still apparent in Dowden's time and addressed in his critical interpretation of Browning's verse. The contrast between the two extracts is remarkable and is one for which the reader can find much more critical evidence throughout Browning's lifetime and beyond.

... Mr. Browning is one of those authors, whom, for the sake of an air of originality, and an apparent disposition to *think*, as a motive for writing,—we have taken more than common pains to understand, or than it may perhaps turn out that he is worth. Our faith in him, however, is not yet extinct,—but our patience *is*. More familiarized as we are, now, with his manner—having conquered that rudiment to the right reading of his productions—we yet find his texts nearly obscure as ever—getting, nevertheless, a glimpse, every now and then, at meanings which it might have been well worth his while to put into English. We have already warned Mr. Browning, that no amount of genius can fling any lights from under the bushel of his affectations. Shakspere himself would, in all probability, have been lost to the world, if he had written in the dead languages. On the present occasion, Mr. Browning's conundrums begin with his very title-page. *Bells and Pomegranates* is the general title given (it is reasonable to suppose Mr. Browning knows why, but certainly we have not yet found out—indeed we 'give it up') to an intended 'Series of Dramatical Pieces,' of which this is the first; and *Pippa Passes* is a very pretty exercise of the reader's ingenuity, which we believe, however, on reading the poem, we may venture to say we have succeeded in solving. A curious part of the matter is, that these 'Dramatical Pieces' are produced in a cheap form (neatly printed in double columns, price sixpence,) to meet and help the large demand—the 'sort of pit-audience'—which Mr. Browning anticipates for them! How many men does Mr. Browning think there are in the world who have time to read this little poem of his? and of these, what proportion does he suppose will waste it, in searching after treasures that he thus unnecessarily and deliberately conceals? 'Of course,' he says, 'such a work as this must go on no longer than it is liked;'—and, therefore, we are speaking of it, now, with that reverence and forbearance which one is accustomed to exercise towards the dead. Still-born, itself, it is also, no doubt, the last of its race—that is, if their being maintained by the public is a positive condition of their being begotten. Yet it has its limbs and lineaments of beauty, and exhibits the traces of an immortal spirit.

The idea of this little drama is, in itself, we think, remarkably beautiful, and well worth working out in language suited to its own simple and healthy moral. One of the daughters of labour, Pippa, a young girl employed in the silk-mills of Asolo, in the Trevisan, rises from her bed, on new-year's morning,—her single holiday of all the year: and, as she pursues the long, but willing, labours of her toilet, the map of its boundless enjoyments unfolds before her imagination. Then, among the light-hearted girl's thoughts, come those which *must* intrude upon the speculations of the poor—the contrasts with her own lowly lot presented by the more fortunate forms of life which she sees everywhere around her. Her neighbours of the little town of Asolo pass in review before her, with their several circumstances of what, to the outward eye, is advantage; and a touch of the envy and ill will, from which even the humble cannot be wholly exempt, mingles with her purer fancies, and dims the brightness of her holiday morning. But, in the breast of this joyous-hearted girl, these feelings soon take a healthier tone,—resolving themselves into reliance upon providence, contentment with her lot, which has in it this *one* chartered day—now only beginning—and a sense that she is a child of God as well as all the others, and has a certain value in the sum of creation, like the rest:—and so, she breaks away out into the sunshine, merry as a May-day queen,—

> Down the grass-path grey with dew,
> Neath the pine-wood blind with boughs,
> Where the swallow never flew
> As yet, nor cicale dared carouse,

with a song expressing such sentiments, and her own joy:

> The year's at the spring,
> And day's at the morn:
> Morning's at seven;
> The hill-side's dew pearled;
> The lark's on the wing,
> The snail's on the thorn;
> God's in his heaven—
> All's right with the world!

And then, the poem, which has no unity of action,—is held together by the single unity of its moral, and is dramatic only because it is written in dialogue-form—introduces us, by a series of changes, into the interiors of certain of those dwellings which the envious thoughts of Pippa had failed to pierce: and we are present at scenes of passion or intrigue, which the trappings, that had dazzled her eye, serve to hide. One of these, between the wife of a rich miser and her paramour,—on the night which conceals the murder of the husband, by the guilty pair, but just as the day is about to dawn upon it—is written with such power of passion and of painting (with a voluptuousness of colour and incident, however, which Mr. Browning may find it convenient to subdue, for an English public) as marks a master-hand,—and makes it really a matter of lamentation, that he should persist in thinking it necessary for a poet to adopt the tricks of a conjuror, or fancy that among the true spells of the former are the mock ones of the latter's mystical words. Into this scene of guilt and passion,—as into all the others to which we are introduced,—breaks the clear voice of a girl, singing in the young sunshine. By each and all of them, 'Pippa passes,'—carolling away her one untiring burthen of gladness,—carrying everywhere her moral that 'God's in his heaven' and the world beneath his eye—scattering sophisms and startling crime. Before this one natural and important truth, taught to a cheerful and lowly heart, the artificialities of life severally dissolve, and its criminals grow pale. Surely, there is something very fine in this! Not only have we the trite, but valuable, moral that happiness is more evenly distributed than it seems, enforced in a new form,—but also that other and less popularly understood one, which it were well the poor should learn,—and still better that the rich should ponder,—that the meanest of them all has his appointed value in God's scheme,—and a higher part may be cast to him who has to play it in rags, than to the puppet of the drama who enacts king, and walks the stage in purple. This despised little silk-weaver, like a messenger from God, knocks at the hearts of all these persons who seem to her so privileged,—and the proudest of them all opens to her. Again, we say, this is very fine;—and Mr. Browning is unjust both to himself and others, when he subjects it to the almost certainty of being lost. Why should an author, who can think such living thoughts as these, persist in making mummies of them?—and why should we, ere we could disengage this high and beautiful truth, have had to go through the tedious and disagreeable process of unwrapping?

—Unsigned, *The Athenæum*,
December 11, 1841, p. 952

A BLOT IN THE 'SCUTCHEON

CHARLES DICKENS (1842)

In this extract from a letter, Charles Dickens, the famous and popular English author, writes with the greatest esteem for Browning's play *A Blot in the 'Scutcheon*. The praise should strike the reader as even more impressive as it comes in a private correspondence where tact and diplomacy are often set aside for brutal honesty. It should be remembered that Dickens's own novels were well known for their scenes of emotion and poignancy, the very effects that the author claims he experiences when witnessing Browning's play; it is often the case that critics and readers find in texts those same things that can be found in their own natures (consider how many extracts defending Browning suggest that accusations of obscurity are based on the readers' own critical expectations). However, even Dickens in this eulogistic letter remarks on a few, minor aspects of the play that he would correct: "broken lines" and the formal ordering of scenes. It would seem that some of those who have only the highest praise for Browning find the same causes for concern as his most critical of detractors.

Browning's play has thrown me into a perfect passion of sorrow. To say that there is anything in its subject save what is lovely, true, deeply affecting, full of the best emotion, the most earnest feeling, and the most true and tender source of interest, is to say that there is no light in the sun, and no heat in blood. It is full of genius, natural and great thoughts, profound, and yet simple and beautiful in its vigour. I know nothing that is so affecting, nothing in any book I have ever read, as Mildred's recurrence to that "I was so young—I had no mother." I know no love like it, no passion like it, no moulding of a splendid thing after its conception, like it. And I swear it is a tragedy that MUST be played; and must be played, moreover, by Macready. There are some things I would have changed if I could (they are very slight, mostly broken lines); and I assuredly would have the old servant *begin his tale upon the scene*; and be taken by the throat, or drawn upon, by his master, in its commencement. But the tragedy I never shall forget, or less vividly remember than I do now. And if you tell Browning that I have seen it, tell him that I believe from my soul there is no man living (and not many dead) who could produce such a work.

—Charles Dickens, letter to John Forster,
November 25, 1842

UNSIGNED (1843)

This unsigned review of *A Blot in the 'Scutcheon* describes the audience's general engagement with the play, its pathos and conception, while still discussing the disagreeable subject matter, the overlong dialogues, and the faulty plot structure. The reviewer summarizes the story and the performances of various actors, giving credit where he feels it is due, and decrying both the author's and actors' craft when he feels it does not satisfy. He is aware that, despite the audience's applause at the curtain, the play might not be long for the stage; Browning's plays had suffered very short runs before, and the artistic problems that the extract describes, whether the case or not, were often those commonly felt by critics of Browning's work, both professional and public.

On Saturday a 'tragic play' in three acts, by Mr. Robert Browning, the author of *Paracelsus*, was produced here, and with doubtful success, though the audience in general certainly went along with the author. And, indeed, it would have been difficult not to do so; for albeit some of the scenes and much of the dialogue are too long, there is a sufficient variety and constant moving in the action, which keeps the mind engaged, and prevents it from detecting and dwelling upon the faultiness of the plot. It requires the pause of reflection to feel the full force of the error, and be aware that human nature, physics, and metaphysics, must be outraged, or there would be no play at all. Allowing Mr. Browning his grounds, we are bound to say there are fine marks of genius in the working-out of his conception, and not a few beautiful touches of genuine pathos and poetry—half lines worth a world of declamation. But the grounds slip from under him—there is no critical *locus standi* for the drama of the *Blot in the 'Scutcheon*. It is, besides, a disagreeable subject. Two young people, but old enough to know better,—Lord Mertoun (Anderson), and Mildred (Miss Faucit), sister of Lord Tresham (Phelps),—have formed an illicit amour; for which the lover makes a lame excuse of extreme youth and profound admiration for his mistress's brother, and to which the lady seems not to be reconciled by any likely process. For the piece opens with Lord Mertoun at last summoning up courage to propose himself as husband to his secret love, and being favourably received by her brother. His joy is excessive, and though late, we hardly care to ask why he did not apply before. His midnight visit to Mildred ensues, and he communicates the happy auspices to her; and then comes the unnatural foundation for all that is to follow. Instead of rejoicing, as all females under similarly untoward circumstances do, that she is about to be made, according to the old saying, "an honest woman," she flies off at a tangent, and declares that she is born to misery and tragedy. It is clear that things are likely to take a bad turn, though the easiest and most certain path is straight to the church, the second or public honeymoon, and a tolerably comfortable life even after the indiscretion of its commencement. An old retainer informs Lord Tresham of Mildred's midnight gallantries, her lamp lighting an unknown stranger to her chamber, and he climbing thereto with Capuletish ardour and alacrity. The "blot" is hit, and the earl is thrown into a vortex of passion. He seeks his sister, and she confesses her frailty, but refuses to give the name of her visitor, simply, as it would seem, because that straight-forward and natural course would have obliged the curtain to drop on a wedding most satisfactory to all parties concerned. Lord Tresham, in consequence, rushes out furiously to inform the other lord of Mildred's infamy (for she has *aggravated* him by offering to receive Mertoun's proposals)—wanders about till night; meets the incognito lover, and hastily slays him; then tells the news to his sister, who dies thereon; and, finally, gives himself to imperishable remorse or death. Such is the outline of a play, in poetical composition far above the mediocrity of our ordinary writers. But its inherent faults are fatal. No man or woman that ever existed, if they fell into the base position, so improbable too, of this noble-minded young lord and most admirably virtuous young lady, would conduct themselves in the way Mr. Browning paints. Mildred has no reason on earth, when detected in and confessing her folly, for not telling her doating brother the whole truth, saving him from paroxysms of passion, herself from the bitterest denunciations, and, in short—the tragedy from its catastrophe. Miss H. Faucit performed the part tenderly and sweetly; and the scene when she sinks senseless to the ground on her brother's reproaches, was very effective. Mr. Phelps was unequal. He has too much of violence to deliver, and it occasionally degenerated into rant and hair-tearing. But some portions were excellently done. Anderson was judicious and effective in spite of a dying scene in which his martyrdom of talking, after being mortally hurt, was enough to try the patience of Job. His conversation with his slayer, intermixed with groans and twistings, became almost ludicrous. Two other characters, cousins of Tresham, and his successors in the family *blotted* out by his rashness, are introduced; but they have not much to do; and so Mrs. Stirling and Mr. Hudson did their best. At the end the applause greatly predominated; but still we cannot promise the Blot that it will not soon be wiped off the stage.

—Unsigned, *The Literary Gazette*
and Journal of the Belles Lettres,
February 18, 1843, pp. 107–108

JOHN FORSTER (1843)

John Forster, one of Browning's first favorable reviewers, continues his support for the poet by reviewing his play *A Blot in the 'Scutcheon* and acclaiming Browning's genius, originality, and capacity to produce such works of "rare beauty." It is interesting to note that Forster suggests it is precisely the quality of rarity that has often led to Browning's being criticized in the press and by the public. The argument that there are simply too many people who cannot appreciate such extraordinary and original work is a familiar one from other extracts in this volume, and Forster does not seem to hold out a great deal of hope that the future run on the stage for *A Blot in the 'Scutcheon* will be a long one; it is the product of a unique soul and, as such, will perhaps have difficulty appealing to a general public overly familiar with the traditions and conventions of the theater.

Mr Browning—a writer whose career we watch with great interest, because we believe him to be a man of genius and a true poet—is the author of a tragedy in three acts, produced at this theatre, on Saturday last, and entitled *A Blot in the 'Scutcheon*. In performance it was successful: a result which it had been hardly safe to predict of a work of so much rare beauty, and of such decisive originality.

These are qualities that seldom, at first starting, make their way in the world, more especially the world theatrical. And we are not sanguine of the chances of continued patronage to the *Blot in the 'Scutcheon*. People are already finding out, we see, that there is a great deal that is equivocal in its sentiment, a vast quantity of mere artifice in its situations, and in its general composition not much to 'touch humanity.' We do not pretend to know what should touch humanity, beyond that which touches our own hearts, but we would give little for the feelings of the man who could read this tragedy without a deep emotion. It is very sad; painfully and perhaps needlessly so; but it is unutterably tender, passionate, and true. It is not copied from this or that existing notion; it is not moulded on this or the other of the old authors; it is the growth of the writer's heart, and has the distinct truth, the animated pathos, the freshness and unexaggerated strength, which spring in that soil alone.

—John Forster, *Examiner*, February 18, 1843, p. 101

HELENA FAUCIT MARTIN "ON SOME OF SHAKESPEARE'S FEMALE CHARACTERS: III. DESDEMONA" (1881)

Helena Faucit Martin was an English actress, famous for her many roles playing Shakespeare's heroines. She was a protégée of the producer William Charles Macready (and purportedly his romantic partner) and had taken one of the leading roles in Macready's production of Browning's early play *Strafford*. In this extract, she recalls how Macready's required absence from the theater during the rehearsals for Browning's play meant that the prompter took over the interpretation of the dialogue for the actors. As a result, and despite the prompter's best efforts, the actors misunderstood the play's meaning and were, Faucit Martin claims, directly responsible for the drama's failure despite its superb artistic promise. It seems that no matter the quality of a drama, the most incidental and seemingly insignificant factors, the absence of Macready in this case, can be cause for failure.

As a rule, Mr Macready always read the new plays. But owing, I suppose, to some press of business, the task was intrusted on this occasion to the head prompter,—a clever man in his way, but wholly unfitted to bring out, or even to understand, Mr Browning's meaning. Consequently, the delicate subtle lines were twisted, perverted, and sometimes even made ridiculous in his hands. My "cruel father" was a warm admirer of the poet. He sat writhing and indignant, and tried by gentle asides to make me see the real meaning of the verse. But somehow the mischief proved irreparable, for a few of the actors during the rehearsals chose to continue to misunderstand the text, and never took the interest in the play which they must have done had Mr Macready read it,—for he had great power as a reader. I always thought it was chiefly because of this *contretemps* that a play, so thoroughly dramatic, failed, despite its painful story, to make the great success which was justly its due.

> —Helena Faucit Martin, "On Some of
> Shakespeare's Female Characters: III.
> Desdemona," *Blackwood's Edinburgh
> Magazine*, March 1881, p. 326

Thomas R. Lounsbury
"A Philistine View" (1899)

Thomas Raynesford Lounsbury was an American literary critic and historian. In this extract from his "philistine" review (a philistine was a cultural illiterate, or one who was ignorant of civilized tastes), he states that Browning's drama was full of passion, enough to carry along the viewer, but that did not disguise the fact that the play did not amount to a unified whole. It had many fine lines of poetry but still fell short in adequately representing life. Lounsbury goes so far as to suggest that the characters do not simply flout what is realistically and artistically expected in their conduct, they consistently and defiantly act improbably. If the pathos of the drama is once more praised as it has been in other extracts, the unreality of the characterization is counted as being aesthetically unacceptable and the major failure of Browning's dramatic art.

⁓⁓⁓   ⁓⁓⁓   ⁓⁓⁓

We are so carried along by the fervor and fire and passion which he puts into his production that we pay no heed to its failure to fulfill the first conditions of dramatic propriety. But a play as a literary product must stand, not upon the excellence of detailed scenes, but upon its perfection as an artistic whole; not upon the beauty of its poetry, but upon its adequate representation of life. The necessities of the drama at times exact, or at least permit, an occasional neglect of probability in the conduct of the characters; but they certainly do not require a persistent defiance of it, as is exhibited throughout this tragedy, which is in no sense a picture of any life that was ever lived. We are in a world of unreal beings, powerfully portrayed; for the situations are exciting, and the pathos of the piece is harrowing. But the action constantly lies out of the realm of the reality it purports to represent, and therefore out of the realm of the highest art.

—Thomas R. Lounsbury, "A Philistine
View," *Atlantic*, December 1899, p. 773

MEN AND WOMEN

DANTE GABRIEL ROSSETTI (1855)

Dante Gabriel Rossetti was an English poet, illustrator, and painter, who, along with Holman Hunt, developed the artistic philosophy of the pre-Raphaelite movement. In this extract from a letter, Rossetti describes Browning's collection *Men and Women* as "magnificent" and fears that the general public's lukewarm reaction to the verse in the collection is an "awful" sign of the condition of contemporary England. Readers might indulge in comparing Rossetti's favorite poems of Browning to their own, and also to those judged to have best stood the critical test of time.

What a magnificent series is *Men and Women!* Of course you have it half by heart ere this. The comparative stagnation, even among those I see, and complete torpor elsewhere, which greet this my Elixir of Life, are awful signs of the times to me—'and I must hold my peace!'—for it isn't fair to Browning (besides, indeed, being too much trouble) to bicker and flicker about it. I fancy we shall agree pretty well on favourites, though one's mind has no right to be quite made up so soon on such a subject. For my own part, I don't reckon I've read them at all yet, as I only got them the day before leaving town, and couldn't possibly read them then,—the best proof to you how hard at work I was for once—so heard them read by William; since then read them on the journey again, and some a third time at intervals; but they'll bear lots of squeezing yet. My prime favourites hitherto (without the book by me) are 'Childe Roland', *Bishop Blougram*, 'Karshish', 'The Contemporary', 'Lippo Lippi', 'Cleon', and 'Popularity'; about the other lyrical ones I can't quite speak yet, and their names don't stick in my head; but I'm afraid 'The Heretic's Tragedy' rather gave me the gripes at first, though I've tried since to think it didn't on finding *The Athenaeum* similarly affected.

—Dante Gabriel Rossetti, letter to
William Allingham, November 25, 1855

John Greenleaf Whittier
(1855)

John Greenleaf Whittier was an American Quaker poet, a member of the New England Fireside Poets group, and a fervent abolitionist. In this extract from one of his letters, Whittier mentions the effect that Browning's collection has on him, describing it as the nineteenth-century equivalent of an electric shock, the verse spasmodic, the power of its passions intense.

***

Elizabeth has been reading Browning's poem *(Men and Women)*, and she tells me it is great. I have only dipped into it, here and there, but it is not exactly comfortable reading. It seemed to me like a galvanic battery in full play—its spasmodic utterances and intense passion make me feel as if I had been taking a bath among electric eels. But I have not read enough to criticise.

—John Greenleaf Whittier, letter to
Lucy Larcom, 1855, cited in Samuel T. Pickard,
Life and Letters of John Greenleaf Whittier,
1895, vol. 1, p. 370

Margaret Oliphant
"Modern Light Literature—Poetry"
(1856)

Margaret Oliphant was a Scottish author and historical writer. In the following review of *Men and Women* for the influential literary journal *Blackwood's Edinburgh Magazine*, Oliphant states that it is difficult to work out what many of the poems mean. The pleasure she derives from the work seems to be in glimpsing Browning himself appearing in patches amid his chaotically difficult style. Like many critics before her, Oliphant praises Browning's dramatic gifts in rendering distinctive human characters.

***

Only very few of his *Men and Women* is it possible to make out: indeed, we fear that the Andrea and the Bishop Blougram are about the only intelligible sketches, to our poor apprehension, in the volumes; but there is a pleasant glimmer of the author himself through the rent and tortured fabric of his poetry, which commends him to a kindly judgment; and, unlike those brothers of his who use the dramatic form with an entire contravention of its principles, this writer of rugged verses has a dramatic gift, the power of contrasting character, and expressing its distinctions.

—Margaret Oliphant, "Modern Light Literature:
Poetry," *Blackwood's Edinburgh Magazine*,
February 1856, p. 137

ANDREW LANG "ADVENTURES AMONG BOOKS" (1891)

Andrew Lang's essay for *Scribner's Magazine* was written from a distance of some forty years after the publication of *Men and Women* and two years after Browning's death. Lang states that to his mind the collection comprises the greatest work that Browning accomplished, that in it he sees the pinnacle of modern English verse, and there are many other critics who agree with this position. The extract reveals that Lang's level of admiration for the collection was so great that after the publication of *Men and Women* he found it difficult to become enthusiastic about Browning's later works.

The book by which Mr. Browning was best known was the two green volumes of Men *and Women.* In these, I still think, is the heart of his genius beating most strenuously and with an immortal vitality. Perhaps this, for its compass, is the collection of poetry the most various and rich of modern English times, almost of any English times. But just as Mr. Fitzgerald cared little for what Lord Tennyson wrote after 1842, so I have never been able to feel quite the same enthusiasm for Mr. Browning's work after *Men and Women.*

—Andrew Lang, "Adventures among Books,"
Scribner's Magazine, November 1891, p. 652

THE RING AND THE BOOK

RICHELIEU (1868)

The following review of Browning's *The Ring and the Book* was published in the British weekly journal *Vanity Fair*. The title of the journal is taken from John Bunyan's *The Pilgrim's Progress*, one of the most popular stories in English literary history. In Bunyan's narrative, his hero "Christian" journeys through the city of "Vanity Fair" where worldliness and materialism leave no room for the spiritual life. The journal was subtitled "A Weekly Show of Political, Social, and Literary Wares," its general purview that of critiquing and mocking contemporary Victorian values; such a tone is obvious in the extract below. The journal's title and subtitle also established a broad appeal to the higher, more noble, and spiritual natures of its readership. It is not surprising, then, that a poet such as Browning was admired by the editors and reviewers of the magazine.

The article describes Browning as a prophet, despised in his own age. The reference to "the voice of one crying in the wilderness" is biblical, the description of John the Baptist, the forerunner of Christ, who was largely ignored and despised by his contemporaries. The author of this extract suggests that the English literary public reads Browning as if he was a foreigner attempting to speak their own language, their patronizing attitude toward his work operating under the guise of down-to-earth "Englishness," almost with pride taken in their lack of comprehension (it has often been claimed that the English middle classes did not trust intellectuals). The author of the review says that Browning simply stands high above the type of damning articles written about his verse and that were prevalent at the time, that his poetry is beyond the imagination of most critics and certainly their comprehension.

The extract's analysis of Browning's poem and its story, its purpose and ideals, is full of praise. It continues the theme of the poet's prophet-like intentions, his high moral purpose, and the vital, spiritual quality of his work. Readers might compare the reviewer's opinions with other extracts dealing with the spiritual foundation and nature of Browning's verse (Edward Dowden's extracts in particular concentrate on such spiritual aspects, as do G.K. Chesterton's) or with those extracts that examine the incapacity and failure of contemporary Victorian society to appreciate Browning's view of mankind (there are many such examples in this volume).

In a few days Mr. Browning will publish another of those great and supposed enigmatical poems at which all Vanity Fair stands aghast—not exactly with terror, but with the half-amused, half-puzzled look of the honest country folk who hear for the first time in their lives a Frenchman or a German speaking in his own language. Once more the critics in plush will be heard echoing and re-echoing the verdict of the critics in kid gloves, and while the moustache is gracefully twirled, or the cigar held in suspense, *The Ring and the Book* will be turned over with a patronising air, and in all the sincerity of supercilious wonderment plaintively pronounced 'monstwously cwude in style, and altogether puzzling "to a fella", you know!' There is no help for this sort of thing. It is not Mr. Browning's fortune to stand on a level with the criticism of the present generation. His voice is 'the voice of one crying in the wilderness', and they who dwell in kings' houses will not go out to hear him, and are little likely to be influenced by his teaching.

By particular favour I have seen enough of Mr. Browning's new poem to be quite prepared for a repetition of the old verdict of *Vanity Fair* upon his choice of a subject and his treatment of it; yet I shall venture to speak of this book as one of the most striking lessons ever read by poet or philosopher in the ears of an evil generation. The story is a pitiful one—more pitiful than Hood's *Bridge of Sighs*, if that be possible. A young girl of Rome, in those old times which Mr. Browning loves to paint—yet not so remote from the present as his middleaged dramas—is married to an Italian count, shortly after which she and her father and mother are found murdered by him—nay, he is taken red-handed almost in the very act of butchery, and is eventually executed for the crime. This is the substance of the story found by Mr. Browning in an old 'Book', how he treats it is to be gathered from his opening apologue of the *Ring*. Some alloy must be mingled with your virgin gold to make it workable, but the goldsmith having finished his design (the 'lilied loveliness' of the ring) the gold is set free from its baser companionship by the last touch of the workman's art. Once more it is pure gold, 'prime nature with an added artistry'. And so understood, the antique goldsmith's ring serves, in the fore-front of the poem, as a symbol or speaking emblem of the poet's method. Say he has a divine message. How shall he utter it? The story of Guido Franceschini and the babe-like woman he made his bride is the answer.

It is not, therefore, to relate this story with such embellishments as his poetic instinct and sense of artistic beauty might suggest, that Mr. Browning has written. There is a deeply-felt purpose in his work of art, and to accomplish that purpose he has mixed the gold with 'gold's alloy/ We are first told of the tragedy in all its naked ghastliness. Then what 'half Rome' said of it, and what the 'other half/ The motives of the different actors in the drama, and all the little incomplete incidents which go to make up its completeness, are thus vividly realised. We pass them all over, to remark on Mr. Browning's aim, or what may be called the gist of his message in the character of Seer. The handwriting on the wall seems to be this, 'Can evil be done and evil not come of it?' Or this, to vary the expression, 'Is the world ruled by man's cunning devices, or by God's laws?' Or, again, this, 'Can a lie be told, and not make itself manifest, sooner or later, as the work of him who is the father of lies?' Yet, *The Ring and the Book* is not a sermon. It is deeply, intensely, human. It is nevertheless, and for that very reason, a burning protest against the atheistic belief that men and women are the creatures of circumstances. It asserts a Presence in the world, before which every lie, spoken or acted, must wither up, and possibly—nay, most certainly—bring destruction upon those who trust in it.

We picture Dante walking, with sad wide-open eyes, through Purgatory and Hades before he reached the shore of the river across which the loving eyes of Beatrice beamed upon him, and he once more took comfort. So through Vanity Fair and its devious ways, crowded with spectres of men and women as mournful to seeing eyes as those which grieved the heart of the Mantuan bard, we follow the steps of the poet who has been entrusted with this message, and who has already given utterance to it in many like parables. All criticism of Mr. Browning's verse which does not recognise this central fact of his relationship to the age as a messenger of truth seems to me worthless. It is true the good folk in Vanity Fair do not like this sort of thing, and it may be there are times when none of us like it. Belshazzar at high festival has no relish for the mystical handwriting on the wall. It is not always pleasant to be in earnest, and, like Mr. Tennyson's 'Lotus Eaters', we rather enjoy floating down the stream; or like the crew in his glorious 'Voyage', we have aims of our own in which it is vexatious to be disturbed. The answer to this objection is that we are not troubled every day, or even every other day, with a great poet's earnest expression of feeling, or with his sense of the living truth of things. No fear that there will not always be space enough in the Fair for vain shows, or, let us say, for harmless mirth and pleasantry. Now and then we may surely pause a moment in the round of ambition or pleasure to hear the Voice of Truth, and to lay up a gracious remembrance for less festive occasions. This, at least, is the kind of appeal which Mr. Browning's new poem makes to the world, be it received how it may.

Were space available for the purpose, it would be easy to prove by quotations that I have not over-estimated the earnestness of Mr. Browning's purpose, or the reality of his Message. Passages of great force and poetic beauty might be cited to this effect. One such I must find room for. It is an invocation addressed to one whom only to name in the poet's hearing were to call up at once a great sorrow and a great sense of joy, both too sacred to be lightly evoked. Hats off, gentlemen! There are few strains of music so touchingly sweet and so deeply felt. The like may be found in Milton's sonnet to his 'late espoused saint', and in some of Mrs. Browning's own intense verse; not often, if at all, elsewhere—

O LYRIC Love, half angel and half bird,
And all a wonder and a wild desire,—
Boldest of hearts that ever braved the sun,
Took sanctuary within the holier blue,
And sang a kindred soul out to his face,—
Yet human at the red-ripe of the heart—
When the first summons from the darkling earth
Reached thee amid thy chambers, blanched their blue,
And bared them of the glory—to drop down,
To toil for man, to suffer or to die,—
This is the same voice: can thy soul know change?
Hail then, and hearken from the realms of help!
Never may I commence my song, my due
To God who best taught song by gift of thee,
Except with bent head and beseeching hand—
That still, despite the distance and the dark,
What was, again may be; some interchange
Of grace, some splendor once thy very thought,
Some benediction anciently thy smile:
—Never conclude, but raising hand and head
Thither where eyes, that cannot reach, yet yearn
For all hope, all sustainment, all reward,
Their upmost up and on,—so blessing back
In those thy realms of help, that heaven thy home,
Some whiteness which, I judge, thy face makes proud,
Some wanness where, I think, thy foot may fall!

While it is impossible to read a poem with such passages in it, without sharing in the solemnity of Mr. Browning's muse, it must not be overlooked that his genius is dramatic—not essentially didactic, any more than Shakespeare's is so. For force of drawing, for fire and strength, for passion reserved until it flashes like a sudden gleam of lightning in a dark sky, Mr. Browning is without his equal among the poets of this age. In a critique of sufficient scope I should be disposed to look for his parallel, if not for his master, in Keats. There is the same intensity in both, the same concentrated fire, the same whiteness of heat, sometimes hidden by a hard metallic crust, but always ready to burst in flame. There is, too, the same marvellous efflorescence of poetic beauty in occasional passages, breaking out like rose-blossoms, often in most unexpected places and on spiny stems. In a philosophical analysis of his genius it would be possible to show that these apparent contrarieties, and what some have weakly pronounced affectations, are simply a necessity of the poet's nature. In allowing the ruggedness of his verse to appear, and glorifying it with an occasional burst of loveliness, he is doing precisely that in his own way which the Poet Laureate confesses to in his—

> Behold, ye speak an idle thing:
> Ye never knew the sacred dust:
> I do but sing because I must,
> And pipe but as the linnets sing.

Mr. Browning, however, should rather be classed with the wild beasts of creation than the birds—strong of limb and tawny of hue, with teeth like iron, and a roar like thunder. He is the spiritual athlete of poetry, descending into the arena as did the Roman gladiator of old, to grapple with terrible realities, and hold death itself in his strong grip. These are the thoughts which his new poem suggests. If people do not want the reality, with the occasional ruggedness of Nature, they had better not trouble themselves to open the book: *non cuivis*, &c., milk for babes may be got elsewhere.

—Richelieu, *Vanity Fair*, November 28, 1868, i, pp. 46–47

DANTE GABRIEL ROSSETTI (1868)

Rossetti, in this extract from a letter, questions the quality of some of the work in *The Ring and the Book* but states that his opinion is "entre nous," between only him and the letter's recipient. Rossetti suggests that while most poets' work suffers the more imaginative their starting point, Browning's becomes less coherent the more everyday his poem's beginning. It would seem that Rossetti queries the story's opening in Browning's poem, calling it not "pure Cognac" (a fine brandy) but the cheapest type of "Seven Dials Gin" (a working-class drink from a crime-ridden neighborhood in London).

P.P.S.—How do you like the *Ring and the Book?* It is full of wonderful work, but it seems to me that whereas other poets are the more liable to get incoherent the more fanciful their starting-point happens to be, the thing that makes Browning drunk is to give him a dram of prosaic reality, and unluckily this time the 'gum tickler' is less like pure Cognac than Seven Dials Gin. Whether the consequent evolutions will be bearable to their proposed extent without the intervening walls of the station-house to tone down their exuberance may be dubious. This *entre nous*.

—Dante Gabriel Rossetti, letter to
William Allingham, December 23, 1868

John Morley
"On *The Ring and the Book*" (1869)

John Morley, later First Viscount Morley of Blackburn, was a British liberal Member of Parliament, journalist, and newspaper editor. In this extract written for the popular journal the *Fortnightly Review*, Morley praises the strength of thought and conviction and the spiritual nobility of Browning's *The Ring and the Book*. Like the *Vanity Fair* review previously quoted, this extract notes that most contemporary poets have a "sterility of thought," whereas Browning's verse displays the originality and nobly human qualities lacking in those others. While he recognizes the often jarring qualities of Browning's method, his vision and verse structures, Morley states that it is the human drama that he displays in his poetry that makes Browning's *The Ring and the Book* of such great worth: It is a stimulus, health giving and courageous, as long as the reader is capable of being "appreciative."

It is certain that by whatever other deficiencies it may be marked the *Ring and the Book* is blameless for the most characteristic of all the shortcomings of contemporary verse, a grievous sterility of thought. And why? Because sterility of thought is the blight struck into the minds of men by timorous and halt-footed scepticism, by a half-hearted dread of what chill thing the truth might prove itself, by unmanly reluctance or moral incapacity to carry the faculty of poetic vision over the whole field; and because Mr. Browning's intelligence, on the other hand, is masculine and courageous, moving cheerfully on the solid earth of an articulate and defined conviction, and careful not to omit realities from the conception of the great drama, merely for being unsightly to the too fastidious eye, or jarring in the ear, or too bitterly perplexing to faith or understanding. It is this resolute feeling after and grip of fact which is at the root of his distinguishing fruitfulness of thought, and it is exuberance of thought, spontaneous, well-marked, and sapid, that keeps him out of poetical preaching, on the one hand, and mere making of music, on the other. Regret as we may the fantastic rudeness and unscrupulous barbarisms into which Mr. Browning's art too often falls, and find what fault we may with his method, let us ever remember how much he has to say, and how effectively he communicates the shock of new thought which was first imparted to him by the vivid conception of a large and far-reaching story. The value of the thought, indeed, is not to be measured by poetic tests; but still the thought has poetic value, too, for it is this which has stirred in the writer that keen yet impersonal interest in the actors of his story and in its situations which is one of the most certain notes of true dramatic feeling, and which therefore gives the most unfailing stimulus to the interest of the appreciative reader.

—John Morley, "On *The Ring and the Book*," *Fortnightly Review*, March 1869, pp. 341–342

ROBERT BUCHANAN (1869)

Robert Buchanan's review for the London journal the *Athenaeum* is full of the highest praise for Browning's *The Ring and the Book*, calling it the greatest work ("*opus magnum*") of the period. Both the content and the form of the verse are described as being of the highest quality, and the reviewer states that he remains so enamored and excited by the poem that he can hardly write calmly and objectively about it. The poem is claimed as the most supreme of its time, the greatest literary and spiritual treasure since Shakespeare's day. As in several previous extracts in this volume, it is Browning's capacity to accurately and unemotionally display human character and its drama—the passions, thought, and inner workings of the mind—that, along with the spiritual truths that are portrayed, make his verse of the greatest contemporary worth.

At last, the *opus magnum* of our generation lies before the world—the 'ring is rounded'; and we are left in doubt which to admire most, the supremely precious gold of the material or the wondrous beauty of the workmanship. The fascination of the work is still so strong upon us, our eyes are still so spell-bound by the immortal features of Pompilia (which shine through the troubled mists of the story with almost insufferable beauty), that we feel it difficult to write calmly and without exaggeration; yet we must record at once our conviction, not merely that *The Ring and the Book* is beyond all parallel the supremest poetical achievement of our time, but that it is the most precious and profound spiritual treasure that England has produced since the days of Shakspeare. Its intellectual greatness is as nothing compared with its trancendent spiritual teaching. Day after day it grows into the soul of the reader, until all the outlines of thought are brightened and every mystery of the world becomes more and more softened into human emotion. Once and for ever must critics dismiss the old stale charge that Browning is a mere intellectual giant, difficult of comprehension, hard of assimilation. This great book *is* difficult of comprehension, *is* hard of assimilation; not because it is obscure—every fibre of the thought is clear as day; not because it is intellectual,—and it is intellectual in the highest sense,—but because the capacity to comprehend such a book must be spiritual; because, although a child's brain might grasp the general features of the picture, only a purified nature could absorb and feel its profoundest meanings. The man who tosses it aside because it is 'difficult' is simply adopting a subterfuge to hide his moral littleness, not his mental incapacity. It would be unsafe to predict anything concerning a production so many-sided; but we quite believe that its true public lies outside the literary circle, that men of inferior capacity will grow by the aid of it, and that feeble women, once fairly initiated into the mystery, will cling to it as a succour passing all succour save that which is purely religious.

We should be grossly exaggerating if we were to aver that Mr. Browning is likely to take equal rank with the supreme genius of the world; only a gallery of pictures like the Shakspearean group could enable him to do that; and, moreover, his very position as an educated modern must necessarily limit his field of workmanship. What we wish to convey is, that Mr. Browning exhibits—to a great extent in all his writings, but particularly in this great work—a wealth of nature and a perfection of spiritual insight which we have been accustomed to find in the pages of Shakspeare, and in those pages only. His fantastic intellectual feats, his verbosity, his power of quaint versification, are quite other matters. The one great and patent fact is, that, with a faculty in our own time at least unparalleled, he manages to create beings of thoroughly human fibre; he is just without judgment, without preoccupation, to every being so created; and he succeeds, without a single didactic note, in stirring the soul of the spectator with the concentrated emotion and spiritual exaltation which heighten the soul's stature in the finest moments of life itself.

—Robert Buchanan, *Athenaeum,*
March 20, 1869, p. 399

Gerard Manley Hopkins (1881)

Gerard Manley Hopkins was an English poet, Roman Catholic convert, and Jesuit priest. In his letter extracted below, Hopkins does not display the same type of reaction to *The Ring and the Book* as seen in others' opinions in this volume. Considering that Hopkins was a Jesuit, and that so many reviewers had praised Browning's poem for its spiritual worth, the reader might expect the priest to be pleased with the verse. But he finds the poem "not edifying" (not spiritually uplifting) and does not even finish reading it, having been told that there are "coarser" events described in scenes to be found later in the work. Hopkins appreciates Browning's skill and the genius shown in his writing multiple perspectives and maintaining them for three volumes, but he finds the detailed descriptions given in the verse pointless and tiresome, a photograph of "still life," useless and unpoetic. Hopkins repeats the critical commonplace that Browning is not really a poet at all, he has all the gifts to be so but lacks the unifying thread of being able to write what is understood to be poetry. His ideas, philosophy, dramatic eye for human character, passion and thought, all these are his gifts; but without the skill of poetic craft, they cannot be tied together to form a beautiful piece of art. Readers should consider just what preconceptions about poetry Hopkins seems to hold to come to these conclusions.

I read some, not much, of *The Ring and the Book,* but as the tale was not edifying and one of our people, who had been reviewing it, said that further on it was coarser, I did not see, without a particular object, sufficient reason for going on with it. So far as I read I was greatly struck with the skill in which he displayed the facts from different points of view: this is masterly, and to do it through three volumes more shews a great body of genius. I remember a good case of 'the impotent collection of particulars' of which you speak in the description of the market place at Florence where he found the book of the trial: it is a pointless photograph of still life, such as I remember in Balzac, minute upholstery description; only that in Balzac, who besides is writing prose, all tells and is given with a reserve and simplicity of style which Browning has not got. Indeed I hold with the oldfashioned criticism that Browning is not really a poet, that he has all the gifts but the one needful and the pearls without the string; rather one should say raw nuggets and rough diamonds. I suppose him to resemble Ben Jonson, only that Ben Jonson has more real poetry.

—Gerard Manley Hopkins, letter to
R.W. Dixon, October 12, 1881

ALEXANDRA ORR (1885)

Alexandra Orr's thoughts on *The Ring and the Book* are extracted from her study of Browning's verse, published in 1885. She, like many other critics, finds the volume to be the poet's greatest, both in terms of its construction and the fineness of its monologues. She describes the story of how Browning happened upon the impetus for his poem trawling a secondhand goods shop in Florence. Finding a record of the murder and trial that would become the plot of *The Ring and the Book*, Browning purchased the chronicle for a tiny sum, publishing his poetic version of the events it catalogued some four years later.

The dramatic monologue repeats itself in the finest poems of the *Men and Women,* and *Dramatis Persona;* and Mr. Browning's constructive power thus remains, as it were, diffused, till it culminates again in *The Ring and the Book:* at once his greatest constructive achievement, and the triumph of the monologue form. From this time onwards, the monologue will be his prevailing mode of expression, but each will often form an independent work. *The Ring and the Book* is thus our next object of interest.

Mr. Browning was strolling one day through a square in Florence, the Piazza San Lorenzo, which is a standing market for old clothes, old furniture, and old curiosities of every kind, when a parchment-covered book attracted his eye, from amidst the artistic or nondescript rubbish of one of the stalls. It was the record of a murder which had taken place in Rome. . . .

The book proved, on examination, to contain the whole history of the case, as carried on in writing, after the fashion of those days: pleadings and counter-pleadings, the depositions of defendants and witnesses; manuscript letters announcing the execution of the murderer; and the "instrument of the Definitive Sentence" which established the perfect innocence of the murdered wife: these various documents having been collected and bound together by some person interested in the trial, possibly the very Cencini, friend of the Franceschini family, to whom the manuscript letters are addressed. Mr. Browning bought the whole for the value of eightpence, and it became the raw material of what appeared four years later as *The Ring and the Book.*

—Alexandra Orr, *A Handbook to the Works of Robert Browning,* 1885, pp. 75–76

WILLIAM DEAN HOWELLS
"CERTAIN PREFERENCES AND EXPERIENCES" (1895)

William Dean Howells was an American author and literary critic. In this extract, he claims to have never been greatly appreciative of Browning's verse apart from *The Ring and the Book*, which he describes as one of his literary passions (the theme of the text from which this extract is taken). He admits that such an impassioned response might well have been the case because he had just returned from Italy when the poem was published and because it reminded him so much of his time in that country. He is not an unconditional admirer of the work, saying he became bored with the repetition of different perspectives on the same events, but the worth of the story itself makes up for the poem's shortcomings. Like other critics, Howells remarks on the nobility of character described in Browning's poem but states that its popularity seems to have declined somewhat in recent years (he was writing six years after Browning's death and almost thirty years after the poem's publication). He suggests that if the poem had been written in the distant literary past or if the psychology evidenced in the verse was not so distinctly modern, *The Ring and the Book* would be classified as one of the greatest dramatic epics ever written. Nevertheless, Howells concedes that Browning's poem will never suffer complete and lasting eclipse; it is too great a work to ever undergo such a fate.

I think I may class the *Ring and the Book* among [my literary passions], though I have never been otherwise a devotee of Browning. But I was still newly home from Italy, or away from home, when that poem appeared, and whether or not it was because it took me so with the old enchantment of that land, I gave my heart promptly to it. Of course, there are terrible *longueurs* in it, and you do get tired of the same story told over and over from the different points of view, and yet it is such a great story, and unfolded with such a magnificent breadth and noble fulness, that one who blames it lightly blames himself heavily. There are certain books of it—"Caponsacchi's story," "Pompilia's story," and "Count Guido's story"—that I think ought to rank with the greatest poetry ever written, and that have a direct, dramatic expression of the fact and character, which is without rival. There is a noble and lofty pathos in the close of Caponsacchi's statement, an artless and manly break from his self-control throughout, that seems to me the last possible effect in its kind; and Pompilia's story holds all of womanhood in it, the purity, the passion, the tenderness, the helplessness. But if I begin to praise this or any of the things I have liked, I do not know when I should stop. Yes, as I think it over, the *Ring and the Book* appears to me one of the great few poems whose splendor can never suffer lasting eclipse, however it may have presently fallen into abeyance. If it had impossibly come down to us from some elder time, or had not been so perfectly modern in its recognition of feeling and motives ignored by the less conscious poetry of the past, it might be ranked with the great epics.

—William Dean Howells, "Certain Preferences and Experiences," *My Literary Passions*, 1895

THE INN ALBUM

HENRY JAMES "BROWNING'S *INN ALBUM*" (1876)

Henry James was an American expatriate living in England and one of the most critically acclaimed novelists of the late Victorian period. In the following extract, James makes his feelings toward Browning's *The Inn Album* clear when he states that it is becoming increasingly difficult for the poet's friends to defend him. It is not that Browning's increased poetic output is leaving him empty of ideas; James says the opposite is the case and that concern is precisely the problem with *The Inn Album*. The verse is described as being like a series of rough notes, not even drafts, and, like the authors of other excerpts in this volume, James refers to the poetry as being full of hieroglyphs that can surely only be decipherable to Browning himself. The work displays Browning's usual flair for the dramatic, but it is utterly formless, to the extent that James says *The Inn Album* cannot even be called a poem; nor can it be said to be prose. James does not know what it should be called.

This is a decidedly irritating and displeasing performance. It is growing more difficult every year for Mr. Browning's old friends to fight his battles for him, and many of them will feel that on this occasion the cause is really too hopeless, and the great poet must himself be answerable for his indiscretions. Nothing that Mr. Browning writes, of course, can be vapid; if this were possible, it would be a much simpler affair. If it were a case of a writer "running thin," as the phrase is, there would be no need for criticism; there would be nothing in the way of matter to criticise, and old readers would have no heart to reproach. But it may be said of Mr. Browning that he runs thick rather than thin, and he need claim none of the tenderness granted to those who have used themselves up in the service of their admirers. He is robust and vigorous; more so now, even, than heretofore, and he is more prolific than in the earlier part of his career. But his wantonness, his wilfulness, his crudity, his inexplicable want of secondary thought, as we may call it, of the stage of reflection that follows upon the first outburst of the idea, and smooths, shapes, and adjusts it—all this alloy of his great genius is more sensible now than ever. *The Inn Album* reads like a series of rough notes for a poem—of hasty hieroglyphics and symbols, decipherable only to the author himself. A great poem might perhaps have been made of it, but assuredly it is not a great poem, nor any poem whatsoever. It is hard to say very coherently what it is. Up to a certain point, like everything of Mr. Browning's, it is highly dramatic and vivid, and beyond that point, like all its companions, it is as little dramatic as possible. It is not narrative, for there is not a line of comprehensible, consecutive statement in the two hundred and eleven pages of the volume. It is not lyrical, for there is not a phrase which in any degree does the office of the poetry that comes lawfully into the world—chants itself, images itself, or lingers in the memory. "That bard's a Browning; he neglects the form!" one of the characters exclaims with irresponsible frankness. That Mr. Browning knows he "neglects the form," and does not particularly care, does not very much help matters; it only deepens the reader's sense of the graceless and thankless and altogether unavailable character of the poem. And when we say unavailable, we make the only reproach which is worth addressing to a writer of Mr. Browning's intellectual power. A poem with so many presumptions in its favor as such an authorship carries with it is a thing to make some intellectual use of, to care for, to remember, to return to, to linger over, to become intimate with. But we can as little imagine a reader (who has not the misfortune to be a reviewer) addressing himself more than once to the perusal of *The Inn Album,* as we can fancy cultivating for conversational purposes the society of a person afflicted with a grievous impediment of speech. . . .

The whole picture indefinably appeals to the imagination. There is something very curious about it and even rather arbitrary, and the reader wonders how it came, in the poet's mind, to take exactly that shape. It is very much as if he had worked backwards, had seen his denouement first, as a mere picture—the two corpses in the inn-parlor, and the young man and his cousin confronted above them—and then had traced back the possible motives and sources. In looking for these Mr. Browning has of course encountered a vast number of deep discriminations and powerful touches of portraiture. He deals with human character as a chemist with his acids and alkalies, and while he mixes his colored fluids in a way that surprises the profane, knows perfectly well what he is about. But there is too apt to be in his style that hiss and sputter and evil aroma which characterize the proceedings of the laboratory. The idea, with Mr. Browning, always tumbles out into the world in some grotesque hind-foremost manner; it is like an unruly horse backing out of his stall, and stamping and plunging as he comes. His thought knows no simple stage—at the very moment of its birth it is a terribly complicated affair. We frankly confess, at the risk of being accused of deplorable levity of mind,   that we have found this want of clearness of explanation, of continuity, of at least superficial verisimilitude, of the smooth, the easy, the agreeable, quite fatal to our enjoyment of *The Inn Album*. It is all too argumentative, too curious and recondite. The people talk too much in long set speeches, at a moment's notice, and the anomaly so common in Browning, that the talk of the women is even more rugged and insoluble than that of the men, is here greatly exaggerated. We are reading neither prose nor poetry; it is too real for the ideal, and too ideal for the real. The author of *The Inn Album* is not a writer to whom we care to pay trivial compliments, and it is not a trivial complaint to say that his book is only barely comprehensible. Of a successful dramatic poem one ought to be able to say more.

—Henry James, "Browning's *Inn Album*,"
The Nation, January 20, 1876, p. 49

A.C. Bradley "Mr. Browning's Inn Album" (1876)

Andrew Cecil Bradley was an English literary critic and later the professor of poetry at Oxford University. The following extract suggests that Browning's imperfect form has become a type of habit or his own personal mannerism. While it is clear, Bradley says, that Browning retains a most imaginative energy in his verse, *The Inn Album* deals with so undignified a subject and has so little form that it can only be short lived in the world of letters. The story functions only as a psychological revelation, but the characters are too ugly, disgusting, or mean to afford the reader any pleasure in their story or an edifying moral in their tale. Readers might compare Bradley's reasons for the poetic failure of *The Inn Album* to the several extracts praising and championing the spiritual quality of Browning's earlier verse: As far as Bradley is concerned, this quality is utterly absent from the poet's latest publication.

After reading such poetry as this, in which the passionate expression is but just touched by the defect we have been noticing, we have little cause to fear that a mannerism, which must help to shorten the fame of Mr. Browning's later poems, has become inevitable to him. Everyone must hope that he will yet produce works not defaced by it. And happily no one can doubt that he has still in him rich stores of poetic energy, and of an energy which is in ceaseless activity in the most diverse directions.

But the imperfection of form is not the only thing which will, we believe, make productions like the *Inn Album* shortlived. Form and matter alike, the poem is pitched at a low level; and not even Mr. Browning's genius is sufficient to dignify a story which contains the elements of so little real pathos, and so painfully little beauty. With all its power, we are not refreshed, nor awed, nor uplifted by the *Inn Album*; it has no form to charm us, little brightness to relieve its gloom, and, except for the dramatic touches we have tried to indicate, the human nature it shows us is too mean, or too commonplace, or too repellent, to excite more than the pleasure of following a psychological revelation.

—A.C. Bradley, "Mr. Browning's *Inn Album*,"
Macmillan's Magazine, February 1876, p. 354

GEORGE HENRY LEWES (1847)

George Henry Lewes was an English philosopher and a literary and theater critic. The following extract, taken from *The British Quarterly Review*, is an early essay on Browning's verse published shortly after the final volume of the poet's *Bells and Pomegranates*. Lewes does not believe Browning to be a distinguished poet but sees in his originality the reason he stands out among his contemporaries. He has the gift of seeing what others cannot and, Lewes argues, is unquestionably original in the manner in which he writes about what he sees in his verse. He already has his own imitators, but Lewes says that Browning is neither a deep thinker nor able to write musically (the latter is the most usual criticism of the poet, although readers should consult other extracts from the period to contrast the many critics who found much that they believed to be profound in Browning's verse). He has not produced in his ten years of publishing anything as popular as his contemporary Lord Alfred Tennyson, nor will he as far as Lewes is concerned. He states that *Paracelsus*, the earliest work discussed in the extract, is still considered to be Browning's most accomplished creation.

He is assuredly not a great poet; he is not even a distinguished poet, whose works will be gathered into future collections; but he is nevertheless a man who stands out in relief from his contemporaries—he is a writer of whom one must speak with the respect due to originality. In an age more favourable to the production of poetry, he might have been conspicuous; for he is endowed with some portion of the great faculty which we may metaphorically call the 'eye to see'. Deficient in some of the great requisites of his art, he has that one primary requisite: the power of seeing for himself and writing in his own language. Robert Browning is Robert Browning—call him sublime or call him feeble, take any view you will of his poems, you must still admit that he is one standing up to speak to mankind in his speech, not theirs—what he thinks, not what they think. We do not say that there are no traces of other poets in his works: he is of his age, and no man can pretend to escape its influence; he has studied poetry, and no man can at all times separate in his mind the acquired from the generated; but we do say emphatically that he is, in our strict and narrow sense of the term, no imitator, but an original thinker and an original writer.

Unfortunately, this high praise demands some qualification, and we are forced to add, that he is neither a deep thinker nor a musical writer. So that, although his originality has created for him an eminent position amongst a race of imitators, he has never yet been able to charm the public—he has never produced anything like 'Mariana at the Moated Grange', 'Locksley Hall', 'Ulysses', 'Œnone', 'Godiva', or the 'Miller's Daughter', (we mention those least resembling each other) with which Tennyson has built himself a name. Nor do we anticipate that he will ever do so. He has now been some years before the public, and in various characters. His first poem, which (unlucky circumstance!) is still regarded as his best, was *Paracelsus*. We well remember its appearance, and the attention it drew on the new poet, who, being young, was held destined to achieve great things. As a first work, it was assuredly remarkable. It had good thoughts, clear imagery, genuine original speech, touches of simple pathos, caprices of fancy, and a power of composition which made one hope that more experience and practice would ripen him into a distinguished poet. There were two objections, which occurred to us at the time. We did not lay much stress upon them, as the author was evidently young. Age and practice, we thought, would certainly remove them. They were the sort of faults most likely to be found in youthful works—viz., a great mistake in the choice of subject, and an abruptness, harshness, and inelegance of versification. It was pardonable in a young man to make a quack his hero; it looked a paradox, tempting to wilful and skilful ingenuity. On the other hand, it also betokened, or seemed to betoken, a want of proper earnestness and rectitude of mind—a love rather of the extraordinary than of the true. Paracelsus was not the hero a young man should have chosen; and yet one felt that he was just the hero a young man would choose. It seems to us that what this betokened has come to pass, and that in his subsequent works we have, if not the *same* fault, yet a fault which springs, we take it, from the same source. His conceptions are either false or feeble. In the work which succeeded *Paracelsus* we noted a repetition of the very error itself—viz., in the attempt to idealize into a hero that great but desperate Strafford, the 'wicked earl', as he was called, and as his actions prove him. Meanwhile the other fault—that, namely, of harshness and abruptness—was carried almost to a ridiculous extent; the language was spasmodic, and tortured almost into the style of Alfred Jingle, Esq., in *Pickwick,* as the Edinburgh Reviewer remarked at the time. Next, after an interval of two or three years, if our memory serves us, came *Sordello.* What the merit or demerit of conception in that poem may be, no one can presume to say; for except the author himself and the printer's reader (in the course of duty), no earthly being ever toiled through that work. Walking on a new-ploughed field of damp clayey soil, would be skating compared to it. Even his staunchest admirers could say nothing to *Sordello.* Great as is the relish for the obscure and the involved in some minds, there was no one found to listen to these Sybilline incoherences. Other dealers in the obscure have at least charmed the ear with a drowsy music, but *Sordello's* music was too grating and cacophonous to admit of the least repose. Whether Browning is to this day convinced of his mistake we know not, but to our ever-renewed surprise we often see *Sordello* advertised. That he has not burnt every copy he could by any means lay hands on, is to be explained only upon the principle which makes a mother cherish more fondly the reprobate or the cripple of her family.

This much, at any rate, is significant; he has ventured on no such experiment on the public patience since *Sordello.* The subsequent poems here collected, as *Bells and Pomegranates,* are always readable, if not often musical, and are not insults to our ears. But, as we hinted, the old objections still remain. He has not yet learned to take due pains with his subject, nor to write clearly and musically. It appears as if he sat down to write poetry without the least preparation; that the first subject which presented itself was accepted, as if any canvass was good enough to be embroidered upon. And respecting his versification, it appears as if he consulted his own ease more than the reader's; and if by any arbitrary distribution of accents he could make the verse satisfy his own ear, it must necessarily satisfy the ear of another. At the same time, he occasionally pours forth a strain of real melody, and always exhibits great powers of rhyming.

—George Henry Lewes, from his unsigned
review, *The British Quarterly Review*,
November 1847, vi, pp. 490–509

THOMAS POWELL (1849)

In the following extract, Thomas Powell reviews Browning's literary career up until *Bells and Pomegranates*, the same period covered by George Henry Lewes in the extract immediately preceding this one. Setting aside Browning's first publication, *Pauline*, as something the author has never publicly acknowledged, Powell suggests that it is *Paracelsus* for which the poet will be remembered in future years. He recalls the attempts by the critic John W.J. Fox to boost Browning's popularity in the initial years of his writing and also the work of William Charles Macready in producing a number of Browning's dramas onstage (readers can examine extracts from these two critics earlier in the volume).

Despite Powell's broad sympathy for Browning's work, he recognizes the complexity of the poet's language and his inclination for choosing the obscure when the poetically conventional (although Browning would name that the clichéd) would be enough. It is for these two reasons that Powell maintains Browning's work has not received greater public acclaim. It is noteworthy in his comments about *Paracelsus* that Powell underlines the distinction between critical and public attitudes toward Browning's poetry: Often critics, as has been shown in this volume, and usually those more antagonistic to the poet's verse were apt to collapse these attitudes into one response to Browning's work. When Powell states that it is with *Pippa Passes*, the first volume of *Bells and Pomegranates*, that Browning's poetic life really begins "as far as the public know him," he is making precisely this distinction; the "critics of the day" believe it likely that *Paracelsus* will be the poet's most remembered work.

Powell also makes interesting comments about the "spiritual grace and purity" of Browning's female characters, placing them favorably alongside those of Shakespeare and the English romantic poet Lord Byron. Readers should consider just how much these comments are a product of Powell's mid-Victorian expectations in regard to women and whether such qualities in Browning's work would be equally valued today. Similarly, his comments on Browning's marriage to Elizabeth Barrett show a more "romantic" attitude than is perhaps common today.

Powell concludes with some telling observations on Browning's character. He describes, as others have done in this volume, Browning's aptitude for intelligent and intelligible conversation, his politeness and social grace, and his distaste for brusque manners. Powell suggests that Browning occasionally becomes almost affected in his behavior, that he is sensitive to criticism of his verse and maintains small regard for his poetic contemporaries. Nevertheless, Powell points out, many of the dedications to Browning's poetry praise those same contemporaries, a contradiction of character ascribed to the rigorously polite manners maintained by the poet.

In his twentieth year he published a poem called *Pauline*, which he has never acknowledged, and of which he now appears to be ashamed. It has little merit beyond a certain faint evidence of sensuous feeling running through it; that kind of murmuring music which ever accompanies a poet in his walk through life.

In 1836 his first acknowledged poem appeared, called *Paracelsus*, and it is the opinion of many of the critics of the day that this will be the work by which he will be the most remembered. A critic has remarked, that one of the finest thoughts of modern times is embalmed in three lines in this poem.

> There are two points in the adventure of a diver,
> First when a beggar he prepares to plunge,
> Then when a prince he rises with his pearl.
> Festus, I plunge!

An eminent poet remarked that Mr. Browning had lost the chief force of the thought by the first line, which he maintained was very prosaic; he suggested that it ought to be altered, as

'There are two moments in a diver's life,' &c.

This is a point for the author. We named this to Mr. Browning, who acknowledged his own line was feeble.

Mr. Browning's *Paracelsus* excited little attention. Mr. Forster, of *The Examiner*, praised it, Mr. Fox, of *The Monthly Repository*, and *Heraud's New Monthly Magazine*—and there was an end of the matter. It, however, gave the poet a quiet pedestal for his future station, and he is now so proud of his young creation that he generally places it as his peculiar characteristic, and calls himself author of *Paracelsus*.

To *Paracelsus* succeeded a tragedy, called *Strafford*, which owing to Mr. Forster's influence with Mr. Macready, was performed. The great tragedian acted Strafford—but all his efforts were unavailing. It was the tragedy of spasms: the want of personal interest is too deeply felt to allow of any doubt, and the work of a strong mentality went to the tomb of the Capulets for want of a physical Romeo. We fear it will be found to be the verdict of the public, that the author of *Sordello* is a noble abstraction; a great spirit, but he lacks the flesh and blood of Shakspere, and the milk of human kindness.

Four years afterwards *Sordello* astonished his friends, and amazed the world—of this work we shall speak more anon....

Mr. Browning's next work was *Pippa Passes*, the first of a series which he has called *Bells and Pomegranates*. Here begins the real poetic life of Browning, so far as the public know him, and out of these singular productions we hope to justify our faith to the world. The idea of Pippa, a poor factory girl, purifying human nature as she passes about on her vocation, is a fine conception, and it is to be lamented that it is not made so intelligible to the common mind as to be capable of a wider appreciation. To the poet, however, it remains what Keats said of Beauty, 'a joy for ever'. After a time Mr. Macready produced another play, and the reception which the *Blot in the 'Scutcheon* had at Drury Lane in 1843, and at Sadler's Wells in 1848, seems to justify the current opinion that the author is only a dramatist for the poet and the critic. He cannot touch the hearts of the million. That he abounds in the esthetic, may be presumed, but the world at large care little for the subtler and more minute works of the human heart. They demand a broader, wider range, a rougher 'guess' at their nature; when it is borne in mind how many words are not heard in a large theatre; how few of the actors know how to deliver a speech intelligibly; it is evident that a tortuous, obscure and condensed style must be so much Greek to a mixed audience who hear a drama for the first time; when, however, you add to these disadvantages, a plot not springing from the every day impulses of the heart, but evolved from some peculiar idiosyncracy of the mind, it is evident you make a very fatiguing and ingenious puzzle, and not a drama to move our tears or smiles.

We have heard Mr. Browning frequently reply in answer to some of the critics who have accused him of an impracticable style, that he is as clear as any poet can be, who uses a new set of symbols; he declares that he is weary of phoenixes, roses, lilies, and the old stock in trade, which with the aid of ten fingers, he enabled mere versifiers to inundate the reading world with a deluge of 'Verse and water'.

For instance, if Mr. Browning wishes to make a simile, and illustrate redness, he will not take the rose, but select some out of the way flower equally red, but of whose name not one in a thousand has ever heard:

this added to a style so condensed and clipt of all aids as to sometimes be unintelligible, has sealed Mr. Browning's works to the many. It is indeed the shorthand of poetry. It requires the author or some duly qualified admirer to interpret it to the world. We feel sure it is a great defect in an author when he requires 'an explanator'. He should be able to converse with his reader without intermediate aid. He should sit face to face, flashing bright thoughts into the gazer's mind.

We must not conclude our notice of Robert Browning without alluding to the exquisite spiritual grace and purity he has thrown around his female characters. We confess that they all seem to belong to one family, although brought up at different colleges (for all his women are great metaphysicians), still there is a purity and unselfishness about them which makes one wish that the world were peopled only with such divine creatures as Shakspere and Browning's heroines are.

Lamb once told a friend that he would any day marry, old as he was, if he could only 'find one of Shakspere's women'. The poet, logician, and metaphysician would, in like manner, look out for some Sordellian creature such as Mildred, Pippa, Anael, or one of her sister heroines. The purity of a poet's heart may frequently be tested by his ideal seraglio. We have only to refer to Byron, Shakspere and Browning, for strong cases in support of our opinion.

It would be unjust to Mr. Browning to give any specimen from his larger works; they should be read by themselves; they do not abound in fine isolated passages, like most poets. All their beauties are so interwoven as to render extracts, to inform the reader, well nigh as absurd as to bring a brick as a specimen of the architecture of any particular building.

In November, 1846, Mr. Browning married Miss Barrett, the celebrated poetess, and shortly after went to Florence, where he now remains. The conjugal union of the first poetess of the age with the author of *Paracelsus* is certainly an unparalleled event in the history of matrimony, and a singular illustration of Shakspere's sonnet.

Let me not to the marriage of pure minds
Admit impediments.

We are happy to add, that the first social production of these highly favoured children of Apollo is a fine boy, born in the sunny south. In person Browning is small, but well made and active; very dark, with a Jewish cast of countenance; has large black whiskers, which he cultivates under his chin; his eyes are dark; complexion almost approaching to sallow. However obscure in his writings, he is intelligible in his conversation; and his dislike to brusquerie often borders on affectation and punctiliousness unworthy of so true a poet. His marriage with Miss Barrett was the result of a short courtship; their correspondence commenced in Greek, and doubtless in that language their love longings were expressed.

Mr. Browning is very susceptible of criticism, although pretending to a great contempt of it. He is a strong disbeliever in the genius of his contemporaries, and is as chary of his critical praise as Shakspere himself. The absurdity of some of his dedications is in striking contrast to this hesitation; as those to Talfourd, Barry Cornwall, &c. abundantly testify. This is a contradiction in his nature we cannot easily explain, and most probably proceeds from that false courtesy which is, perhaps, his solitary blemish; in other respects he is a gentleman and an undoubted poet. His political principles are republican. He is in his thirty-seventh year.

Mr. Browning's writings are numerous.

> —Thomas Powell, from his "Robert Browning,"
> *The Living Authors of England,* 1849, pp. 71–85.

WALTER BAGEHOT "WORDSWORTH, TENNYSON, AND BROWNING; OR, PURE, ORNATE, AND GROTESQUE ART IN ENGLISH POETRY" (1864)

Walter Bagehot was a prolific English journalist and essayist, predominantly writing literary criticism and studies on political economy. In the following extract, Bagehot is suggesting three distinct styles in English verse as typified by the poets William Wordsworth, Lord Alfred Tennyson, and Browning. Wordsworth had been arguably the most famous poet in England since the late eighteenth century and had been England's poet laureate, succeeded in that position on his death in 1850 by Tennyson. Thus, Bagehot has brought together two laureates to critique alongside Browning.

Bagehot's fundamental premise is that, unlike the styles of "pure" and "ornate" poetry, the "grotesque" deals with the unnatural, not the portrayal of ideal nature, as the former two styles do. The grotesque does not reveal the perfect form but suggests it by depicting the imperfect, allowing the reader to deduce the perfect from that which it is not. Browning, Bagehot states, is the master of this grotesque style. Browning's ability and mind are praised; his capacity for bringing together ideas and images in an original way is recognized. Bagehot is at pains to state at the outset that any criticisms he has to make about Browning's verse are made not about the effort of the poet but in the interest of the art of poetry. The author of the extract is thus claiming to be writing from a position of objectivity with an unbiased and fair attitude; the reader might almost sense that Bagehot is apologizing for what he is about to say concerning Browning's verse.

In his extract from Browning's *Caliban upon Setebos*, Bagehot gives an example of what he means by the grotesque, using extensive quotation to show how readers might often be disinclined to pursue such a difficult piece of writing. Bagehot finds the lines he quotes to be a fairly typical example of Browning's style and theme and summarizes the poet's chief consideration in his verse as being the "mind in difficulties" (an interesting suggestion that readers might pursue in their review of many of Browning's works).

Bagehot maintains that for a number of readers the grotesque simply does not appeal, and he makes the astute (if controversial) claim that, while giving pleasure is not the chief aim of poetry, it should nevertheless be pleasing. Browning's verse, Bagehot claims, pleases few readers by nature of its grotesque subject matter. Readers should note Bagehot's excellent (and repeated) allusions to the "material" nature of Browning's thought as revealed in his poetry, its lack of idealism and grounding in reality, its concrete examples rather than abstract conceits. The general impression is of a distinctly "earthy" verse but, nevertheless, one that affords profound insights into life and living.

There is, however, a third kind of art which differs from these (ornate art and pure art) on the point in which they most resemble one another. Ornate art and pure art have this in common, that they paint the types of literature in as good perfection as they can. Ornate art, indeed, uses undue disguises and unreal enhancements; it does not confine itself to the best types; on the contrary it is its office to make the best of imperfect types and lame approximations; but ornate art, as much as pure art, catches its subject in the best light it can, takes the most developed aspect of it which it can find, and throws upon it the most congruous colours it can use. But grotesque art does just the contrary. It takes the type, so to say, *in difficulties*. It gives a representation of it in its minimum development, amid the circumstances least favourable to it, just while it is struggling with obstacles, just where it is encumbered with incongruities. It deals, to use the language of science, not with normal types but with abnormal specimens; to use the language of old philosophy, not with what nature is striving to be, but with what by some lapse she has happened to become.

This art works by contrast. It enables you to see, it makes you see, the perfect type by painting the opposite deviation. It shows you what ought to be by what ought not to be; when complete, it reminds you of the perfect image by showing you the distorted and imperfect image. Of this art we possess in the present generation one prolific master. Mr. Browning is an artist working by incongruity. Possibly hardly one of his most considerable efforts can be found which is not great because of its odd mixture. He puts together things which no one else would have put together, and produces on our minds a result which no one else would have produced, or tried to produce. His admirers may not like all we may have to say of him. But in our way we too are among his admirers. No one ever read him without seeing not only his great ability but his great *mind*. He not only possesses superficial useable talents, but the strong something, the inner secret something, which uses them and controls them; he is great, not in mere accomplishments, but in himself. He has applied a hard strong intellect to real life; he has applied the same intellect to the problems of his age. He has striven to know what is: he has endeavoured not to be cheated by counterfeits, not to be infatuated with illusions. His heart is in what he says. He has battered his brain against his creed till he believes it. He has accomplishments too, the more effective because they are mixed. He is at once a student of mysticism and a citizen of the world. He brings to the club sofa distinct visions of old creeds, intense images of strange thoughts: he takes to the bookish student tidings of wild Bohemia, and little traces of the *demi-monde*. He puts down what is good for the naughty and what is naughty for the good. Over women his easier writings exercise that imperious power which belongs to the writings of a great man of the world upon such matters. He knows women, and therefore they wish to know him. If we blame many of Browning's efforts, it is in the interest of art, and not from a wish to hurt or degrade him.

If we wanted to illustrate the nature of grotesque art by an exaggerated instance, we should have selected a poem which the chance of late publication brings us in this new volume. Mr. Browning has undertaken to describe what may be called *mind in difficulties*—mind set to make out the universe under the worst and hardest circumstances. He takes 'Caliban,' not perhaps exactly Shakespeare's Caliban, but an analogous and worse creature; a strong thinking power, but a nasty creature—a gross animal, uncontrolled and unelevated by any feeling of religion or duty. The delineation of him will show that Mr. Browning does not wish to take undue advantage of his readers by a choice of nice subjects.

'Will sprawl, now that the heat of day is best,
Flat on his belly in the pit's much mire,
With elbows wide, fists clenched to prop his chin.
And, while he kicks both feet in the cool slush,
And feels about his spine small eft-things course,
Run in and out each arm, and make him laugh;
And while above his head a pompion-plant,
Coating the cave-top as a brow its eye,
Creeps down to touch and tickle hair and beard,
And now a flower drops with a bee inside,
And now a fruit to snap at, catch and crunch,—

This pleasant creature proceeds to give his idea of the origin of the universe, and it is as follows. Caliban speaks in the third person, and is of opinion that the maker of the universe took to making it on account of his personal discomfort:—

Setebos, Setebos, and Setebos!
'Thinketh, He dwelleth i' the cold o' the moon.
'Thinketh He made it, with the sun to match,
But not the stars; the stars came otherwise;
Only made clouds, winds, meteors, such as that;
Also this isle, what lives and grows thereon,
And snaky sea which rounds and ends the same.
'Thinketh, it came of being ill at ease:
He hated that He cannot change His cold,
Nor cure its ache. 'Hath spied an icy fish
That longed to 'scape the rock-stream where she lived,
And thaw herself within the lukewarm brine
O' the lazy sea her stream thrusts far amid,
A crystal spike 'twixt two warm walls of wave;
Only she ever sickened, found repulse
At the other kind of water, not her life,
(Green-dense and dim-delicious, bred o' the sun)
Flounced back from bliss she was not born to breathe,
And in her old bounds buried her despair,
Hating and loving warmth alike: so He.

'Thinketh, He made thereat the sun, this isle,
Trees and the fowls here, beast and creeping thing.
Yon otter, sleek-wet, black, lithe as a leech;
Yon auk, one fire-eye, in a ball of foam,
That floats and feeds; a certain badger brown
He hath watched hunt with that slant white-wedge eye
By moonlight; and the pie with the long tongue
That pricks deep into oakwarts for a worm,
And says a plain word when she finds her prize,
But will not eat the ants; the ants themselves
That build a wall of seeds and settled stalks
About their hole—He made all these and more,
Made all we see, and us, in spite: how else?

It may seem perhaps to most readers that these lines are very difficult,
and that they are unpleasant. And so they are. We quote them to illustrate,
not the *success* of grotesque art, but the *nature* of grotesque art. It shows
the end at which this species of art aims, and if it fails it is from over-
boldness in the choice of a subject by the artist, or from the defects of
its execution. A thinking faculty more in difficulties—a great type—an
inquisitive, searching intellect under more disagreeable conditions, with
worse helps, more likely to find falsehood, less likely to find truth, can
scarcely be imagined. Nor is the mere description of the thought at all bad:
on the contrary, if we closely examine it, it is very clever. Hardly anyone
could have amassed so many ideas at once nasty and suitable. But scarcely
any readers—any casual readers—who are not of the sect of Mr. Browning's
admirers will be able to examine it enough to appreciate it. From a defect,
partly of subject, and partly of style, many of Mr. Browning's works make
a demand upon the reader's zeal and sense of duty to which the nature of
most readers is unequal. They have on the turf the convenient expression
'staying power': some horses can hold on and others cannot. But hardly
any reader not of especial and peculiar nature can hold on through such
composition. There is not enough of 'staying power' in human nature. One
of his greatest admirers once owned to us that he seldom or never began
a new poem without looking on in advance, and foreseeing with caution
what length of intellectual adventure he was about to commence. Whoever
will work hard at such poems will find much mind in them: they are a sort
of quarry of ideas, but whoever goes there will find these ideas in such a
jagged, ugly, useless shape that he can hardly bear them.

We are not judging Mr. Browning simply from a hasty recent production. All poets are liable to misconceptions, and if such a piece as 'Caliban upon Setebos' were an isolated error, a venial and particular exception, we should have given it no prominence. We have put it forward because it just elucidates both our subject and the characteristics of Mr. Browning. But many other of his best known pieces do so almost equally. . . .

It is very natural that a poet whose wishes incline, or whose genius conducts him, to a grotesque art, should be attracted towards mediaeval subjects. There is no age whose legends are so full of grotesque subjects, and no age where real life was so fit to suggest them. Then, more than at any other time, good principles have been under great hardships. The vestiges of ancient civilisation, the germs of modern civilisation, the little remains of what had been, the small beginnings of what is, were buried under a cumbrous mass of barbarism and cruelty. Good elements hidden in horrid accompaniments are the special theme of grotesque art, and these mediaeval life and legends afford more copiously than could have been furnished before Christianity gave its new elements of good, or since modern civilisation has removed some few at least of the old elements of destruction. A *buried* life like the spiritual mediaeval was Mr. Browning's natural element, and he was right to be attracted by it. His mistake has been, that he has not made it pleasant; that he has forced his art to topics on which no one could charm, or on which he, at any rate, could not; that on these occasions and in these poems he has failed in fascinating men and women of sane taste.

We say 'sane' because there is a most formidable and estimable *insane* taste. The will has great though indirect power over the taste, just as it has over the belief. There are some horrid beliefs from which human nature revolts, from which at first it shrinks, to which, at first, no effort can force it. But if we fix the mind upon them they have a power over us just because of their natural offensiveness. They are like the sight of human blood: experienced soldiers tell us that at first men are sickened by the smell and newness of blood almost to death and fainting, but that as soon as they harden their hearts and stiffen their minds, as soon as they *will* bear it, then comes an appetite for slaughter, a tendency to gloat on carnage, to love blood, at least for the moment, with a deep, eager love. It is a principle that if we put down a healthy instinctive aversion, nature avenges herself by creating an unhealthy insane attraction. For this reason, the most earnest truth-seeking men fall into the worst delusions; they will not let their mind alone; they force it towards some ugly thing, which a crotchet of argument, a conceit of intellect recommends, and nature punishes their disregard of her warning by subjection to the ugly one, by belief in it. Just so, the most industrious critics get the most admiration. They think it unjust to rest in their instinctive natural horror: they overcome it, and angry nature gives them over to ugly poems and marries them to detestable stanzas.

Mr. Browning possibly, and some of the worst of Mr. Browning's admirers certainly, will say that these grotesque objects exist in real life, and therefore they ought to be, at least may be, described in art. But though pleasure is not the end of poetry, pleasing is a condition of poetry. An exceptional monstrosity of horrid ugliness cannot be made pleasing, except it be made to suggest—to recall—the perfection, the beauty, from which it is a deviation. Perhaps in extreme cases no art is equal to this; but then such self-imposed problems should not be worked by the artist; these out-of-the-way and detestable subjects should be let alone by him. It is rather characteristic of Mr. Browning to neglect this rule. He is the most of a realist, and the least of an idealist, of any poet we know. He evidently sympathises with some part at least of Bishop Blougram's apology. Anyhow this world exists. 'There *is* good wine—there *are* pretty women—there *are* comfortable benefices—there *is* money, and it is pleasant to spend it. Accept the creed of your age and you get these, reject that creed and you lose them. And for what do you lose them? For a fancy creed of your own, which no one else will accept, which hardly anyone will call a "creed," which most people will consider a sort of unbelief.' Again, Mr. Browning evidently loves what we may call the realism, the grotesque realism, of Orthodox Christianity. Many parts of it in which great divines have felt keen difficulties are quite pleasant to him. He must *see* his religion, he must have an 'object-lesson' in believing. He must have a creed that will *take*, which wins and holds the miscellaneous world, which stout men will heed, which nice women will adore. The spare moments of solitary religion—the 'obstinate questionings,' the 'high instincts,' the 'first affections,' the 'shadowy recollections,'

> Which, be they what they may,
> Are yet the fountain light of all our day,
> Are yet a master light of all our seeing;

the great but vague faith—the unutterable tenets—seem to him worthless, visionary; they are not enough 'immersed in matter;' they move about 'in worlds not realised.' We wish he could be tried like the prophet once; he would have found God in the earthquake and the storm; he would have deciphered from them a bracing and a rough religion: he would have known that crude men and ignorant women felt them too, and he would accordingly have trusted them; but he would have distrusted and disregarded the 'still small voice;' he would have said it was 'fancy'—a thing you thought you heard to-day, but were not sure you had heard to-morrow: he would call it a nice illusion, an immaterial prettiness; he would ask triumphantly, 'How are you to get the mass of men to heed this little thing?' he would have persevered and insisted, 'My *wife* does not hear it.'

But although a suspicion of beauty, and a taste for ugly reality, have led Mr. Browning to exaggerate the functions, and to caricature the nature of grotesque art, we own, or rather, we maintain, that he has given many excellent specimens of that art within its proper boundaries and limits. Take an example, his picture of what we may call the *bourgeois* nature in *difficulties;* in the utmost difficulty, in contact with magic and the supernatural. He has made of it something homely, comic, true; reminding us of what *bourgeois* nature really is. By showing us the type under abnormal conditions, he reminds us of the type under its best and most satisfactory conditions.

—Walter Bagehot, "Wordsworth, Tennyson,
and Browning; or, Pure, Ornate, and Grotesque Art
in English Poetry," 1864, *Collected Works,* ed.
Norman St. John-Stevas, 1965, vol. 2, pp. 352–361

ALFRED AUSTIN
"THE POETRY OF THE PERIOD" (1869)

Alfred Austin was an English poet and was appointed poet laureate after the death of Lord Alfred Tennyson in 1896. In the following essay extracted from the literary magazine the *Temple Bar*, Austin attempts to assess the position of Browning among his contemporaries in the world of letters, and most notably Austin examines Browning's position relative to that of Tennyson. The article suggests that just as poetic thought is naturally presented in poetic language (or "music"), so philosophical thought is presented in prose. According to this division, Austin does not believe Browning to be a poet at all, and he states that this is, in large part, the problem that many readers have with Browning's work: They are not confronted with the type of language relevant to their (correct) expectations. Not only does Browning essentially write in metrical prose, but his thought is philosophical, and this strange hybrid of thought and language leaves many readers in a quandary. Austin does, however, grant that the thoughts are profound, Browning's wit precise, and the poet an acute analyzer.

Austin examines a heading from Browning's *Sordello* as exemplifying the poet's conception of his estate, no matter whether the opinion is incorrect or not. Browning, Austin says, conceives his artistic function to be that of portraying the development of the soul, of depicting the inner progress of character from a psychological perspective. But Browning does not accomplish the synthetic aspect of his conception of the poet's office, does not show the characters presenting their own souls' development in verse; Browning only analyzes and, Austin says, fails to proceed any further. His poetry is akin to the dissections of the anatomist. Shakespeare is presented as the greatest of synthetic artists, as having the capacity to make his characters come alive in his drama and to reflect on their own being; he was not an analyst like Browning, this to his benefit, unraveling character into its constitutive parts and examining those separate parts one by one. Austin states that in the confusion of the role of a philosophical analyst, no matter that he is great in this role, Browning has written obscure, jargon-ridden prose in the form of poetry, a form that is suited neither to his thought nor to his analytical intellect.

Austin then turns in detail to the manner of Browning's language, what the poet had called "half-words." Austin says that it was simple necessity that required Browning to speak in this way, for if he had written in clear language, the fact that he was a prose writer and that his use of metrical form was superfluous to his thought would have become abundantly apparent. Browning's writing does not have the music nor the clarity required of true verse for Austin. He argues that many critics who acclaim Tennyson as the greatest poet of the age also find him wanting in "loftiness" of thought, and now those same critics see in Browning that which Tennyson lacks. They are consequently making the mistake of replacing Tennyson with Browning in their critical estimation. Austin agrees that Tennyson lacks elevation of thought, but he carefully distinguishes Browning for the "depth" or profundity of his ideas and claims the critics erroneously presume that the latter can satisfy the want of the former.

Austin's own poetry was not held in particularly high esteem, and much of his criticism of both Browning and Tennyson might be read as a retaliation for his own lack of critical acclaim. Certainly the book from which this extract is taken was generally considered to be immoderate in its attacks by his contemporaries and broadly uncritical in its positions (in the sense of being overly opinionated and extreme in its sentiments). However, to be fair to Austin, his extract provides a rationale that has combined the critical concerns of many scholars about Browning's verse with the general public's quandaries as to what to make of it. If the tone is caustic, Austin does not limit his praise for what he considers Browning's greatness (even if it is not in the realm he defines as poetry): He assigns plaudits where he believes them due and is equally obliging in his (il)liberal lodging of criticisms.

———⁓⁓⁓—— ——⁓⁓⁓—— ——⁓⁓⁓——

Whether Mr. Browning keeps a Commonplace Book, we have no means of knowing; but we have every means of knowing that he thinks in prose, for the prose thoughts are there before us, gratuitously turned by some arbitrary whim, which we confess completely puzzles us, into metre. Mr. Browning is, as we have said, a profound thinker, and nearly all his thoughts have the quality of depth. Now, probably all thoughts to which this quality of depth can be ascribed, arrive at the portals of the brain in this prose—their natural vesture; whilst, on the contrary, lofty thoughts, their antitheses, usually enter it in the subtle garb of music. Here we have a clear difference in kind; prose thoughts, so to speak, from below—poetical thoughts, so to speak, from above. If we suppose a permeable plane dividing these two regions of thought, we can easily understand how there comes to be what we may call a sliding scale of poets, and a sliding scale of philosophical thinkers; some of the latter, to whom the faculty of philosophising cannot be denied, being rather shallow—some of the former, whose claims to poetical status cannot fairly be questioned, not being very soaring; and we can further understand how the natural denizens of one sphere may ever and anon cross the permeable plane, invade the other sphere, and seem to belong to it in the sense in which foreigners belong to a country they are constantly visiting. But for all that there ever remains a substantial difference between the two spheres and between their respective native inhabitants, between the country of poetry and the country of prose, between poetical power and instinct and philosophical power and proclivity. Accordingly, where a man talks the language of the sphere to which he properly belongs—in other words, when a philosophical thinker publishes his thoughts in prose, or a poetical thinker addresses us in verse—our task is comparatively simple. All we have got to do is to decide whether the former be profound or shallow, and whether the latter have a lofty or a lagging pinion. It is when a man affects to talk the language of the sphere to which he does not essentially belong, that he deceives some people, and puzzles us all. This is precisely what Mr. Browning has done. Hence most people scarcely know what to make of this poetico-philosophical hybrid, this claimant to the great inheritance of bardic fame, whose hands are the hands of Esau, but whose voice is the voice of Jacob. Several, whose eyes, like those of

Isaac, are dim, and who therefore cannot see, admit the claim—hesitatingly, it is true, again like Isaac—of the hands, and accept him as a poet. But it is the true resonant voice, not the made-up delusive hand, which is the test of the singer; and to those whose sight is not dim, Mr. Browning is not a poet at all—save in the sense that all cultivated men and women of sensitive feelings are poets—but a deep thinker, a profound philosopher, a keen analyser, and a biting wit. With this key to what to most persons is a riddle—for, despite the importunate attempts of certain critics who, as we have already said, having placed Mr. Tennyson on a poetical pedestal considerably too high for him, are now beginning to waver in their extravagant creed, and are disposed to put him on one a trifle lower, placing Mr. Browning there instead, the general public has not yet become quite reconciled to the operation—we think we shall be able to rid them of their perplexities. At any rate, we will keep applying it as we go along.

Let us revert to *Paracelsus* and take our start from it, as Mr. Browning himself did. His lyrical pieces apart—of which something anon—and the humoristic faculty which has since developed itself in him, Mr. Browning in *Paracelsus* is what Mr. Browning is in all the many so-called poetical works he has since given to the world. He is Mr. Browning, naturally not yet grown to his full size; not yet quite so deep, shrewd, obscure, fantastical, unmusical; but with the exceptions we have just made, what manner and matter of mental man he is may there be satisfactorily scrutinised. He is at his never-abandoned natural task of thinking deep thoughts in prose, and his artificial trick of turning them into verse. He is, as he imagines, working like a dramatist, just as he has since imagined himself to be working as a dramatist in such pieces as *Bishop Blougram's Apology*, "Caliban on Setebos," &c. Indeed, he has let us into the secret of his method in *Sordello*, written very shortly after *Paracelsus*, in the following lines; which we quote, though at the risk perhaps of most of our readers declaring that they have not the faintest notion as to what they mean:

> How I rose,
> And how you have advanced! since evermore
> Yourselves effect what I was fain before
> Effect, what I supplied yourselves suggest,
> What I leave bare yourselves can now invest.
> How we attain to talk as brothers talk,
> In half-words, call things by half-names, no balk
> From discontinuing old aids. To-day

Takes in account the work of Yesterday:
Has not the world a Past now, its adept
New aids? A single touch more may enhance,
A touch less turn to insignificance,
Those structures' symmetry the Past has strewed
The world with, once so bare. Leave the mere rude
Explicit details! 'tis but brother's speech
We need, speech where an accent's change gives each
The other's soul—no speech to understand
By former audience: need was then to expand,
Expatiate—hardly were we brothers! true—
Nor I lament my small remove from you,
Nor reconstruct what stands already. Ends
Accomplished turn to means: my art intends
New structure from the ancient.

It must not be supposed that we quote this passage with approbation. Not only do we think it not poetry, but we think it detestable gibberish, even if we look at it as prose. Had Mr. Browning been writing bona-fide prose, he would have put it very differently and much more intelligibly; but talking, to revert to our metaphor, in a foreign language over which he has not obtained due mastery, he is shockingly unintelligible, or at least painfully difficult to understand. By dint of great trouble we have arrived at understanding the above passage, and will endeavour briefly to explain its meaning. Our readers have no doubt heard the vulgar proverb, "A nod is as good as a wink to a blind horse." Mr. Browning wishes to intimate that a nod or a wink is really and seriously as good to an intelligent man of the nineteenth century as formal speech. Shakespeare and such unfortunate individuals, having had to deal with an inferior set of people, were compelled to use "rude explicit details." Mr. Browning's "art intending new structure from the ancient," has only to "talk in half-words, call things by half-names," and if they do not understand him, the fault is theirs of course, not his. They are not his brothers. In this same *Sordello*, from which we are quoting, over each page stands a prose heading, which is a continuation of the foregoing one. Over the passage from which we have made the above extract, the following headings occur: "He asserts the poet's rank and right, Basing these on their proper ground, Recognizing true dignity in service, Whether successively that of Epoist, *Dramatist or, so to call him, analyst*, Who turns in due course synthesist."

Now the last two headings are of great importance, just as is the passage in verse below them which we have quoted, because, however false may be their matter, and however deplorable their manner, they contain Mr. Browning's own estimate of his office, and his own account of his method. As such, they are invaluable to us. Just one more brief confession on his part will complete for us the idea, as understood by himself, of his functions as a poet. In the Dedication of *Sordello* to Mr. Milsand, written in 1863, or twenty-three years after it was first published, Mr. Browning writes: "The historical decoration was purposely of no more importance than a background requires; and my stress lay on the incidents in the development of a soul: *little else is worth study. I, at least, always thought so.*" Thus Mr. Browning's office, according to his own account, is that of an analyst who turns in due course synthesist and develops a soul by half-words; or, as we should put it, it is to get inside an imaginary or historical personage, and evolve him for the benefit of the intelligent public by nods and winks. This is how his "new art intends new structure from the ancient."

We hope our readers understand us; for, if they do not, they will certainly never understand Mr. Browning, and it is highly desirable that they should understand so much of him as the foregoing, both in order to be able to measure him as he asks to be measured, and to appreciate our account of him, which a very little reflection shows to be in perfect harmony with, and indeed substantially the same as, his own account of himself. What is his own account of himself? An analyst who turns in due course synthesist, whose subject matter is souls, and whose method of communication with the outer world is half-words arranged in metre. What is our account of him? A subtle, profound, conscious psychologist, who scientifically gets inside souls, and, having scrutinised their thoughts and motives in a prose and methodical fashion, then makes them give the result, as if they had been scrutinising themselves, in verse. This latter operation Mr. Browning evidently imagines is synthesis. There never was a more ludicrous mistake. It is, in reality, nothing more than the analysis completed and stated, and is no more synthesis than a lecture by Professor Huxley on the *vertebrata* is an animal. Mr. Browning labours under the greatest possible delusion when he imagines that he ever "turns in due course synthesist." That is precisely what he never does. He remains a mere analyst to the end of the chapter, pottering about among the brains and entrails of the souls he has dissected, and utterly unable to do anything with them, except to call attention to the component parts he has skilfully laid bare with his knife. It would be wonderful if he could do anything more; just as wonderful as it would be if the anatomical professor could put together again the poor carcass of the dog he has reduced to so many inanimate members. He can galvanise them, it is true, for a moment, into simulating life. So can Mr. Browning. But that is the range of the synthesis of both of them. If Mr. Browning wants to know of a dramatist who is a real synthesist, we can easily tell him of one. His name is Shakespeare. But, then, Shakespeare was, luckily, not so great in analysis as Mr. Browning. Speaking properly, Shakespeare never analyses at all in our presence, and probably never did so even in the presence of his own consciousness, any more than millions of men who speak grammatically analyse the construction of their sentences before they utter them. Every real drama—indeed every real work of plastic (as opposed to mere technic) art—is an organism, a growth, a vitality, just as much as is a bird, a tree, or a mammal. Not only is it true that a poet is born, not made, but it is equally true that his poem is born, not made.[1] In his brain, heart, soul, whatever we like to call it—in his being would be, perhaps, the best word—exists the seed or germ of a poem or of many poems; and all that external conditions, sights, sounds, experiences, can do for this seed or germ is to foster or to check it. But the thing itself, the real living, poetic protoplasm, is not to be had or got *ab extra*. Going about seizing upon objects and submitting them to analysis, even though synthesis be then superadded, will by no means produce poetry, or any work of plastic art—using the word art properly, as opposed to craft. Otherwise a chemist, who finds out what a particular kind of gunpowder is made of, and then makes it, would be a poet. For to him is peculiarly applicable Mr. Browning's definition of "dramatist"— terrible dramatist indeed! "or, so to speak, analyst, who turns in due course synthesist." But we assure Mr. Browning there is an impassable difference between dramas and detonating powder, and also between the processes by which they are to be produced. We freely grant—indeed, we more than grant, we insist—that Mr. Browning, whatever may be said against his synthetical powers (and, as we have seen, even if he had them to perfection, he would not necessarily be a poet), is great as an analyst. But the analysed goose of the fable laid no more golden eggs; and analysed souls are just as little likely ever again to speak golden words. It is not the province of the poet to perform any such operation. It is the province of such men as Hartley, James Mill, and Professor Bain, and admirably do they perform their work. But we have not got any poems from them, nor is it likely that from the only living one of the illustrious trio we ever shall. Having a distinct comprehension of their office and its limits, they have accordingly kept within the sphere—the sphere of deep prose thoughts as opposed to that of lofty poetical thoughts, of which we have spoken—to which their talents and task naturally belonged. Hence their labours have been of inestimable service to the world. But Mr. Browning has perversely flitted from one sphere to the other, insisted on making himself at home where he is a perfect stranger, uttered profound thoughts in would-be poetic idiom, an idiom foreign to them and to him, and involved them accordingly in such abominable jargon that, when he and his affected admirers have passed away, they will be utterly lost to the world—for they *will* be a loss, on account of their depth—and buried in permanent oblivion. Should he possibly be remembered at all, it will be because posterity, condensing this our judgment, will inscribe on his grave the words of Martial:

Carmina scribis et Apolline nullo Laudari debes.
Anglice:
You kept on twanging at your lyre, Though no Apollo did inspire.

So much for Mr. Browning's *novum organum,* or new method of making poetry. Having considered the subject-matter of his work, and the process by which he labours on it, we have now only to examine the form in which he presents it, when finished, to the public gaze. In other words, having scrutinised his matter and method, we have now to look at his manner, or, to speak still more plainly, his expression—those "half-words," as he has himself called them, whereby he communicates with intelligent readers. Now, why does Mr. Browning communicate his thoughts in this fashion of half-words? The answer is exceedingly simple. Because, if he communicated them in full ones—i.e. explicitly and clearly—though still in verse, their prose nature would be seen at a glance by everybody; and everybody, the simplest person as well as the most pedantic, could not fail to perceive that the author was whimsically and gratuitously measuring them out into certain lengths, instead of unaffectedly not caring how many metrical feet there were in them, or whether they formed feet at all. For there is no difficulty in putting anything into verse, as may be seen in the versified rules of the "Gradus ad Parnassum," or in the advertisements of Mr. Moses, the cheap outfitter. It would require very little ingenuity to turn "Euclid" into metre, and, for anything we know, it may already have been done. But, as in these instances the primary object is to be understood, the reader sees at once that he is not reading, or supposed to be reading, poetry, but only metre, so employed for mnemonic or for catchpenny purposes. In Mr. Browning's case the unsophisticated reader really does not know what it is he is reading. It is printed in arbitrary lengths, and therefore looks as if it cannot well be prose; yet it does not, as a rule, read like verse, and in nearly all cases its meaning is obscure, and in none very obvious. It if were, Mr. Browning would be found out without more ado. We do not mean to say that he consciously deceives his readers; he deceives his readers and himself too. He is the real M. Jourdain, who has been writing prose all his life without knowing it; very bad prose, it is true, as half-words arranged in lengths necessarily must be, but prose all the same. It would be idle to quote instances of this, for his works are one long almost uninterrupted instance of it. You may open any one of his volumes at any page you like for proof of the assertion. Surely the two passages we have already quoted from him, though for a totally different purpose, will suffice as instances. If

> Since evermore
> Yourselves effect what I was fain before Effect, what I
> supplied yourselves suggest, What I leave bare yourselves
> can now invest

does not strike everybody as very bad prose, consisting of half-words arranged in lengths, we own ourselves completely beaten, or at least baffled, in our demonstration. And what is true of these passages is true of Mr. Browning's compositions *passim*. For poetic thought has its natural utterance or expression, just as everything else has, and you cannot make it express itself differently save by travestying it. To put the case as extremely as possible, yet without travelling one hair's breadth beyond the limits of the strictest truth, a living tree expresses itself in foliage not more necessarily than does poetic thought express itself in a certain and inevitable kind and form of diction. But what is the diction of poetry? Is it half-words arranged in lengths? Is it obscure diction of any sort? Is the diction of poetry anything but diction that is at once clear—*that,* it shares with other diction—lofty, and musical? Who are the clearest and most musical poets? Unquestionably the great poets. Whose blank verse is fit to be mentioned, even for mere sound, after Shakespeare's? Only Milton's; and his, *longo intervallo*. Mr. Tennyson's, smooth as it is, is the poorest stuff compared with the blank verse of Shakespeare or Milton. It is melodious enough, no doubt (just as Moore, in rhyme, is the perfection of melody); but where is its harmony—where are the infinite harmonies in it? They are wanting. For melody is not the only thing in music. All the wonderful combinations that come of an innate familiarity with the use of fugue and counterpoint make something very different from mere melody. Shakespeare and Milton betray this innate familiarity in blank verse; Spenser and Byron betray it in rhyme; and so, whilst they are the greatest of our poets in other respects, they are, when one once knows what music really means and is, the most musical. Similarly they are the most clear. Poor Mr. Browning is both muddy and unmusical to the last degree. In fact, his style may fairly be described as the very incarnation of discordant obscurity. Is it wonderful? He has no voice, and yet he wants to sing. He is not a poet, and yet he would fain write poetry. We have no right to be surprised if he is inarticulate, and if we get only half-words cut into lengths. The wonder would be if we got anything else. In reading Mr. Browning, we are perpetually reminded of those lines in Mr. Bailey's *Festus*:

> The dress of words,
> Like to the Roman girl's enticing garb,
> Should let the play of limb be seen through it.

> . . . A *mist of words,*
> Like halos round the moon, though they enlarge
> The seeming *size of thoughts, make the light less.*[2]

But, it will be urged, there is occasionally something else in Mr. Browning, which, if not poetry, is at least something very like poetry. Exactly: there is. But when? When Mr. Browning ceases to be Mr. Browning proper, when his *differentia* disappears, and he is no longer Mr. Browning "the dramatist, or, so to call him, analyst," but Mr. Browning the man pure and simple. It will be remembered that we have already incidentally said that Mr. Browning is not a poet save in the sense that all cultivated men and women of sensitive feelings are poets; and we made the statement deliberately and with the intention of reverting to it here. It would therefore be strange indeed if in the course of thirty-five years' obstinate practice of writing verse Mr. Browning had not once or twice deviated into penning something that resembled poetry, and was so much on the borderland of poetry or even across it that it ought to bear that name. Be it so. All that we are arguing for is that Mr. Browning is not specifically a poet, but is specifically something quite different. The poetic temperament and intellect are not the *proprium* of Mr. Browning, but only the *accidens*. But let us see what is the highest result, when the latter has, so to speak, the upper hand, or the command of him.

> Oh! to be in England
> Now that April's there;
> And whosoever wakes in England
> Sees, some morning, unaware,
> That the lowest boughs and the brush-wood sheaf

Round the elm-tree bole are in tiny leaf,
While the chaffinch sings on the orchard bough In England—now!
(Lyrics.)

Love like mine must have return, I thought: no river starts but to some
sea. (*A Soul's Tragedy.*)

Is this poetry? If it is, it is of a very commonplace sort, rather above than below
average Magazine verse, and we could produce many examples of it from Mr.
Browning if we had space, inasmuch as he perpetually, indeed invariably,
lapses into commonplace when he allows himself to think, on the poetic
side, naturally. Often, as though conscious that what poetic utterance he has
in common with ordinary cultivated men and women of sensitive feelings
is of this complexion, he will not allow himself to think naturally, but strains
at being original whilst still wanting to remain poetical. Then the result is
lamentable; is, in fact, spasmodic. For instance:

Earth is a wintry clod:
But spring-wind, like a dancing psaltress, passes Over its
breast to waken it.
(*Paracelsus.*)

The sprinkled isles, Lily on lily, that o'erlace the
sea, And laugh their pride when the light wave lisps,
'Greece.'
(*Cleon.*)
One wave,
Feeling the foot of Him upon its neck, Gaped as a snake
does, lolled out its large tongue, And licked the whole
labour flat.
(*Dramatis Personae*)

Is it better in May? I ask you. You've summer all at once;
In a day he leaps complete with a few strong April suns!
'Mid the sharp short emerald wheat, scarce risen three fingers well,
The wild tulip, at end of its tube, blows out its great red bell,
Like a thin clear bubble of blood, for the children to pick and sell.
(*Up at a Villa—Down in the City.*)

These are pure spasms; specimens of the mental action of a man who is striving earnestly to be an original poet, and who for the life of him cannot be—since no striving will make a man such, any more than it will give him wings. Mr. John Stuart Mill has in one of his admirable *Dissertations and Discussions* made the unfortunate remark that probably any man of good abilities might by determination and persistence end by becoming as great a poet as Wordsworth—he himself thinking very highly of Wordsworth as a poet. In any philosophical question we should differ from Mr. Mill with great diffidence; but we have not a moment's hesitation in saying that such an assertion, save as applied to—say—one-half of Wordsworth's compositions, which, as we have already remarked, are perhaps not poetry at all, but only verse, must be described, despite the reverence we feel for Mr. Mill, as fundamentally erroneous. Accepted, however, to the limited extent we have prescribed to it, the assertion is true enough, and it is singularly applicable to Mr. Browning. Any ordinarily cultivated person of sensitive feelings who could write verse might have written the first two commonplace passages we have just quoted from Mr. Browning, and, being resolved to be original, might have strained himself till he concocted the last four. The former are examples of such natural versified speech as might be attained by almost anybody. The latter are instances of that artificial, acquired, laborious, *foreign* speech which is necessarily fallen into by people who are clumsily translating complex thoughts into an alien tongue. As for such pieces as "Marching Along," and "How They Brought the Good News from Ghent," they cannot be classed, at the very highest estimate, save with Macaulay's *Lays of Rome,* to which surely no impartial person can doubt they are very inferior—and yet no one talks or thinks of Macaulay as specifically a poet—and ought more fairly to be classed with the Cavalier Songs of Mr. Walter Thornbury, whom no one has ever dreamt of alluding to save as a very spirited versifier.

Thus, as far as we have inquired, we find Mr. Browning, in his attempted *role* of poet, to be doing three things, and generally the first of them. Either playing the part of analyst, getting inside souls, and developing them to the reader by half-words, which is not writing poetry at all; or writing simple intelligible verse, which, if it is to be considered poetry, must honestly be described as commonplace poetry, both easy and by no means infrequent of production; or, in dread and dislike of being commonplace, writing what has so happily been termed spasmodic poetry, poetry that comes of violent straining after effect, and which ought, on no account, to be written by anybody, since it sins against that eternal truth, so well put in the same passage in *Festus* from which we have already quoted:

Simplicity
Is nature's first step, and the last of art.

Which quotation we may supplement, for the benefit of Mr. Browning and his admirers, by another from a still higher authority, and in itself still more suggestive and instructive:

This is an art
Which doth mend nature, change it rather, but
The art itself is nature.
(*Winter's Tale*, iv. 3.)

That is just the art which Mr. Browning has not got.

But how about "Andrea del Sarto," "Fra Lippo Lippi," "A Death in the Desert," "Caliban on Setebos," and *Bishop Blougram's Apology?* What have we to say about these? This much. That, with the exception of "Caliban on Setebos"—which, on account of its rendering certain prevailing modes of thought on theological questions, has been very much overestimated—they are productions betraying the possession of peculiar imagination, of mordant wit of almost the highest kind, of a delicious sense of humour, and, in "Andrea del Sarto," of deep tenderness. But neither tenderness, nor humour, nor wit, nor even imagination, nor indeed all these together, will constitute a man a poet. Laplace, Bacon,[3] Copernicus, Newton, Mr. Darwin, all have immense imagination; and we might, of course, extend the list indefinitely. We think we have allowed it to be seen that we regard Mr. Browning's intellectual powers as very considerable indeed. *Bishop Blougram's Apology* is an astonishing production, which we invariably read almost throughout with unflagging zest. But it is not poetry. There is not a line of poetry in it from first to last, and we confess we prefer it to all Mr. Browning's compositions. Suppose he had never written anything else, would it have occurred to anybody that he was a poet, or even aspiring to be a poet? In order still further to illustrate our meaning, suppose Mr. Tennyson had never written anything but "The Northern Farmer"—a piece we chuckle over with inexpressible delight—again, would it have occurred to anybody that Mr. Tennyson was a poet, or was pretending to be such? Of course not; no more than it would have occurred to his contemporaries to have regarded Cowper as a poet if he had never written anything but *John Gilpin,* whose pre-eminent success positively annoyed its author? So with *Bishop Blougram's Apology,* and all of Mr. Browning's compositions, or passages in his compositions, which are *ejusdem generis* with it. They are witty, wise, shrewd, deep, true, wonderful—anything or everything but poetry. It is the greatest, though apparently the commonest, mistake in the world to suppose that the quality of verse, provided the thoughts it expresses are excellent thoughts, involves for those thoughts and their expression the quality of poetry. This has been Mr. Browning's ignis fatuus through life; and the absurd chase it has led him he in turn has led those who have not found out what it is he has all along been following. In a word, Mr. Browning's so-called Muse is a *lusus naturae*, a sport, to use gardeners' language; but certain sapient critics have been exulting over it, as though it were a new and finer specimen of the old true poetic stock. Moreover, Mr. Browning's undoubted faculty of depth has bewitched and bewrayed them. Despite their protestations of being perfectly content with Mr. Tennyson as the great poet who justifies the period, they are not content with him. They have all along more or less consciously felt what we insisted on in our article last month—his want of loftiness. Now, in Mr. Browning they have found something that unquestionably is not in Mr. Tennyson, and they have begun to fancy that that something may possibly supply Mr. Tennyson's shortcomings. That comes of not having thought the matter out with regard to either of these authors.[4] They know Mr. Tennyson wants something or other: they know Mr. Browning has something or other. But from lack of patient reflection and investigation they fail to perceive for themselves that what Mr. Tennyson wants is height, and what Mr. Browning has is depth. This once clearly perceived, it is obvious that the latter characteristic cannot mend the imperfection of the former characteristic. You might just as well try to make a mountain higher by excavating round it, or make swallows fly more soaringly by yourself descending a coal-pit. We have already very explicitly given our estimate of Mr. Tennyson as a poet; and though it is such as thousands of men who have fancied themselves beloved of the Muses would have given anything to have honestly formed of them, it is far removed from that in which his more ardent admirers at times affect to indulge. One thing, however, is certain. They need be in no fear lest Mr. Tennyson should be displaced by any critic in his sound senses to make way for Mr. Browning. When men desire to behold the flight of an eagle, and cannot get it, they do not usually regard the tramp of an elephant as a substitute. We therefore beg of the general public to return to the bent of its own original judgment, and, unbewildered by those who would fain be its guides, to treat Mr. Browning's *Poetical Works* as it treated *Paracelsus, &c.,* on its first appearance—as though they were non-existent. We know it has now much to contend against. When the academy and the drawing-room, when pedantry and folly, combine to set a fashion, it requires more self-confidence than the meek public commonly possesses to laugh the silly innovation down.

To Mr. Tennyson's credit be it spoken, he has never gone looking for fame. The ground we tread on is delicate; and we will, therefore, only add that we should have been better pleased if the author, who is now so ridiculously obtruded as his rival, had imitated him in that particular. Small London literary coteries, and large fashionable London salons, cannot crown a man with the bays of Apollo. They may stick their trumpery tinsel wreaths upon him, but these will last no longer than the locks they encircle. They may confer notoriety, but fame is not in their gift. All they can bestow is as transitory as themselves. Let the sane general public, therefore, we say, take heart, and bluntly forswear Mr. Browning and all his works. It is bad enough that there should be people, pretending to authority among us, who call a man a great poet when, though unquestionably a poet, he has no marks of greatness about him. But that is a venial error, and a trifling misfortune, compared to what would be the misery of living in an age which gibbetted itself beforehand for the pity of posterity, by deliberately calling a man a poet who—however remarkable his mental attributes and powers—is not specifically a poet at all. We hope we shall be spared this humiliation. At any rate, we must protest against being supposed willingly to participate in it.

P.S.—It will be observed that we have abstained from all mention of *The Ring and the Book*. Our readers must not, however, suppose that the foregoing paper was written before that work appeared. Not at all. But *The Ring and the Book* throws no new light on the subject; and what we have said of Mr. Browning's aim, method, and manner, whilst examining his other compositions, holds equally good of his latest, wonderful but unpoetical, production. We have refrained from scrutinising it, only because conscientious criticism of art, like art itself, is long, and Magazine articles are short.

Notes

1. Hence the difficulty of defining poetry, just as there exists the well-known difficulty of defining life. But just as despite the latter difficulty we can always say in any particular instance what is *not* life, so despite the former one we can say in any particular instance what is not poetry.

2. Could we allow, which we cannot, that Mr. Browning is to be classed among poets, instead of among a totally different order of intellects, Mr. Bailey is the poet with whom we should be compelled to compare him; and were the comparison possible, it would certainly have to be pronounced that the author of *Festus* is, poetically speaking, immeasurably the superior of the author of *Paracelsus, Sordello,* &c, with which the former has occasionally many points in common. Mr. Bailey is unquestionably a

poet. How is it he has for years persisted in silence? Is the following passage in *Festus* the explanation?—

> *Student.* Say, did thy friend
> Write aught beside the work thou tell'st of?
> *Festus.*   Nothing.
> After that, like to the burning peak, he fell
> Into himself, and was missing ever after.

3. A brief extract from Mr. Bain upon the nature of Bacon's genius will throw some light on this subject. "Although Bacon's imagery," says that profound and accurate writer, "sometimes rises to poetry, this is not its usual character; his was not a poetic sense of Nature, but a broad general susceptibility, partaking more of the natural historian than of the poet, by which all the objects coming before his view or presented to his imagination took a deep hold, and, by the help of his intense attraction of similarity, were recalled on the slightest similitude. Many great writers in English literature have had this strong susceptibility to the sensible world at large without a special poetic sense, while some have had the poetic sense superadded. These last are our greatest poets." This is nearly as good an account of Mr. Browning's "sense of Nature" as it is of Bacon's.

4. To illustrate the lax nonsense that is written on this subject, take the following propositions from the *Spectator*. "Mr. Browning would perhaps make a great dramatist," using the word dramatist in the sense of writer for the stage. The critic who hazards such an assertion can either know nothing really of Mr. Browning or nothing of the very elements of dramatic representation. Again: "Though not the widest, the most powerful, or the freest, we hold Tennyson the deepest, by far (Clough perhaps excepted, above whom, of course, in almost all other respects he must rank), of all English poets after Shakespeare, and superior to Byron in every characteristic of a poet, except one of the greater characteristics, fire." The only epithet that properly describes this sentence, which mainly consists of a series of clashing indefinite adjectives, is muddle-speeched. The writer, who signs himself "Ed. Spectator," obviously does not even know what he himself thinks on the subject. In other words, he has never thought the matter out. Why will the *Spectator* persist in always serving up its thoughts *raw?*

—Alfred Austin, "The Poetry of the
Period," *Temple Bar,* June 1869, pp. 320–333

RICHARD HENRY STODDARD (1871)

Richard Henry Stoddard was an American critic and poet. In this extract from the literary magazine *Appletons' Journal*, Stoddard suggests that the fundamental problem with Browning's poetry is that his characters are not "actualities," rather they are "possibilities." Whereas the poetic individuals in Shakespeare's drama are immediately accessible to us, speaking in a language we comprehend and presenting us with thought processes we understand, Browning's depth of vision into human psychology and the inner workings of individuals is often so profound as to render his characters too "deep" to seem actual.

Browning's talent for plumbing the depths of character would seem to be the idea behind Stoddard's beginning the extract stating that the poet will never be popular in the literary world: He simply does not appeal to the general reader because of his profundity (an idea seen expressed in various ways in many of the earlier extracts in this volume). Browning's major achievement, and Stoddard says he knows of no other poet who surpasses him in this ability, including Shakespeare, is to have his poetic characters reveal themselves to the reader when they themselves seem unaware of the truth about their own situations and motivations. Stoddard suggests that it is in his *Dramatic Lyrics* rather than in his dramas that Browning displays this skill most ably.

———

Mr. Browning has never been a popular poet, and never can be. Perhaps he does not desire to be. Certainly, it is not much to desire just now. There is one thing to be said for Mr. Browning, and that is that if when we have finished one of his dramas, or dramatic soliloquies, we have leisure—I will not say to think it over, for that does not help the matter, but leisure to let his work explain and justify itself, some things that were obscure in reading become tangible in memory-taking, or making shapes out of the clouds in which they were diffused; in short, orbing themselves into stars of greater or lesser brilliancy and distinctness.

To be a little more explicit, I must return to Shakespeare, if his scholars will pardon my momentary invasion of their province. Shakespeare's characters are all actualities, and the passions they exhibit and develop are such as we find in the men and women we know. We understand them when they speak, and when they act. Mr. Browning's characters are possibilities, perhaps, but we have never met with them. We cannot follow them in their talk, and their actions puzzle us. They are too subtle, too metaphysical, too remote, from mankind. It is wise for a poet to work 'from within outward,' but he should not work from so far within as never to come to the surface. There is a world of surfacework in Shakespeare, as in Homer, but how delightful it is! Mr. Browning disdains it, except in his *Dramatic Lyrics*, which will live when his dramas are forgotten. He excels Shakespeare, I think, in the art—if it be art—with which he makes his characters betray what they really are. They may deceive themselves, but they cannot deceive us. 'My Last Duchess' is a fine instance of this art, and 'Andrea Del Sarto' another. Nothing in literature is more masterly than the faultless painter's unconscious betrayal of his unknown shame. I know of nothing like this in Shakespeare—nothing so profound in any poet.

—Richard Henry Stoddard,
"Robert Browning," *Appletons' Journal*,
November 11, 1871, vi, pp. 533–536

ARTHUR GALTON "MR. BROWNING" (1885)

Arthur Galton's extract expresses the same idea as that of Alfred Austin in his commentary: that Browning is an anatomist more than he is an artist. The fact that the two extracts were written sixteen years apart is evidence that Browning drew similarly expressed critical attacks on his poetry throughout the period of his life when his fame was increasing. Galton's extract is much less vehement in its criticism than Austin's, and he does not use the "anatomist" metaphor as a means to attack Browning, specifically referring to the poet as a "master" mental anatomist and the majority of his poetry as being a "skilful" and "subtle" mental anatomy. For Galton, it is this very skill that makes Browning's drama unsuccessful, the dramatic action being overcome and submerged beneath the minute observation of character. In Browning's poetry, however, this acute scrutiny (and Galton finds *The Ring and the Book* best exemplifies this point) is a fine quality, allowing the reader an intimate knowledge of the inner thoughts and deliberations of the individuals described in the work.

Galton makes the usual critical complaints about Browning's language and intellect, saying that the former is "uncouth" and the latter often obscure. Readers might consider just what presumptions those critics like Galton have made who find Browning's use of language lacking in grace; they generally seem to have a preconceived notion of what should constitute "poetic" diction. Using the metaphor of the sculptor, Galton says that Browning's material is precious like marble, but he leaves it too often roughly worked rather than beautifully carved. Galton cannot excuse the poet this failure, as he says others have done because of those of Browning's poetic qualities that *are* great. The critic can find many examples of finely worked sentences in the poet's work where the rhythm, alliteration, and dynamism are more than could be hoped for; thus, Browning has no excuse in Galton's opinion. He allows that poets should have a certain freedom when it comes to their art but that art itself must abide within certain parameters to maintain its identity *as* art. Browning's writing all too often lacks two important criteria intrinsic to poetry: music and beauty. Austin had suggested the same criticism in his previous extract in this volume, but unlike Austin, Galton takes some time to praise Browning's verse for two other qualities: its power and insight. Like Richard Henry Stoddard in the passage immediately preceding this one, Galton suggests that, while we might know Shakespeare's characters better than those of Browning, the former great poet does not dissect them with the precision and skill of the latter, Victorian bard. Browning's poetry has stood the test of time because it is "real" and grounded in the poet's great observations into human character; but Browning's verse will continue to suffer in the estimation of critics and the public alike because it does not satisfy the principles of fine art: It seldom portrays beauty, and its language too often lacks music.

—————   —————   —————

Mr. Browning is not so much an artist as an anatomist. The greatest poets are like sculptors: they show us a lovely work of art, whose growth we do not think of, and can hardly guess at. But Mr. Browning is like a man of science, who builds up an antediluvian monster, bone by bone. He differs only from the geologist in that his constructions are not bodies only, but bodies with minds; Mr. Browning can construct a mind, as the geologist does a skeleton. And this simile gives us the clue to all his poetry; he is a mental anatomist. His power and his skill, in his own peculiar province, are undeniable; and among his English contemporaries unequalled. Though, in spite of his unrivalled power of describing character, we cannot call him a great dramatist; that is, if we mean by dramas, complete plays: because Mr. Browning's anatomical instincts, the minuteness of his dissection of individual characters, spoil his plays as wholes. His dramas, like most of his lyrics, are revelations of individual minds; and his searching power of showing single characters prevents him from completing his plays; he is a subtle dramatic poet, then, but not a great dramatist.

So that we may describe the bulk of his work, by calling it mental anatomy; and in this art of his, Mr. Browning is a most skilful master. His reading must be large, and the grasp of his mind much larger; and his mind is certainly both keen and strong. While he has an amazing power of realizing the spirit of other days; so that his pictures of bygone ages are living and forcible. His characters are taken from many sources, Eastern and Western, modern, mediaeval and classical, but undoubtedly his firmest, truest drawing has been of people of the Italian Renascence: and from this source, his masterpieces are types of ecclesiastical life.

The greatest of his works, as a whole, is *The Ring and the Book,* in which is told the story of a Roman trial for murder, in the seventeenth century. Mr. Browning shows us the most intimate feelings and motives of the murderer, the victim, the judges, the advocates on either side; the arguments of partisans, the prejudices of the people; all these are expressed with a master-hand. Such pictures of the workings of many minds, from different standpoints, and on so large a scale, are marvellous for their subtlety and force. The work is more than a narrative, but we cannot call it either a drama or an epic, though it inclines to be both, with a leaning towards the epic. Still, it is chiefly a series of wonderful sketches of character; and we are always, in Mr. Browning's work, driven back to our definition; he is a master of mental anatomy.

But while doing homage to Mr. Browning's greatness, we must not be blind to his faults, and they are many and serious. His thought is too often abrupt and jerky, so much so, that at times it is difficult to follow. This difficulty is caused by his obscurity rather than his depth, for generally when most deep, where his thought is greatest, he is singularly clear.

His words match his thoughts, and are too often rugged and uncouth; though this again is only because he chooses to be odd, for his expression, when he likes, can be transparently limpid. Since this is so, he must bear the penalty; the workmanship of many of his poems is frightful. Poetry should teach us, but should always minister to pleasure and to beauty; and there are times when Mr. Browning affords neither. A poet's work should be like a sculptor's, he should chisel his marble into forms of beauty. Mr. Browning has marble—marble most precious—but it is only rough-hewn from the quarry; or, to make a better comparison, he has gold to give us, jewels of the finest gold, but it is formless and unrefined, as it is encumbered still with minerals and dross. It is given to few readers to remove these, few have the patience, and fewer the skill; so that Mr. Browning's disciples are few. While his thought is so keen, and so deep, that of those who reach it, a part only can grasp it. His greatness may make us overlook, but not forgive, his want of workmanship; even the power of his style in some of his poetry makes it harder for us to pardon his carelessness in the rest.

Many of his lines are so magnificent in their energy, their rhythm, their alliteration, that we cannot possibly suppose Mr. Browning has not the fulness of the poetical gift, if he likes to make use of it. Genius, it is true, is beyond rules; greatness must be unfettered; we cannot confine the sea in bottles, or, with all due deference to Mr. Ruskin, the clouds either; nor can we measure the mountains with compasses. We do not judge Shakespeare by foolish rules of grammar and pedantry; and we are quite willing to allow Mr. Browning an almost equal freedom of defiance; though there are certain bounds which are not pedantic, but are true in the nature of things. Art cannot be violated and remain artistic. Poetry which has not beauty may have force, or keenness, or coarseness, or weakness, but it cannot be artistic if it is not beautiful. Now, form is a quality about which there are many discussions, and these are not always wise or moderate. Form may even be insisted on too much, or striven for too much; but still, good form is an excellence in poetry. It is an essential to the best poetry; and if a writer has not cultivated form, it cannot be true criticism to say he is the greater for his neglect, or that his work will not bear refinement. Surely it is his business to make it bear refinement, or if it will not, to utter it in prose. The strength of a great artist must be hidden, veiled by his beauty, as Raphael's strength is hidden. We should not call him a greater painter if he were coarser in his work, all his other qualities remaining the same; neither should we say Mr. Browning is not less great because he has not given his work the last touches of finish. His admirers cannot, in much of his work, call him beautiful; the wildest of them cannot, in much of his work, call him musical; so that two important qualities of good poetry are not found always in his. It is undoubtedly far better to have thought like Mr. Browning's, than the most exquisite wording if it is empty of meaning; and it takes a greater man to give us such thought. But when we concede this to the enthusiasts of the Browning Society, we should remind ourselves that those poets whom the world considers the greatest are conspicuous for their form, for their splendid workmanship. All their mental powers might remain, but had they expressed their minds less well, we should certainly not rank them so high as artists. Style, then, is not a mere luxury; it is an essential of classical poetry; and since the poets who are classics would have suffered, had their style been less excellent, we may conclude that no poet, not even the greatest, can afford to despise style; so that we cannot allow even Mr. Browning to despise style. His greatness is undoubted, his poetry, we may even say, is wonderful; but we must always hold that it would be greater and more splendid had its utterance been more beautiful.

Two qualities, then, of good poetry, beauty and music, are frequently absent from Mr. Browning's; but two others are always present, power and insight. When a third is found in his work, clearness, Mr. Browning is a forcible wielder of words. To compare him with other poets would be almost idle, even if comparison were our purpose; he is so unlike any of them, that we are stopped on the threshold by his peculiar manner. Even to compare his characters with those of other poets is not easy, they are treated so differently. We know Shakespeare's characters even better than we know Mr. Browning's, but Shakespeare's are never dissected.

Mr. Browning shows us his men and women as a watchmaker shows the wheels of a clock, with all its springs and machinery laid bare. His characters are very real or they would not bear the process and live; and his people are very living. And they are worth knowing, even when we know them through and through. . . .

Mr. Browning's enemies are not those who are willing to pay every due homage to his enormous greatness, but a reasonable homage. They are those who will praise him for that in which he is not great; or who set up new ideals of poetry to suit their fancies, and the eccentricities of their poet. But, in spite of his feeble enemies, the defenders of a meaningless form; in spite of his false friends, who admire him wrongly; Mr. Browning's fame must grow. His work is so real, so solid, and so great, that those who have once learnt to know it, will like it more and more. They will forget its shortcomings when they think of its strength and solidity. And his poetry wears well, it stands the test of time and use. Though acknowledging all this, we cannot overlook its serious faults; and we must not forget that, perhaps, to us, its faults are less serious than they will be to future readers. If any age had been represented to us, in poetry like Mr. Browning's, we might think it was serious and searching in its aims, and that it meant well: but we should not have a high idea of its sense of art and beauty. So that Mr. Browning must suffer, because he has violated the principles of perfect art.

Misshapen monsters have their uses: they bring out the beauty of the perfect type. Earthquakes, volcanoes, and thunderings, have their uses: they clear the air, and show us the power which underlies the calm beauty of nature. And Mr. Browning's workmanship is like a monster: it shows us how beautiful the true types are. His spirit, too, has the uses of a storm: it shows us the power which should underlie a poet's beauty, if his words are not to be mere tinkling cymbals. Let us hope that like other storms he will clear the air, that he will help to drive away the clinging mists of luxuriant but senseless words which threaten to enfold us.

If disgust at his ruggedness leads our writers to study more those deathless masters of perfect verse, whose great thoughts are enshrined in forms of faultless art, and expressed in tones of godlike music, he will be a great literary benefactor. But this work is more likely to be done by their followers, than by one whose poetry shows too little of their touch; though we must always remember how largely it is dowered with some of their other and their highest gifts.

—Arthur Galton, "Mr. Browning,"
Urbana Scripta, 1885, pp. 59–76

ANDREW LANG "ESOTERIC BROWNINGISM" (1888)

Andrew Lang, the prolific Scottish novelist, poet, and literary critic, considers in this extract the future of Browning's poetry in the estimation of the general public. His essay, from which this passage is extracted, was written the year before Browning's death and is, therefore, a good vantage point from which readers can estimate critical feeling about the poet at the conclusion of his life.

Lang seems to fear the critical commentary, or "dissertations," that have grown up around Browning's poetry: In attempting to explain the complexity of Browning's verse, they are in danger of making the present generation forget the quality of the verse itself (a warning to all critics, one should add). Lang believes much of Browning's work is as clear to a boy of sixteen as it is to any scholarly critic and requires no translation to be understood. It is for this reason that Lang has attempted to praise those things in Browning's verse that are imperishable, for he feels concern that there are readers who will turn away from all Browning's work when they come across a particularly difficult text. There are those who simply read Browning's verse because commentators state that it is great; there are those who take pleasure in treating Browning's work as one long riddle to be unraveled. All these, Lang says, will lose for themselves the great pleasure and benefit that many poems of Browning might afford them. There is much that Browning wrote that should be handled and its pages turned over, not simply kept in libraries and on shelves because critics have praised its worth. Lang applauds Browning, then, as a poet to be read and for the continued worth of his verse in and of itself, not for the reams of critical praise and commentary it has accumulated over the poet's lifetime.

. . . It may not need all this quoting of passages and numbering of names to remind readers that Mr. Browning is something other than a scientific analyst of souls, using a jargon worse than scientific. It should be superfluous to repeat that he is as full of magic, of charm, of art; that he has raised and can raise as many phantoms, fair or terrible, as ever Faust beheld in the magic mirror. He has interpreted every one of our emotions from divine love to human friendship, from the despair of the soul to the depths of personal hatred. He has unravelled with delicate fingers the words of Andrea del Sarto, and has not disdained beauty, but has made

A common greyness silver everything.

He has piped to children, like his own Pied Piper, and they have followed him as willingly as they of Hamelin. All these poems, and scores of others, need no interpreter, no commentator; any boy of sixteen who cares for verse can read them as easily as he can read Longfellow.

This later generation is in danger of forgetting the real poet in the multitude of dissertations about poems which need explaining. It is for this reason that one has attempted, however weakly, to praise that in Mr. Browning's work which is divine and imperishable. It is not that one undervalues *The Ring and the Book*, or *Balaustion's Adventure*, or *Pippa Passes*. But time, that sifts poets like wheat, will almost certainly treat much that Mr. Browning has written as time has treated the dark pieces of George Chapman or the *Cassandra* of Lycophron. They will survive, indeed, but rather because a poet wrote them than because they are poetry. They can hardly survive, as Theocritus hoped one of his idyls would do, 'on the lips of all, and chiefly on those of the young.' There is, however, no reason why the central and perfect poems of Mr. Browning should not survive thus, in men's pockets, not only on their shelves; in men's hands, not only in scholar's libraries. But there is at present this danger, that young readers, just waking to poetry, may be lost in *Red Cotton Night-Cap Country*, and may emerge with difficulty, as from a Sleepy Hollow haunted by nightmares—may emerge and may never again choose to enter even that demesne which is peopled by *Men and Women*. In that event great would be their loss, nor less great if, by way of approving themselves clever and 'cultured,' they try to heat themselves into an enthusiasm for the poems commended by commentators, and for the riddles which are their despair and delight.

—Andrew Lang, from "Esoteric Browningism,"
Forum, November 1888, vi, 300–310

UNSIGNED (1890)

This unsigned review was written on the publication of the sixteen-volume edition of Browning's collected works that appeared only a month after his death. The reviewer begins with praise for Browning that summarizes his many poetic gifts: his ear for music (although readers should note that the reviewer specifies the verse's musicality is apparent only when Browning takes patient care to produce it); his capacity for thought ranging from the classical to the medieval and conditioned by a thoroughly modern sensibility; and, of course, his sympathetic imagination, his insight into the lot of the human individual.

The review states that Browning's poetry will not disappear as long as there are individuals who speak English but also recognizes that there are those who only know Browning by name rather than for his poetry or actually sneer along with those parodists who have mocked the poet and his verse. The Browning Society, the "cult of Browning" as it is described in earlier extracts in this volume, has done little to foster his popularity. The members behave as if they are part of a select group with a special understanding of Browning's poetry, and the general public resents their attitude, turning away from the poet's works in larger numbers.

In speaking of the collected verse, the review suggests that, unlike the English poet Lord Byron, Browning does not deploy his characters as projections of his own voice: He eschews revealing his own soul to the reader. Quoting the Roman poet Terence, who said that "I am a man; and I consider nothing that concerns mankind a matter of indifference to me," the review's author maintains that Browning allowed his poetic characters to speak in their own voices, a vast array of men and women in different situations, figures from various cultures and from many historical moments. Nevertheless, the reviewer recognizes that Browning's verse is occasionally obscure. He does not fault the complexity of a poem's theme in causing this, stating that often the poet's most complicated ideas are translated brilliantly in his verse. The initial suggestion made in the review about Browning's care and patience in writing, although there related to the musicality of his verse, might perhaps also be considered to be the cause of his sometimes unintelligible poetry.

It is now five-and-fifty years since Robert Browning came before the world with his surprising youthful poem, *Paracelsus*; it is full fifty years since he put forth to his countrymen that rare poetic riddle which he called *Sordello*, and which remains yet an unsolved riddle for the multitude. To-day his publishers give us their Uniform Edition of his Complete Works, and show us in its sixteen compact volumes how productive have been all these long years, how full of a restless, fruitful energy; how little this poet lies open to the charge of having buried his golden talent in the earth. At least, it is not as a slothful servant that he can be condemned.

Nor, among the select company of his readers, will any be found to deny the splendour of the gift so liberally put to use for the world's service. It is not our own time that will show us a poet more royally equipped for his work. Alive to all the rich harmonies of form and colour in the poet's sphere of working, he has the word-painter's faculty of flashing on you what picture he will from the great gallery of his imagination. He has also, when he lists to use it patiently and with loving intensity of care and consciousness, the highly educated musical sensibility that can teach how to make verse tread with the airy foot of a dancer, swing lightly as a bird upon a bough, or move with the massive march of an army, the solemn sweep of a procession. More and better than even these, he has the quick-divining observation, the large intuitive sympathy that, looking under the human mask, discerns the truth about his fellows in their sorrow, their joy, even their guilt, and, comprehending much, scorns little; while a certain robust and sturdy common-sense, a saving salt of manliness, never allows this sympathetic tolerance to sicken into sentimentalism. The seeing eye, the hearing ear, the understanding heart, are his in sovereign measure, not less than the poet's special dower, 'the hate of hate, the scorn of scorn, the love of love.' To those friendly fortune has added a large and liberal culture, artistic as well as literary, comprehending alike classic lore and modern thought; and, to aid in the attaining of all needful accomplishment, there has been added to these greater things a wordly position so well assured that this poet may write and publish as seems him good, never needing either to sell great thoughts for bread, or to toil at uncongenial work because it brings the better price.

To one so excellently gifted, and so favoured by fortune, we look rightly for good and lasting work. Nor are we disappointed. Marvellous as are the mutations of earthly fame, large as are the poetic treasures which the world's weary memory is ever letting slip, there is much of Robert Browning which will hardly perish while men continue to speak the language in which he has written, much which the world should not and scarcely can let die. Yet, strange as it might seem, it is true that to a large majority of the English-reading public, including not a few gifted and accomplished persons, this kingly poet remains a name only, and for certain of them not even that, being actually known to some eager thinkers and readers solely through the parodist's sneer at him in the clever piece of mockery, where he figures as one who

> Loves to dock the smaller parts of speech, As men curtail the already curtailed

the imitation being ridiculously good enough to prove effective in deterring from the study of the original.

Nor does the half-adoring enthusiasm of the poet's sworn admirers avail very greatly against the vague distaste of a public, much out of love with depth and difficulty in the works it reads for delight. The ardent devotees of Browning are too apt to speak in the style of the elect, to whom alone out of a wicked world it has been granted to penetrate into certain holy mysteries, which, nevertheless, they are willing to expound to the outside crowd, if they will humbly listen; but the wicked world resents their tone of superiority, and inclines to go on its way heedless of their lore.

That this should be so cannot but at times irritate some, themselves admirers of Browning, who are concerned that no good influence should be wasted, and wishful that as many as are worthy should share in the heritage of delight of which this true poet can make them free. For hardly is there a living writer to whose pages the understanding reader may turn with such a certainty of finding in many of them the keen and stimulating pleasure that arises from high and deep thoughts arrayed in splendid imagery, while his message for the world, when the world can understand it, is full often one well worthy to be heard.

To be angry, however, that the immediate circle of Browning's influence is but narrow, is idle enough. Indirectly that influence is widely diffused, filtering through many a receptive writer who has the art of re-imparting it to the average reader in such measure and in such guise as are fitting. This must content us perforce, since the mastersinger has not cared to learn that humble art himself. Even the brief survey of his life-work that we are about to make will show us that he has in full measure *les défauts de ses qualités*, subtlety degenerating sometimes into obscurity, strength becoming mere ruggedness, and both tending to produce peculiarities of form and of diction the reverse of attractive.

There is nothing necessarily unpopular in the predominatingly impersonal character which Browning has chosen to confer on his poems—poems, to a very great extent, 'dramatic in principle'—as their writer has said 'so many utterances of so many imaginery persons, *not me.*' He has willed rather to project himself into the minds of others, and to express *their* thoughts, than to give language to his own; avoiding the error of Byron, most undramatic because least sympathetic of writers, whose personages, one and all, are mere hollow masks and brazen mouthpieces for sending forth to the world the magnified echoes of their creator's single soul, his special personal hopes and fears and despairs, loves and hates, his hates more particularly.

This Byron-method finds small favour with Browning, who refuses very definitely to take the world so deep into his confidence, who will not be lured into 'sonnet-writing about himself,' even by Shakspeare's example.

> With this same key
> Shakspeare unlocked his heart, once more?
> Did Shakspeare? If so, the less Shakspeare he!

is his blunt answer to the plea that he, too, would so unfold himself, 'unlock his heart with a sonnet-key.' An earthquake, indeed, may shake your house, shiver it from top to bottom, leave it gaping so that the malign curiosity of the mob may explore all its domestic secrets; that you cannot help; but why throw your house open with your own hand? Such over-frankness our poet abjures, preferring to speak in parables and enforce his beliefs and convictions by life-like examples, not his own. And, certainly, if infinite variety in his list of *dramatis personæ* could defend him against overmuch self-revelation, that safety would be his. Here in his pageant you see moving the figures of not a few historic men and women, mingling with a cloud of fictitious personages, typical of many classes: Paracelsus, the charlatan of genius; Sordello, Dante's precursor, amid his Guelf and Ghilbellin contemporaries; Strafford, the great earl, and the master who betrayed him, and the men of the Long Parliament, greater than both; kings, bishops, popes; musician, painter, Dervish, spiritualist; Arab physician, Jewish rabbi, Christian martyr, and hero-king of Israel, womanhood, beautiful, forlorn, innocent, or guilty; manhood, noble, debased, sceptical, or believing; Caliban, half-human brute, exponent of the devil-worshipping tendency of the savage; Rabbi Ben Ezra, exemplifying the divinest aspiration of the Hebrew. Has not our poet acted well up to the saying of that Latin play wright who was also an African freedman—*Homo sum; humani nihil a me alienum puto?*

But how has he succeeded in his chosen work? Many are the poems in which he has aimed deliberately—as in Sordello—at setting forth 'incidents in the development of a soul', considering, as he avows, that 'little else is worth study'. Therefore we find him bringing his mind to bear on the doings of men and women, trying to 'uncombine motive from motive', and to show what forces may be at work on the human spirit, determining belief, influencing conduct, moulding character, deciding whether this or that immortal soul shall rise heavenward or sink towards the abyss. Has he seen clearly and judged rightly in these matters?—and has he, led by a happy intuition, chosen always the best vehicle for his thought, that mode of expression which most certainly would impress other minds with his opinion, compel them to see and judge as he does? In endeavouring to deal with such questions, relating to the effort and achievement of a master-poet, it behoves us to walk modestly and warily.

Wishful, therefore, to avoid such oracular decisiveness of tone as might befit those inner-court worshippers, the illuminati of the Browning Society, and desirous above all to speak with the humility befitting mere outsiders, we yet do not fear to say that Browning has often succeeded magnificently in his difficult self-imposed task, while sometimes, so far as the mass of his readers is concerned, he has attained only an amazing failure. A failure it assuredly is, when the sacred Vates, the appointed messenger of Heaven's truth to men, is all but unintelligible to his hearers. The secret of this disparity in the poet's work is not to be found in the nature of the themes he has handled, in their varying degrees of grandeur or difficulty. Some of his most daring *tours de force* are just those which conquer admiration most thoroughly, which compel us to say, 'This is how it really was; this was the true meaning of the life; this was the innermost secret of the man's thought and action; thus the event must have appeared to such an observer; and thus, to such another one'.

—Unsigned, *The London Quarterly*
Review, January 1890, lxxiii, pp. 205–225

UNSIGNED (1890)

This unsigned review for the American journal *The Atlantic Monthly,* and like the review preceding this one, affords the reader a snapshot of attitudes about Browning's position and verse almost immediately upon his death. The view that the poet's work will suffer due to its lack of artistry (or craft) is stated to be likely, even after so many years of publication (and the publication the month before of the collected works in sixteen volumes). He is praised as the most "realist" writer since Shakespeare, a skilled lyricist, and a mystical talent for giving form to the indistinct in life. The review suggests that Browning delivered a "few" original poems (not a significant number from sixteen volumes!) that in their lyricism and dramatic realism show his poetic power (but yet they do not make him one of England's finest poets). The review concludes with an interesting critical statement, seeing Browning and

Lord Alfred Tennyson as the second stage of English romanticism, giving to that poetic movement a sense of realism presumably lacking in its
earlier idealism. Today critics often tend to see Tennyson and Browning
as representing a distinct (Victorian) period in and of themselves; while
certainly in their youthful period the two poets were inevitably influenced by romanticism, Browning at least is now considered as slough-
ing its influences in favor of the type of experimentation in free verse
and psychological content that has more in common with the modern-
ist movement of the twentieth century.

The prevalent opinion even now is that Browning, notwithstanding the rare
intellectual power which enriches much of his inferior work, will suffer very
seriously from his defective art. Nevertheless, he must rank as the most
powerful realist in the representation of human life who has appeared in
England since Shakespeare. He also possessed a lyrical gift which, in its
best expression, entitles him to a place only below the first. He had, too, a
peculiar felicity in rendering mysticism, in giving form to vague feeling, and
in expressing the moods of indefinite suggestion that music awakens. He had
an estate in the borderland of thought and feeling, on the confines of our
knowledge, in the places that look to the promised land. This faculty yielded
to him a few characteristic and original poems, in which there is a kind of
exaltation at times, and at times of sorcery. The fascination in these, together
with his dramatic realism and his lyrical movement, constitute his power as
a poet, apart from all consideration of what he said. They do not place him
among the few supreme poets of his country.

It was fortunate that long life was given him, so that he made the most of
his gifts. The romantic movement thus found in him one of its most original
and striking products, and gained by his strong sense of reality and his wide-
ranging intellect. It completes in him and in Tennyson its second stage of
development.

—Unsigned, *The Atlantic Monthly*,
February 1890, lxv, pp. 243–248

HENRY JAMES "BROWNING
IN WESTMINSTER ABBEY" (1890)

Henry James here describes Browning's interment in Westminster Abbey's
Poets' Corner, finding in the ceremony an original means of discussing

Browning as a poet and also his poetic method. James imagines what Browning himself might have made of the ceremony, delightfully imagining the possibility of a dramatic discussion among those great figures in English life already buried there as to the worthiness of the latest addition to their company. Readers might contrast Arthur Waugh's much more romantic description of Browning's interment given in a previous extract in this volume.

James, unlike the author of the extract immediately preceding this one, sees Browning as a "modern" writer, not as representing the second stage of romanticism. He imagines the other poets buried there puzzling over Browning's place among them. In a wonderful phrase about those other writers in relation to Browning, James states that "none of the odd ones have been so great and none of the great ones so odd." There is no other writer of verse, James claims, from whom so many would withhold the title of a great poet, but the simple fact of Browning's interment, and the passage of the years, will finally remove the uncertainty about the rightness of the poet's place in such select company. James also makes an unusual and interesting suggestion about Browning's oft-cited formal failures: Rather than seeing them as poetic shortcomings, James claims them to be an overflowing of Browning's distinctive qualities, an excess, rather than something lacking.

James concludes by saying that Browning, for all his cosmopolitan themes, was still distinctly "English," did not find in himself his nation's common character submerged beneath the foreign situations he described, and was very much, despite his "moderness," part of the great tradition of English verse. Browning will, inevitably, make it easier for more of these "modern" writers to find their place among the greats recognized in the abbey's Poets' Corner (and James is perhaps thinking here of himself and of his own distinctively modern outlook in his novels).

The lovers of a great poet are the people in the world who are most to be forgiven for an imaginative way of thinking of him, for they have before them, in his genius and work, an irresistible example of the application of that method to a thousand subjects. Certainly, therefore, there are many confirmed admirers of Robert Browning to whom it will not have failed to occur that the consignment of his ashes to the great temple of fame of the English race was exactly one of those occasions in which his own analytic spirit would have rejoiced, and his irrepressible faculty for looking at human events in all sorts of oblique lights have found a Signal opportunity. If he had been taken with it as a subject, if it had moved him to the confused and comprehensive utterance of which he was master, we can immediately guess at some of the sparks he would have scraped from it, guess how splendidly, in the case, the pictorial sense would have intertwined itself with the metaphysical. For such an occasion would have lacked, for the author of *The Ring and the Book,* none of the complexity and convertibility that were dear to him. Passion and ingenuity, irony and solemnity, the impressive and the unexpected, would each have forced their way through; in a word, the author would have been sure to take the special, circumstantial view (the inveterate mark of all his speculation) even of so foregone a conclusion as that England should pay her greatest honour to one of her greatest poets. At any rate, as they stood in the Abbey on Tuesday last, those of his admirers and mourners who were disposed to profit by his warrant for inquiring curiously, may well have let their fancy range, with its muffled step, in the direction which *his* fancy would probably not have shrunk from following, even perhaps to the dim corners where humour and the whimsical lurk. Only, we hasten to add, it would have taken Robert Browning himself to render the multifold impression.

One part of it on such an occasion is, of course, irresistible—the sense that these honours are the greatest that a generous nation has to confer, and that the emotion that accompanies them is one of the high moments of a nation's life. The attitude of the public, of the multitude, at such hours, is a great expansion, a great openness to ideas of aspiration and achievement; the pride of possession and of bestowal, especially in the case of a career so complete as Mr. Browning's, is so present as to make regret a minor matter. We possess a great man most when we begin to look at him through the glass plate of death; and it is a simple truth, though containing an apparent contradiction, that the Abbey never strikes us so benignantly as when we have a valued voice to commit to silence there. For the silence is articulate after all, and in worthy instances the preservation great. It is the other side of the question that would pull most the strings of irresponsible reflection—all those conceivable postulates and hypotheses of the poetic and satiric mind to which we owe the picture of how the Bishop ordered his tomb in St. Praxed's. Macaulay's "temple of silence and reconciliation"—and none the less perhaps because he himself is now a presence there—strikes one, as one stands in it, not only as a place but as a society, a sort of corporate company; so thick, under its high arches, its dim transepts and chapels, is the population of its historic names and figures. They are a company in possession, with a high standard of distinction, of immortality, as it were; for there is something serenely inexpugnable even in the position of the interlopers. As they look out, in the rich dusk, from the cold eyes of statues and the careful identity of tablets, they seem, with their converging faces, to scrutinise decorously the claims of each new recumbent glory, to ask each other how he is to be judged as an accession. How difficult to banish the idea that Robert Browning would have enjoyed prefiguring and disintegrating the mystifications, the reservations, even perhaps the slight buzz of scandal in the Poets' Corner, to which his own obsequies might give rise! Would not his great relish, in so characteristic an interview with his crucible, have been his perception of the bewildering modernness, to much of the society, of the new candidate for a niche? That is the interest and the fascination, from what may be termed the inside point of view, of Mr. Browning's having received, in this direction of becoming a classic, the only official assistance that is ever conferred upon English writers.

It is as classics, on one ground and another—some members of it perhaps on that of not being anything else—that the numerous assembly in the Abbey holds together, and it is as a tremendous and incomparable modern that the author of *Men and Women* takes his place in it. He introduces to his predecessors a kind of contemporary individualism which, surely, for many a year, they had not been reminded of with any such force. The tradition of the poetic character as something high, detached and simple, which may be assumed to have prevailed among them for a good while, is one that Browning has broken at every turn; so that we can imagine his new associates to stand about him, till they have got used to him, with rather a sense of failing measures. A good many oddities and a good many great writers have been entombed in the Abbey; but none of the odd ones have been so great and none of the great ones so odd. There are plenty of poets whose right to the title may be contested, but there is no poetic head of equal power—crowned and re-crowned by almost importunate hands—from which so many people would withhold the distinctive wreath. All this will give the marble phantoms at the base of the great pillars and the definite personalities of the honorary slabs something to puzzle out until, by the quick operation of time, the mere fact of his lying there among the classified and protected makes even Robert Browning lose a portion of the bristling surface of his actuality.

For the rest, judging from the outside and with his contemporaries, we of the public can only feel that his very modernness—by which we mean the all-touching, all-trying spirit of his work, permeated with accumulations and playing with knowledge—achieves a kind of conquest, or at least of extension, of the rigid pale. We cannot enter here upon any account of either that or any other element of his genius, though surely no literary figure of our day is a more challenging one to attempt to paint. The very imperfections of this original are fascinating, for they never present themselves as weaknesses—they are boldnesses and overgrowths, rich roughnesses and humours—and the patient critic need not despair of digging to the primary soil from which so many disparities and contradictions spring. He may finally even put his finger on some explanation of the great mystery, the imperfect conquest of the poetic form by a genius in which the poetic passion had such volume and range. He may successfully say how it was that a poet without a lyre—for that is practically Browning's deficiency: he had the scroll, but not often the sounding-strings—was nevertheless, in his best hours, wonderfully rich in the magic of his art, a magnificent master of poetic emotion. He will justify, on behalf of a multitude of devotees, the great position assigned to a writer of verse of which the nature or the fortune has been (in proportion to its value and quantity) to be treated rarely as quotable. He will do all this and a great deal more beside; but we need not wait for it to feel that something of our latest sympathies, our latest and most restless selves, passed the other day into the high part—the show part, to speak vulgarly—of our literature. To speak of Mr. Browning only as he was in the last twenty years of his life, how quick such an imagination as his would have been to recognise all the latent or mystical suitabilities that, in the last resort, might link to the great Valhalla by the Thames a figure that had become so conspicuously a figure of London! He had grown to be intimately and inveterately of the London world; he was so familiar and recurrent, so responsive to all its solicitations, that, given the noble evocations that he stands for to-day, he would have been missed from the congregation of worthies whose memorials are the special pride of the Londoner. Just as his great sign, to those who knew him, was that he was a force of health, of temperament, of tone, so what he takes into the Abbey is an immense expression of life—of life rendered with large liberty and free experiment, with an unrespecting intellectual eagerness to put himself in other people's place, to participate in complications and consequences—a restlessness of psychological research that might well alarm any pale company for their formal orthodoxies.

But the illustrious whom he rejoins may be reassured, as they will not fail to discover; in so far as they are representative, it will clear itself up that, in spite of a surface unsuggestive of marble and a reckless individualism of form, he is quite as representative as any of them. For the great value of Browning is that at bottom, in all the deep spiritual and human essentials, he is unmistakably in the great tradition—is, with all his Italianisms and cosmopolitanisms, all his victimisation by societies organised to talk about

him, a magnificent example of the best and least dilettantish English spirit.
That constitutes indeed the main chance for his eventual critic, who will have
to solve the refreshing problem of how, if subtleties are not what the English
spirit most delights in, the author of, for instance, *Any Wife to Any Husband*
made them his perpetual pasture and yet remained typically of his race.
He was indeed a wonderful mixture of the universal and the alembicated.
But he played with the curious and the special, they never submerged
him, and it was a sign of his robustness that he could play to the end. His
voice sounds loudest, and also clearest, for the things that, as a race, we
like best—the fascination of faith, the acceptance of life, the respect of its
mysteries, the endurance of its charges, the vitality of the will, the validity of
character, the beauty of action, the seriousness, above all, of the great human
passion. If Browning had spoken for us in no other way he ought to have been
made sure of, tamed and chained as a classic, on account of the extraordinary
beauty of his treatment of the special relation between man and woman. It
is a complete and splendid picture of the matter, which somehow places it,
at the same time, in the region of conduct and responsibility. But when we
talk of Robert Browning's speaking "for" us, we go to the end of our privilege,
we say all. With a sense of security, perhaps a certain complacency, we
leave our complicated modern conscience, and even our heterogeneous
modern vocabulary, in his charge among the illustrious. There will possibly
be moments in which these things will seem to us to have widened the
allowance, to have made the high abode more comfortable for some of those
who are yet to enter it.

— Henry James, "Browning in Westminster
Abbey," *Speaker,* January 4, 1890, pp. 10–12

George Edward Woodberry
"On Browning's Death" (1890)

George Edward Woodberry was an American poet, academic, and literary critic, a member of the American Academy of Arts and Letters, and
one of the first recipients of a Frost Medal for lifetime achievement in
poetry. In the following extract, Woodberry examines Browning's likely
legacy, finding faults where other critics have done so but also taking
time to explore the spiritual qualities of Browning's verse to a greater
degree. Woodberry sees a literary age coming to an end with the poet's

death and views Browning's work as uniquely representative of his historical moment, in both positive and negative ways.

Woodberry suggests that with Browning's earliest publication, *Pauline*, it is critically clear that the young poet had an easy ability with the poetic medium and an unusual fluency with language; his next publication, *Paracelsus*, displayed Browning's ready intelligence and powers of reasoning in verse. But, Woodberry adds, these two capacities were also the main sources of Browning's poetic flaws: His language could become diffuse and opaque, and the matter of his verse become vague and overly metaphysical in its nature. Browning's *Sordello* is described as monstrous by Woodberry for these reasons. The poetic gifts on display in *Pauline* and *Paracelsus* become in *Sordello* the horrible flaws of that later work.

Woodberry states that what is important in *Sordello* is the suggestion of Browning himself that his theme as a poet is to portray the "history of a soul," and Woodberry makes a crucial point that it is "a" soul and not "the" soul that is of interest to the poet not only in *Sordello* but for the rest of his poetic career. It is this focus on the motivation and psychology of individuals in different situations, the human character in his or her particular moment, that makes Browning a realist and sets him in opposition to the idealistic Lord Alfred Tennyson, whose subject matter is the human as a type.

Woodberry maintains that every sort of character is of interest to Browning, for in each he sees the "spark" and worth of the human soul. It is this stance by the poet that marks him as being essentially a humanitarian and a liberal, a democrat and a representative of the spirit of his age. Human life is relative to Browning, and individuals are capable of developing their souls in ways specific to their character, station, and situation; indeed, Woodberry suggests that in Browning's verse and philosophy great wickedness can develop the soul's immortality as much as great good can, the intensity of the individual's will and energy being of the utmost importance to the poet. If, then, Browning's poetry has a distinctly spiritual quality, it is not of the traditional Christian type where judgment and righteousness are mainstays; rather, forgiveness and understanding are keys to an understanding of his characters, and this liberality in attitude marked the poet as being at one with the general attitude of his contemporary period.

Woodberry claims that Browning's lyrical gifts far surpass his dramatic ones, giving the example of *Pippa Passes* as evidence that the poet's talents denied him the capacity to write for the stage. Browning's interest in intense moments and in inner turmoil meant that traditional dramatic action became unimportant in his plays and that the fragmentary nature of their structures destroyed the quality of his writing for the theater. It is with his dramatic monologues written in the middle period of his poetic career that Woodberry believes Browning will achieve enduring fame. In his later years, the review suggests, the poet would again fall foul of those long passages of ponderous, metaphysical thought that detracted from the quality of his earliest poetry. He would simultaneously become more interested in the grotesque character and the bizarre situation as fit subjects for his verse. Notwithstanding these problems, Woodberry maintains that the lyrics of Browning's middle period are accomplished and should endure. The critic concludes his review essay by comparing Browning with the English poets John Dryden and Ben Jonson, seeing in all three a rugged intellect, not without grace, but more interested in intellectual thought than the poetic form of its delivery. Woodberry declares that time will sift the worthy art from the inadequate; as it has with Dryden's and Jonson's, so it will do with Browning's.

Woodberry's review is of great interest to readers for a variety of reasons. The critic suggests a number of relationships between Browning and his own period, seeing in the poet's verse a confluence of attitudes struck and developed that reflect those of his contemporary age; the spiritual quality of Browning's verse is examined in detail and with a great deal of insight; a sensitive analysis of the broad scope of Browning's achievements is presented, separating the good from the bad but seeing in each the same root causes of language and thought. These same problems have been suggested by many other critics in this volume, but Woodberry sees Browning's fluency and comfort with language and his philosophizing intellect as being both his strengths and weaknesses as a poet. Most other critics have taken one side or the other, but this review is subtle enough to offer the reader a perhaps more compelling interpretation of the complexity of Browning's verse and thought. Readers familiar with the culture of the 1890s and the ideals of the Decadent movement might also consider how many of Woodberry's ideas operate in reaction to his own historical moment and how many of his problems with Browning seem to be based on those same critical and cultural reactions against Decadence's ideals: suggestions of antinomianism, aesthetic experimentation in fractured forms, the primacy of the uniquely individual subject and of human will, and the grotesque as a fit subject for artists.

The death of Browning brings one stage nearer the too plainly approaching end of a literary age which will long be full of curious interest to the student of the moods of the mind of man. Time has linked his name with that of Tennyson, and the conjunction gives to England another of those double stars of genius in which her years are rich, and by which the spirit of an age has a twofold expression. The old opposition, the polarity of mind, by virtue of which the Platonist differs from the Aristotelian, the artist from the thinker, Shakespeare from Jonson, shows its efficacy here, too, in the last modern age, and divides the poets and their admirers by innate preferences. It is needful to remember this contrast, though not to insist upon it unduly, in order to approach the work of Browning rightly, to be just to those who idolize him without offense to those who are repelled by him. The analysis of his powers, the charting of his life and work, are not difficult; but the value of his real achievement is more uncertain. Interest centres entirely in his poetry, for his career has been without notable incident, and is told when it is said that he has lived the life of a scholar and man of letters in England and Italy amid the social culture of his time. For the world, his career is the succession of books he has put forth, and this is as he would have it; publicity beyond this he did not seek, but refused with violence and acrimony.

In his earliest poem, youthful in its self-portraiture, its literary touch, and its fragmentary plan, the one striking quality is the flow of language. Here was a writer who would never lack for words; fluent, as if inexhaustible, the merely verbal element in *Pauline* shows no struggle with the medium of the poet's art. This gift of facility was, as is usual, first to show itself. In *Paracelsus* the second primary quality of Browning was equally conspicuous,—the power of reasoning in verse. These two traits have for a poet as much weakness as strength, and they lie at the source of Browning's defects as a master of poetic art. His facility allowed him to be diffuse in language, and his reasoning habit led him often to be diffuse in matter. In *Sordello* the two produced a monstrosity, both in construction and expression, not to be rivaled in literature. Picturesque detail, intellectual interest, moral meaning, struggle in vain in that tale to make themselves felt and discerned through the tangle of words and the labyrinth of act and reflection. But already in these poems Browning had shown, to himself, if not to the world, that he had come to certain conclusions, to a conception of human life and a decision as to the use of his art in regard to it, which were to give him substantial power. He defined it by his absorption in *Paracelsus* with the broad ideas of infinite power and infinite love, which in his last poem still maintain their place in his system as the highest solvents of experience and speculation; and in *Sordello* he stated the end of art, which he continued to seek, in his maxim that little else is worth study except the "history of a soul." His entire poetic work, broadly speaking, is the illustration of this short sentence. Such prepossessions with the spiritual meaning of life as these poems show made sure the predominance in his work of the higher interests of man; and he won his audience finally by this fact, that he had something to say that was ethical and religious. The development, however, of both the theory and practice of his mind had to be realized in far more definite and striking forms than the earlier poems before the attention of the world could be secured.

It would seem natural that a man with such convictions as Browning acknowledged, should be preeminently an idealist, and that his point of weakness should prove to be the tendency to metaphysical and vague matter not easily putting on poetical form. But he was, in fact, a realist,—one who is primarily concerned with things, and uses the method of observation. His sense for actual fact is always keen. In that poem of *Paracelsus*, which is a discussion in the air if ever a poem was, it is significant to find him emphasizing the circumstance that he had taken very few liberties with his subject, and bringing books to show evidence of historical fidelity. But, little of the dramatic spirit as there is in *Paracelsus*, there was much in Browning when it should come to be released, and it belongs to the dramatist to be interested in the facts of life, the flesh and blood reality, in which he may or may not (according to his greatness) find a soul. Browning was thus a realist, and he chose habitually the objective method of art—but to set forth "the history of a soul." Had he been an idealist, his subject would have been "the history of *the* soul;" his method might or might not have been different. This change of the particle is a slight one, but it involves that polarity of mind which sets Browning opposite to Tennyson. He deals with individuals, takes in imagination their point of view, assumes for the time being their circumstances and emotions; and one who does this in our time, with a preoccupation with the soul in the individual, cannot escape from one overpowering impression, repeated from every side of the modern age,—the impression, namely, of the relativity of human life.

This is the lesson which is spread over Browning's pages, with line on line and precept on precept. By it he comes into harmony with the very spirit of the century on its intellectual side, and represents it. The "history of a soul" differs very greatly according to circumstance, native impulses, the needs of life at different stages of growth, the balance of faculties and desires in it, the temperament of its historical period, the access to it of art or music or thought, and in a thousand ways; and Browning devotes himself oftentimes to the exposition of all this web of circumstance, in order that we may see the soul as it was under its conditions, instead of leaping to a conclusion by a hard-and-fast morality based upon the similarity of the soul in all men. The task happily falls in with his fine gift of reasoning, and increases by practice the suppleness and subtlety of this faculty of his. One might say, indeed, without close computation, that the larger part of his entire poetic work is occupied with such reasoning upon psychological cases, in the manner of a lawyer who educes a client's justification from the details of his temptation. Many of the longer poems are only instances of special pleading, and have all the faults that belong to that form of thought. *The Ring and the Book* is such an interminable argument, marvelous for intellectual resource, for skill in dialectic, for plausibility. *Bishop Blougram, Mr. Sludge, Prince Hohenstiel-Schwangau,* and others, readily occur to mind as being in the same way "apologies;" and in these one feels that, while it is well to know what the prisoner urges on his own behalf, it is the shabby, the cowardly, the criminal, the base, the detestable, that is masking under a too well-woven cloak of words, and that the special pleader is pursuing his game at the risk of a higher honesty than consists in the mere understanding of the mechanism of motive and act. Yet this catholicity, which seems to have for its motto, "Who understands all, forgives all," is a natural consequence in a mind so impressed with the doctrine of the relativity of human life as was Browning's. The tendency of the doctrine is to efface moral judgment, and to substitute for it intellectual comprehension; and usually this results in a practical fatalism, acquiesced in if not actively held. Here, too, Browning's mental temperament has another point of contact with the general spirit of the age, and allows him to take up into his genius the humanitarian instinct so powerful in his contemporaries. For the perception of the excuses for men's action in those of low or morbid or deformed development liberalizes the mind, and the finding of the spark of soul in such individuals does mean to the Christian the finding of that immortal part which equalizes all in an equal destiny, however the difference may look between men while the process of life is going on. Browning came very early to this conviction, that in all men, however weak or grossly set this spark may be, it is to be sought for. In this he is consistently philanthropic and democratic, Christian in spirit and practice, comprehensive in tolerance, large in charity, intellectually (but not emotionally) sympathetic. It is perhaps unnecessary to add that his love of righteousness is not so striking a trait.

But what in all this view of life is most original in Browning is something that possibly perplexes even his devoted admirers. Life, he says, no matter what it may be in its accidents of time, or place, or action, is the stuff to make the soul of. In the humblest as the noblest, in Caliban as in Prospero, the life vouchsafed is the means (adequate, he seems to say, in all cases) of which the soul makes use to grow in. He thus avoids the deadening conclusions to which his doctrine of relativity might lead, by asserting the equal and identical opportunity in all to develop the soul. He unites with this the original theory—at least one that he has made his own—that whatever the soul seeks it should seek with all its might; and, pushing to the extreme, he urges that if a man sin, let him sin to the uttermost of his desire. This is the moral of the typical poem of this class, "The Statue and the Bust," and he means more by this than that the intention, sinning in thought, is equivalent to sinning in act,—he means that a man should have his will. No doubt this is directly in accord with the great value he places on strength of character, vitality in life, on resolution, courage, and the braving of consequences. But the ignoring of the immense value of restraint as an element in character is complete; and in the case of many whose choice is slowly and doubtfully made in those younger years when the desire for life in its fullness of experience is strongest, and the wisdom of knowledge of life in its effects is weakest, the advice to obey impulse at all costs, to throw doubt and authority to the winds, and "live my life and have my day," is of dubious utility. Over and over again in Browning's poetry one meets with this insistence on the value of moments of high excitement, of intense living, of full experience of pleasure, even though such moments be of the essence of evil and fruitful in all dark consequences. It is probable that a deep optimism underlies all this; that Browning believed that the soul does not perish in its wrong-doing, but that through this experience, too, as through good, it develops finally its immortal nature, and that, as in his view the life of the soul is in its energy of action, the man must act even evil if he is to grow at all. Optimism, certainly, of the most thorough-going kind this is; but Browning is so consistent an optimist in other parts of his philosophy that this defense may be made for him on a point where the common thought and deepest conviction of the race, in its noblest thinkers and purest artists, are opposed to him, refusing to believe that the doing of evil is to be urged in the interest of true manliness.

The discussion of Browning's attitude towards life in the actual world of men has led away from the direct consideration of the work in which he embodied his convictions. The important portion of it came in middle life, when he obtained mastery of the form of poetic art known as the dramatic monologue. A realist, if he be a poet, must resort to the drama. It was inevitable in Browning's case. Yet the drama, as a form, offered as much unfitness for Browning's genius as it did fitness. The drama requires energy, it is true, and interest in men as individuals; and these Browning had. It also requires concentration, economy of material, and constructive power; and these were difficult to Browning. He did not succeed in his attempts to write drama in its perfect form. He could make fragments of intense power in passion; he could reveal a single character at one critical moment of its career; he could sum up a life history in a long soliloquy; but he could not do more than this and keep the same level of performance. Why he failed is a curious question, and will doubtless be critically debated with a plentiful lack of results. His growth in dramatic faculty, in apprehension of the salient points of character and grasp in presenting them, in perception of the value of situation and power to use it to the full, can readily be traced; but there comes a point where the growth stops. Superior as his mature work is to that of his youth in all these qualities, it falls short of that perfect and complex design and that informing life which mark the developed dramatist. In the monologues he deals with incidents in a life, with moods of a personality, with the consciousness which a man has of his own character at the end of his career; but he seizes these singly, and at one moment. His characters do not develop before the eye; he does not catch the soul in the very act; he does not present life so much as the results of life. He frequently works by the method of retrospect, he tells the story, but does not enact it. In all these he displays the governing motive of his art, which is to reveal the soul; but if the soul reveals itself in his verses, it is commonly by confession, not presentation. He has, in fact, that malady of thought which interferes with the dramatist's control of his hand; he is thinking *about* his characters, and only indirectly *in* them, and he is most anxious to convey his reflections upon the psychical phenomenon which he is attending to. In other words, he is, primarily, a moralist; he reasons, and he is fluent in words and fertile in thoughts, and so he loses the object itself, becomes indirect, full of afterthought and parenthesis, and impairs the dramatic effect. These traits may be observed, in different degrees, in many of the poems, even in the best. In the dramas themselves the lack of constructive power is absolute. *Pippa Passes* is only a succession of dramatic fragments artificially bound together, and in the others the lack of body and interdependent life between the parts is patent to all. In "A Balcony," certainly one of his finest wrought poems, is only an incident. He is at his best when his field is most narrow—in such a poem as "The Laboratory."

There is a compensation for these deficiencies of power in that the preference of his mind for a single passion or mood or crisis at its main moment opens to him the plain and unobstructed way to lyrical expression. His dramatic feeling of the passion and the situation supplies an intensity which finds its natural course in lyrical exaltation. It may well be thought, if it were deemed necessary to decide upon the best in Browning's work, that his genius is most nobly manifest in those lyrics and romances which he called dramatic. The scale rises from his argumentative and moralizing verse, however employed, through those monologues which obey the necessity for greater concentration as the dramatic element enters into them, up to those most powerful and direct poems in which the intensity of feeling enforces a lyrical movement and lift; and akin to these last are the songs of love or heroism into which the dramatic element does not enter. Indeed, Browning's lyrical gift was more perfect than his dramatic gift; he knew the secret of a music which has witchery in it independent of what the words may say, and when his hand fell on that chord, he mastered the heart with real poetic charm. It was seldom, however, that this happy moment came to him, ennobling his language and giving wing to his emotion; and, such poems being rare, it remains true that the best of his work is to be sought in those pieces, comprehending more of life, where his dramatic power takes on a lyrical measure. Such work became more infrequent as years went on, and he declined again into that earlier style of wordy ratiocination, of tedious pleading as of a lawsuit, of mere intellectuality as of the old hair-splitting schoolmen, though he retained the strength and definiteness of mind which mere growth had brought to him, and he occasionally produced a poem which was only less good than the best of his middle age. The translations from the Greek with which he employed his age stand in a different class from his original poems, and were a fortunate resort for his vigorous but now feebly creative mind. At the end he still applied himself to the interpretation of individual lives, but in choosing them he was attracted even more uniformly by something exceptional, often grotesque, in them, and hence they are more curious and less instructive than the earlier work of the same kind.

The mass of Browning's writings which has been glanced at as the expression of the reasoning, the dramatic, or the lyrical impulse in his genius has attracted attention as wide as the English language, and it has been intimated that this success has been won in some degree on other than poetic grounds. It is fair to say, in view of the facts, that many who have felt his appeal to them have found a teacher rather than a poet. Two points in which he reflects his age have been mentioned, but there is a third point which has perhaps been more efficacious than his sense of the relativity of human life or his conviction of the worth of every human soul: he adds to these cardinal doctrines a firm and loudly asseverated religious belief. It is the more noteworthy because his reasoning faculty might in his time have led him almost anywhere rather than to the supreme validity of truth arrived at by intuition. This makes his character the more interesting, for the rationalizing mind which submits itself to intuitive faith exactly parallels in Browning the realist with a predominating interest in the soul. There is no true contradiction in this, no inconsistency; but the combination is unusual. It is natural that, in a time of decreasing authority in formal religion, a poet in Browning's position should wield an immense attraction, and owe something, as Carlyle did, to the wish of his audience to be reassured in their religious faith. Browning had begun with that resolution of the universe into infinite power and infinite love of which something has already been said, and he continued to teach that through nature we arrive at the conception of omnipotence, and through the soul at the conception of love, and he apparently finds the act of faith in the belief that infinite power will finally be discerned as the instrument and expression of infinite love. This is pure optimism; and in accordance with it he preaches his gospel, which is that each soul should grow to its utmost in power and in love, and in the face of difficulties—of mysteries in experience or thought—should repose with entire trust on the doctrine that God has ordered life beneficently, and that we who live should wait with patience, even in the wreck of our own or others' lives, for the disclosure hereafter which shall reconcile to our eyes and hearts the jar with justice and goodness of all that has gone before. This is a system simple enough and complete enough to live by, if it be truly accepted. It is probable, however, that Browning wins less by these doctrines, which are old and commonplace, than by the vigor with which he dogmatizes upon them; the certainty with which he speaks of such high matters; the fervor, and sometimes the eloquence, with which, touching on the deepest and most secret chords of the heart's desire, he strikes out the notes of courage, of hope and vision, and of the foretasted triumph. The energy of his own faith carries others along with it; the manliness of his own soul infects others with its cheer and its delight in the struggle of spiritual life on earth; and all this the more because he is learned in the wisdom of the Rabbis, is conversant with modern life and knowledge in all its range, is gifted with intellectual genius, and yet displays a faith the more robust because it is not cloistered, the more credible because it is not professional.

The character of Browning's genius, his individual traits, the general substance of his thought, do not admit of material misconception. It is when the question is raised upon the permanent value of his work that the opportunity for wide divergence arises. That there are dreary wastes in it cannot be gainsaid. Much is now unreadable that was excused in a contemporary book; much never was readable at all; and of the remainder how much will the next age in its turn cast aside? Its serious claim to our attention on ethical, religious, or intellectual grounds may be admitted, without pledging the twentieth century, which will have its own special phases of thought, and thinkers to illustrate them. Browning must live, as the other immortals do, by the poetry in him. It is true he has enlarged the field of poetry by annexing the experience that belongs to the artist and the musician, and has made some of his finest and most original poems out of such motives; and his wide knowledge has served him in other ways, though it has stiffened many a page with pedantry and antiquarianism. It is true that there is a grotesque quality in some of his work, but his humor in this kind is really a pretense; no one laughs at it; it arouses only an amazed wonder, like the stone masks of some mediaeval church. In all that he derived from learning and scholarship there is the alloy of mortality; in all his moralizing and special pleading and superfine reasoning there enters the chance that the world may lose interest in his treatment of the subject; in all, except where he sings from the heart itself or pictures life directly and without comment save of the briefest, there is some opportunity for time to breed decay. The faith he preached was the poetical complement of Carlyle's prose, and proceeded from much the same grounds and by the same steps: believe in God, and act like a man—that was the substance of it. But Carlyle himself already grows old and harsh. The class of mind to which Browning belongs depends on its matter for its life; unless he has transformed it into poetry, time will deal hardly with it.

To come to the question which cannot be honestly set aside, although it is no longer profitable to discuss it, Browning has not cared for that poetic form which bestows perennial charm, or else he was incapable of it. He fails in beauty, in concentration of interest, in economy of language, in selection of the best from the common treasure of experience. In those works where he has been most indifferent, as in the *Red Cotton Night-Cap Country,* he has been merely whimsical and dull; in those works where the genius he possessed is most felt, as in "Saul," "A Toccata of Galuppi's," "Rabbi Ben Ezra," "The Flight of the Duchess," "The Bishop Orders His Tomb in St. Praxed's Church," "Herve Riel," "Cavalier Tunes," "Time's Revenges," and many more, he achieves beauty or nobility or fitness of phrase such as only a poet is capable of. It is in these last pieces and their like that his fame lies for the future. It was his lot to be strong as the thinker, the moralist with "the accomplishment of verse," the scholar interested to rebuild the past of experience, the teacher with an explicit dogma to enforce in an intellectual form with examples from life, the anatomist of human passions, instincts, and impulses in all their gamut, the commentator on his own age; he was weak as the artist, and indulged, often unnecessarily and by choice, in the repulsive form—in the awkward, the obscure, the ugly. He belongs with Jonson, with Dryden, with the heirs of the masculine intellect, the men of power not unvisited by grace, but in whom mind is predominant. Upon the work of such poets time hesitates, conscious of their mental greatness, but also of their imperfect art, their heterogeneous matter; at last the good is sifted from that whence worth has departed.

—George Edward Woodberry, "On Browning's
Death," *Studies in Letters and Life*, 1890, pp. 276–296

George Santayana "The Poetry of Barbarism: III. Robert Browning" (1900)

George Santayana was a Spanish-born and American-educated poet, novelist, philosopher, and literary critic. He is generally considered to be an American man of letters. In the following extract, Santayana attempts to give a "just" review of Browning's work a decade after the poet's death and at the turn of the twentieth century. Santayana compares the American poet Walt Whitman and Browning bearing two facts in mind: the poets' capacities to directly express passionate experience and their failure to approach any ultimate comprehension of the human condition. Where Whitman is regarded by Santayana as a "savage" (or as primitive as they come) in terms of his poetry's music and philosophy, Browning is called a "barbaric" genius, and it is this barbarism that is the theme of the essay.

Browning's failures are cataloged, and many are by now familiar claims to readers of this volume: the structural shortcomings of his poems, the turgid nature of his verse, the often obscure and long-winded philosophizing, and the fascination with individuals' character traits rather than the human type in general; but Santayana suggests that there are confused misapprehensions about Browning's incapacities as a poet and seeks to plumb their depths in his essay. Those who see in the poet's verse a passionate call to spiritual awakening are confusing the depiction of reality with an initiation into its meaning. Santayana believes it necessary to express his rational dissatisfaction with Browning's philosophy, for he sees it as no philosophy at all; it is a passionate engagement with life perhaps but not the expression of its deeper meaning. Giving the example of the characterizations of Shakespeare's Iago, Hamlet, and Falstaff, Santayana suggests that a poet, without being a philosopher, can stand above the passions he depicts and reflect on them, allowing his readers to at least speculate on, perhaps to be better prepared for, life itself. Browning lacks this capacity of distancing himself from his characters' passions and uses them as a means of self-expression rather than as subjects for his poetic studies. Santayana claims that Browning never learned the secret of contemplative satisfaction: the love of a form as a thing of beauty in itself. The poet was never able to detach himself from that which he had created, to examine it from a position of rational distance, for he was always swept along in and by the passion and feeling of his own characters. Santayana proceeds to give an excellent, close reading of Browning's verse, showing how the poet's depiction of the passion of love is an example of his failure as expressed in the essay.

Santayana summarizes his position in respect to Browning's poetry thus: The work of reason is to transform the raw material of emotion into thought and the passionate into objects fit for, and agreeable to, intellectual reflection. The failure to do so is the work of a barbarous mind, a mind such as Browning's. To Santayana, it is remarkable that the poet, the product of such a wealth of cultural heritage, should have produced the type of verse he did. When Browning said that his time in Italy had provided him with his education, Santayana said he did not sit with the best teachers, consequently misapprehending the civilization in which he found himself. The poet's fascination with the Renaissance was not grounded on an appreciation of the religious spirit that supported it. While many critics in this volume have praised Browning's spirituality, Santayana criticizes it (although readers should distinguish between spirituality and religion): He says that the poet's "faith" amounted to a liberal optimism in an indefinite life, giving humanity the time to turn all faults to the good, and that as a consequence our lives here shall be held to no account (readers might consult the previous extract in this volume by George Woodberry to cite criticism of Browning's spirituality from a similar, if less philosophical, perspective). Browning's belief in the infinite variety of life and its experiences leaves existence unjustified and makes a philosophical nonsense of his poetry's "development of a soul." Santayana states that "development" must be understood philosophically as being the process of a definite and definable nature, the coming into existence of a particular idea: Browning's belief in the indefinite and infinite capacity of the human individual makes any depiction of a soul's "development" impossible. As a consequence, the poet's intellectual delight in the indefinite finds its natural counterpart in the undefined forms of his poetry and its content. Browning's verse reveals little apart from the minutiae of particular individuals' traits, and Santayana suggests that even the poet's contemporaries Lord Alfred Tennyson and Matthew Arnold (and there is no suggestion that the critic thought particularly highly of either of these poets) did not make the mistake of studying human consciousness for itself but rather for the sake of those objects it revealed.

Santayana concludes by saying that there are those sentimental people who favor Browning because he affords them an imaginative outlet in their lives when traditional religious forms no longer appeal. The critic states that this speaks well of mankind, revealing the human tendency for self-study and a desire to contemplate its destiny. The essay ends by saying that simply because people take Browning's verse to be worth more than it really is, because they do not see its limitations, does not detract from its achievement, nor does it render the poetry worthless.

Readers might well find Santayana's essay a difficult analysis, but it should be remembered that he was a philosopher; as a consequence his approach to Browning is unusual in this volume. While much literary criticism can indulge in imaginative flights or the language of hyperbole, Santayana's thoughts are rigorously marshaled and controlled, as befits his philosophical calling. But those readers who see no flaws in Santayana's argument might contrast other critical extracts and remember that all arguments proceed from certain premises. What existing premises inform Santayana's approach to Browning's verse? What seems to be Santayana's personal stance in regard to the function of poetry and the requisite forms it must take? What seems to be his own views on religion and the spiritual? With the answers to these questions, Santayana's essay and the positions it holds may become more accessible to criticism. For those readers at a loss, this volume's final extract by G.K. Chesterton takes up Santayana's ideas and reinterprets his argument.

—⫸⟨⫶⟩⫷— —⫸⟨⫶⟩⫷— —⫸⟨⫶⟩⫷—

If we would do justice to Browning's work as a human document, and at the same time perceive its relation to the rational ideals of the imagination and to that poetry which passes into religion, we must keep, as in the case of Whitman, two things in mind. One is the genuineness of the achievement, the sterling quality of the vision and inspiration; these are their own justification when we approach them from below and regard them as manifesting a more direct or impassioned grasp of experience than is given to mildly blatant, convention-ridden minds. The other thing to remember is the short distance to which this comprehension is carried, its failure to approach any finality, or to achieve a recognition even of the traditional ideals of poetry and religion.

In the case of Walt Whitman such a failure will be generally felt; it is obvious that both his music and his philosophy are those of a barbarian, nay, almost of a savage. Accordingly there is need of dwelling rather on the veracity and simple dignity of his thought and art, on their expression of an order of ideas latent in all better experience. But in the case of Browning it is the success that is obvious to most people. Apart from a certain superficial grotesqueness to which we are soon accustomed, he easily arouses and engages the reader by the pithiness of his phrase, the volume of his passion, the vigour of his moral judgment, the liveliness of his historical fancy. It is obvious that we are in the presence of a great writer, of a great imaginative force, of a master in the expression of emotion. What is perhaps not so obvious, but no less true, is that we are in the presence of a barbaric genius, of a truncated imagination, of a thought and an art inchoate and ill-digested, of a volcanic eruption that tosses itself quite blindly and ineffectually into the sky.

The points of comparison by which this becomes clear are perhaps not in every one's mind, although they are merely the elements of traditional culture, aesthetic and moral. Yet even without reference to ultimate ideals, one may notice in Browning many superficial signs of that deepest of all failures, the failure in rationality and the indifference to perfection. Such a sign is the turgid style, weighty without nobility, pointed without naturalness or precision. Another sign is the "realism" of the personages, who, quite like men and women in actual life, are always displaying traits of character and never attaining character as a whole. Other hints might be found in the structure of the poems, where the dramatic substance does not achieve a dramatic form; in the metaphysical discussion, with its confused prolixity and absence of result; in the moral ideal, where all energies figure without their ultimate purposes; in the religion, which breaks off the expression of this life in the middle, and finds in that suspense an argument for immortality. In all this, and much more that might be recalled, a person coming to Browning with the habits of a cultivated mind might see evidence of some profound incapacity in the poet; but more careful reflection is necessary to understand the nature of this incapacity, its cause, and the peculiar accent which its presence gives to those ideas and impulses which Browning stimulates in us.

There is the more reason for developing this criticism (which might seem needlessly hostile and which time and posterity will doubtless make in their own quiet and decisive fashion) in that Browning did not keep within the sphere of drama and analysis, where he was strong, but allowed his own temperament and opinions to vitiate his representation of life, so that he sometimes turned the expression of a violent passion into the last word of what he thought a religion. He had a didactic vein, a habit of judging the spectacle he evoked and of loading the passions he depicted with his visible sympathy or scorn.

Now a chief support of Browning's popularity is that he is, for many, an initiator into the deeper mysteries of passion, a means of escaping from the moral poverty of their own lives and of feeling the rhythm and compulsion of the general striving. He figures, therefore, distinctly as a prophet, as a bearer of glad tidings, and it is easy for those who hail him as such to imagine that, knowing the labour of life so well, he must know something also of its fruits, and that in giving us the feeling of existence, he is also giving us its meaning. There is serious danger that a mind gathering from his pages the raw materials of truth, the unthreshed harvest of reality, may take him for a philosopher, for a rationalizer of what he describes. Awakening may be mistaken for enlightenment, and the galvanizing of torpid sensations and impulses for wisdom.

Against such fatuity reason should raise her voice. The vital and historic forces that produce illusions of this sort in large groups of men are indeed beyond the control of criticism. The ideas of passion are more vivid than those of memory, until they become memories in turn. They must be allowed to fight out their desperate battle against the laws of Nature and reason. But it is worth while in the meantime, for the sake of the truth and of a just philosophy, to meet the varying though perpetual charlatanism of the world with a steady protest. As soon as Browning is proposed to us as a leader, as soon as we are asked to be not the occasional patrons of his art, but the pupils of his philosophy, we have a right to express the radical dissatisfaction which we must feel, if we are rational, with his whole attitude and temper of mind.

The great dramatists have seldom dealt with perfectly virtuous characters. The great poets have seldom represented mythologies that would bear scientific criticism. But by an instinct which constituted their greatness they have cast these mixed materials furnished by life into forms congenial to the specific principles of their art, and by this transformation they have made acceptable in the aesthetic sphere things that in the sphere of reality were evil or imperfect: in a word, their works have been beautiful as works of art. Or, if their genius exceeded that of the technical poet and rose to prophetic intuition, they have known how to create ideal characters, not possessed,

perhaps, of every virtue accidentally needed in this world, but possessed of
what is ideally better, of internal greatness and perfection. They have also
known how to select and reconstruct their mythology so as to make it a true
interpretation of moral life. When we read the maxims of Iago, Falstaff, or
Hamlet, we are delighted if the thought strikes us as true, but we are not less
delighted if it strikes us as false. These characters are not presented to us in
order to enlarge our capacities of passion nor in order to justify themselves
as processes of redemption; they are there, clothed in poetry and imbedded
in plot, to entertain us with their imaginable feelings and their interesting
errors. The poet, without being especially a philosopher, stands by virtue of his
superlative genius on the plane of universal reason, far above the passionate
experience which he overlooks and on which he reflects; and he raises us for
the moment to his own level, to send us back again, if not better endowed for
practical life, at least not unacquainted with speculation.

With Browning the case is essentially different. When his heroes are
blinded by passion and warped by circumstance, as they almost always are,
he does not describe the fact from the vantage-ground of the intellect and
invite us to look at it from that point of view. On the contrary, his art is all self-
expression or satire. For the most part his hero, like Whitman's, is himself;
not appearing, as in the case of the American bard, *in puns naturalibus,* but
masked in all sorts of historical and romantic finery. Sometimes, however,
the personage, like Guido in *The Ring and the Book* or the "frustrate ghosts"
of other poems, is merely a Marsyas, shown flayed and quivering to the
greater glory of the poet's ideal Apollo. The impulsive utterances and the
crudities of most of the speakers are passionately adopted by the poet as
his own. He thus perverts what might have been a triumph of imagination
into a failure of reason.

This circumstance has much to do with the fact that Browning, in spite
of his extraordinary gift for expressing emotion, has hardly produced works
purely and unconditionally delightful. They not only portray passion, which is
interesting, but they betray it, which is odious. His art was still in the service of
the will. He had not attained, in studying the beauty of things, that detachment
of the phenomenon, that love of the form for its own sake, which is the secret
of contemplative satisfaction. Therefore, the lamentable accidents of his
personality and opinions, in themselves no worse than those of other mortals,
passed into his art. He did not seek to elude them: he had no free speculative
faculty to dominate them by. Or, to put the same thing differently, he was
too much in earnest in his fictions, he threw himself too unreservedly into
his creations. His imagination, like the imagination we have in dreams, was

merely a vent for personal preoccupations. His art was inspired by purposes less simple and universal than the ends of imagination itself. His play of mind consequently could not be free or pure. The creative impulse could not reach its goal or manifest in any notable degree its own organic ideal.

We may illustrate these assertions by considering Browning's treatment of the passion of love, a passion to which he gives great prominence and in which he finds the highest significance.

Love is depicted by Browning with truth, with vehemence, and with the constant conviction that it is the supreme thing in life. The great variety of occasions in which it appears in his pages and the different degrees of elaboration it receives, leave it always of the same quality—the quality of passion. It never sinks into sensuality; in spite of its frequent extreme crudeness, it is always, in Browning's hands, a passion of the imagination, it is always love. On the other hand it never rises into contemplation: mingled as it may be with friendship, with religion, or with various forms of natural tenderness, it always remains a passion; it always remains a personal impulse, a hypnotization, with another person for its object or its cause. Kept within these limits it is represented, in a series of powerful sketches, which are for most readers the gems of the Browning gallery, as the last word of experience, the highest phase of human life.

> The woman yonder, there's no use in life
> But just to obtain her! Heap earth's woes in one
> And bear them—make a pile of all earth's joys
> And spurn them, as they help or help not this;
> Only, obtain her!
> When I do come, she will speak not, she will stand,
> Either hand
> On my shoulder, give her eyes the first embrace
> Of my face,
> Ere we rush, ere we extinguish sight and speech
> Each on each. . . .
> O heart, O blood that freezes, blood that burns!
> Earth's returns
> For whole centuries of folly, noise, and sin—
> Shut them in—
> With their triumphs and their follies and the rest.
> Love is best.

In the piece called "In a Gondola" the lady says to her lover:—

> Heart to heart
> And lips to lips! Yet once more, ere we part,
> Clasp me and make me thine, as mine thou art.

And he, after being surprised and stabbed in her arms, replies:—

> It was ordained to be so, sweet!—and best
> Comes now, beneath thine eyes, upon thy breast:
> Still kiss me! Care not for the cowards; care
> Only to put aside thy beauteous hair
> My blood will hurt! The Three I do not scorn
> To death, because they never lived, but I
> Have lived indeed, and so—(yet one more kiss)—
> can die.

We are not allowed to regard these expressions as the cries of souls blinded by the agony of passion and lust. Browning unmistakably adopts them as expressing his own highest intuitions. He so much admires the strength of this weakness that he does not admit that it is a weakness at all. It is with the strut of self-satisfaction, with the sensation, almost, of muscular Christianity, that he boasts of it through the mouth of one of his heroes, who is explaining to his mistress the motive of his faithful services as a minister of the queen:—

> She thinks there was more cause
> In love of power, high fame, pure loyalty?
> Perhaps she fancies men wear out their lives
> Chasing such shades.
> I worked because I want you with my soul.

Readers of the fifth chapter of this volume ("Platonic Love in Some Italian Poets") need not be reminded here of the contrast which this method of understanding love offers to that adopted by the real masters of passion and imagination. They began with that crude emotion with which Browning ends; they lived it down, they exalted it by thought, they extracted the pure gold of it in a long purgation of discipline and suffering. The fierce paroxysm which for him is heaven, was for them the proof that heaven cannot be found on earth, that the value of experience is not in experience itself but in the ideals which it reveals. The intense, voluminous emotion, the sudden, overwhelming self-surrender in which he rests was for them the starting-point of a life of rational worship, of an austere and impersonal religion, by which the fire of love, kindled for a moment by the sight of some creature, was put, as it were, into a censer, to burn incense before every image of the Highest Good. Thus love ceased to be a passion and became the energy of contemplation: it diffused over the universe, natural and ideal, that light of tenderness and that faculty of worship which the passion of love often is first to quicken in a man's breast.

Of this art, recommended by Plato and practised in the Christian Church by all adepts of the spiritual life, Browning knew absolutely nothing. About the object of love he had no misgivings. What could the object be except somebody or other? The important thing was to love intensely and to love often. He remained in the phenomenal sphere: he was a lover of experience; the ideal did not exist for him. No conception could be farther from his thought than the essential conception of any rational philosophy, namely, that feeling is to be treated as raw material for thought, and that the destiny of emotion is to pass into objects which shall contain all its value while losing all its formlessness. This transformation of sense and emotion into objects agreeable to the intellect, into clear ideas and beautiful things, is the natural work of reason; when it has been accomplished very imperfectly, or not at all, we have a barbarous mind, a mind full of chaotic sensations, objectless passions, and undigested ideas. Such a mind Browning's was, to a degree remarkable in one with so rich a heritage of civilization.

The nineteenth century, as we have already said, has nourished the hope of abolishing the past as a force while it studies it as an object; and Browning, with his fondness for a historical stage setting and for the gossip of history, rebelled equally against the Pagan and the Christian discipline. The *Soul* which he trusted in was the barbarous soul, the "Spontaneous Me" of his half-brother Whitman. It was a restless personal impulse, conscious of obscure depths within itself which it fancied to be infinite, and of a certain vague sympathy with wind and cloud and with the universal mutation. It was the soul that might have animated Attila and Alaric when they came down into Italy, a soul not incurious of the tawdriness and corruption of the strange civilization it beheld, but incapable of understanding its original spirit; a soul maintaining in the presence of that noble, unappreciated ruin all its own lordliness and energy, and all its native vulgarity.

Browning, who had not had the education traditional in his own country, used to say that Italy had been his university. But it was a school for which he was ill prepared, and he did not sit under its best teachers. For the superficial ferment, the worldly passions, and the crimes of the Italian Renaissance he had a keen interest and intelligence. But Italy has been always a civilized country, and beneath the trappings and suits of civilization which at that particular time it flaunted so gayly, it preserved a civilized heart to which Browning's insight could never penetrate. There subsisted in the best minds a trained imagination and a cogent ideal of virtue. Italy had a religion, and that religion permeated all its life, and was the background without which even its secular art and secular passions would not be truly intelligible. The most commanding and representative, the deepest and most appealing of Italian natures are permeated with this religious inspiration. A Saint Francis, a Dante, a Michael Angelo, breathe hardly anything else. Yet for Browning these men and what they represented may be said not to have existed. He saw, he studied, and he painted a decapitated Italy. His vision could not mount so high as her head.

One of the elements of that higher tradition which Browning was not prepared to imbibe was the idealization of love. The passion he represents is lava hot from the crater, in no way moulded, smelted, or refined. He had no thought of subjugating impulses into the harmony of reason. He did not master life, but was mastered by it. Accordingly the love he describes has no wings; it issues in nothing. His lovers "extinguish sight and speech, each on each"; sense, as he says elsewhere, drowning soul. The man in the gondola may well boast that he can die; it is the only thing he can properly do. Death is the only solution of a love that is tied to its individual object and inseparable from the alloy of passion and illusion within itself. Browning's hero, because he has loved intensely, says that he has lived; he would be right, if the significance of life were to be measured by the intensity of the feeling it contained, and if intelligence were not the highest form of vitality. But had that hero known how to love better and had he had enough spirit to dominate his love, he might perhaps have been able to carry away the better part of it and to say that he could not die; for one half of himself and of his love would have been dead already and the other half would have been eternal, having fed—

On death, that feeds on men;
And death once dead, there's no more dying then.

The irrationality of the passions which Browning glorifies, making them the crown of life, is so gross that at times he cannot help perceiving it.

How perplexed
Grows belief! Well, this cold clay clod

Was man's heart:
Crumble it, and what comes next? Is it God?

Yes, he will tell us. These passions and follies, however desperate in themselves and however vain for the individual, are excellent as parts of the dispensation of Providence:—

Be hate that fruit or love that fruit,
It forwards the general deed of man,
And each of the many helps to recruit
The life of the race by a general plan,
Each living his own to boot.

If we doubt, then, the value of our own experience, even perhaps of our experience of love, we may appeal to the interdependence of goods and evils in the world to assure ourselves that, in view of its consequences elsewhere, this experience was great and important after all. We need not stop to consider this supposed solution, which bristles with contradictions; it would not satisfy Browning himself, if he did not back it up with something more to his purpose, something nearer to warm and transitive feeling. The compensation for our defeats, the answer to our doubts, is not to be found merely in a proof of the essential necessity and perfection of the universe; that would be cold comfort, especially to so uncontemplative a mind. No: that answer, and compensation are to come very soon and very vividly to every private bosom. There is another life, a series of other lives, for this to happen in. Death will come, and—

I shall thereupon
Take rest, ere I be gone
Once more on my adventure brave and new,
Fearless and unperplexed,
When I wage battle next,
What weapons to select, what armour to endue
For sudden the worst turns the best to the brave,
The black minute's at end,
And the element's rage, the fiend-voices that rave
Shall dwindle, shall blend,
Shall change, shall become first a peace out of pain,
Then a light, then thy breast,
O thou soul of my soul! I shall clasp thee again
And with God be the rest!

Into this conception of continued life Browning has put, as a collection of further passages might easily show, all the items furnished by fancy or tradition which at the moment satisfied his imagination—new adventures, reunion with friends, and even, after a severe strain and for a short while, a little peace and quiet. The gist of the matter is that we are to live indefinitely, that all our faults can be turned to good, all our unfinished business settled, and that therefore there is time for anything we like in this world and for all we need in the other. It is in spirit the direct opposite of the philosophic maxim of regarding the end, of taking care to leave a finished life and a perfect character behind us. It is the opposite, also, of the religious *memento mori,* of the warning that the time is short before we go to our account. According to Browning, there is no account: we have an infinite credit. With an unconscious and characteristic mixture of heathen instinct with Christian doctrine, he thinks of the other world as heaven, but of the life to be led there as of the life of Nature.

Aristotle observes that we do not think the business of life worthy of the gods, to whom we can only attribute contemplation; if Browning had had the idea of perfecting and rationalizing this life rather than of continuing it indefinitely, he would have followed Aristotle and the Church in this matter. But he had no idea of anything eternal; and so he gave, as he would probably have said, a filling to the empty Christian immortality by making every man busy in it about many things. And to the irrational man, to the boy, it is no unpleasant idea to have an infinite number of days to live through, an infinite number of dinners to eat, with an infinity of fresh fights and new love-affairs, and no end of last rides together.

But it is a mere euphemism to call this perpetual vagrancy a development of the soul. A development means the unfolding of a definite nature, the gradual manifestation of a known idea. A series of phases, like the successive leaps of a water-fall, is no development. And Browning has no idea of an intelligible good which the phases of life might approach and with reference to which they might constitute a progress. His notion is simply that the game of life, the exhilaration of action, is inexhaustible. You may set up your tenpins again after you have bowled them over, and you may keep up the sport for ever. The point is to bring them down as often as possible with a master-stroke and a big bang. That will tend to invigorate in you that self-confidence which in this system passes for faith. But it is unmeaning to call such an exercise heaven, or to talk of being "with God" in such a life, in any sense in which we are not with God already and under all circumstances. Our destiny would rather be, as Browning himself expresses it in a phrase which Atilla or Alaric might have composed, "bound dizzily to the wheel of change to slake the thirst of God."

Such an optimism and such a doctrine of immortality can give no justification to experience which it does not already have in its detached parts. Indeed, those dogmas are not the basis of Browning's attitude, not conditions of his satisfaction in living, but rather overflowings of that satisfaction. The present life is presumably a fair average of the whole series of "adventures brave and new" which fall to each man's share; were it not found delightful in itself, there would be no motive for imagining and asserting that it is reproduced *in infinitum.* So too if we did not think that the evil in experience is actually utilized and visibly swallowed up in its good effects, we should hardly venture to think that God could have regarded as a good something which has evil for its condition and which is for that reason profoundly sad and equivocal. But Browning's philosophy of life and habit of imagination do not require the support of any metaphysical theory. His temperament is perfectly self-sufficient and primary; what doctrines he has are suggested by it and are too loose to give it more than a hesitant expression; they are quite powerless to give it any justification which it might lack on its face.

It is the temperament, then, that speaks; we may brush aside as unsubstantial, and even as distorting, the web of arguments and theories which it has spun out of itself. And what does the temperament say? That life is an adventure, not a discipline; that the exercise of energy is the absolute good, irrespective of motives or of consequences. These are the maxims of a frank barbarism; nothing could express better the lust of life, the dogged unwillingness to learn from experience, the contempt for rationality, the carelessness about perfection, the admiration for mere force, in which barbarism always betrays itself. The vague religion which seeks to justify this attitude is really only another outburst of the same irrational impulse.

In Browning this religion takes the name of Christianity, and identifies itself with one or two Christian ideas arbitrarily selected; but at heart it has far more affinity to the worship of Thor or of Odin than to the religion of the Cross. The zest of life becomes a cosmic emotion; we lump the whole together and cry, "Hurrah for the Universe!" A faith which is thus a pure matter of lustiness and inebriation rises and falls, attracts or repels, with the ebb and flow of the mood from which it springs. It is invincible because unseizable; it is as safe from refutation as it is rebellious to embodiment. But it cannot enlighten or correct the passions on which it feeds. Like a servile priest, it flatters them in the name of Heaven. It cloaks irrationality in sanctimony; and its admiration for every bluff folly, being thus justified by a theory, becomes a positive fanaticism, eager to defend any wayward impulse.

Such barbarism of temper and thought could hardly, in a man of Browning's independence and spontaneity, be without its counterpart in his art. When a man's personal religion is passive, as Shakespeare's seems to have been, and is adopted without question or particular interest from the society around him, we may not observe any analogy between it and the free creations of that man's mind. Not so when the religion is created afresh by the private imagination; it is then merely one among many personal works of art, and will naturally bear a family likeness to the others. The same individual temperament, with its limitations and its bias, will appear in the art which has appeared in the religion. And such is the case with Browning. His limitations as a poet are the counterpart of his limitations as a moralist and theologian; only in the poet they are not so regrettable. Philosophy and religion are nothing if not ultimate; it is their business to deal with general principles and final aims. Now it is in the conception of things fundamental and ultimate that Browning is weak; he is strong in the conception of things immediate. The pulse of the emotion, the bobbing up of the thought, the streaming of the reverie—these he can note down with picturesque force or imagine with admirable fecundity.

Yet the limits of such excellence are narrow, for no man can safely go far without the guidance of reason. His long poems have no structure—for that name cannot be given to the singular mechanical division of *The Ring and the Book*. Even his short poems have no completeness, no limpidity. They are little torsos made broken so as to stimulate the reader to the restoration of their missing legs and arms. What is admirable in them is pregnancy of phrase, vividness of passion and sentiment, heaped-up scraps of observation, occasional flashes of light, occasional beauties of versification,—all like

the quick sharp scratch
And blue spurt of a lighted match.

There is never anything largely composed in the spirit of pure beauty, nothing devotedly finished, nothing simple and truly just. The poet's mind cannot reach equilibrium; at best he oscillates between opposed extravagances; his final word is still a *boutade*, still an explosion. He has no sustained nobility of style. He affects with the reader a confidential and vulgar manner, so as to be more sincere and to feel more at home. Even in the poems where the effort at impersonality is most successful, the dramatic disguise is usually thrown off in a preface, epilogue or parenthesis. The author likes to remind us of himself by some confidential wink or genial poke in the ribs, by some little interlarded sneer. We get in these tricks of manner a taste of that essential vulgarity, that indifference to purity and distinction, which is latent but pervasive in all the products of this mind. The same disdain of perfection which appears in his ethics appears here in his verse, and impairs its beauty by allowing it to remain too often obscure, affected, and grotesque.

Such a correspondence is natural: for the same powers of conception and expression are needed in fiction, which, if turned to reflection, would produce a good philosophy. Reason is necessary to the perception of high beauty. Discipline is indispensable to art. Work from which these qualities are absent must be barbaric; it can have no ideal form and must appeal to us only through the sensuousness and profusion of its materials. We are invited by it to lapse into a miscellaneous appreciativeness, into a subservience to every detached impression. And yet, if we would only reflect even on these disordered beauties, we should see that the principle by which they delight us is a principle by which an ideal, an image of perfection, is inevitably evoked. We can have no pleasure or pain, nor any preference whatsoever, without implicitly setting up a standard of excellence, an ideal of what would satisfy us there. To make these implicit ideals explicit, to catch their hint, to work out their theme, and express clearly to ourselves and to the world what they are demanding in the place of the actual—that is the labour of reason and the task of genius. The two cannot be divided. Clarification of ideas and disentanglement of values are as essential to aesthetic activity as to intelligence. A failure of reason is a failure of art and taste.

The limits of Browning's art, like the limits of Whitman's, can therefore be understood by considering his mental habit. Both poets had powerful imaginations, but the type of their imaginations was low. In Whitman imagination was limited to marshalling sensations in single file; the embroideries he made around that central line were simple and insignificant. His energy was concentrated on that somewhat animal form of contemplation, of which, for the rest, he was a great, perhaps an unequalled master. Browning rose above that level; with him sensation is usually in the background; he is not particularly a poet of the senses or of ocular vision. His favourite subject-matter is rather the stream of thought and feeling in the mind; he is the poet of soliloquy. Nature and life as they really are, rather than as they may appear to the ignorant and passionate participant in them, lie beyond his range. Even in his best dramas, like A *Blot in the 'Scutcheon* or *Colombe's Birthday,* the interest remains in the experience of the several persons as they explain it to us. The same is the case in *The Ring and the Book,* the conception of which, in twelve monstrous soliloquies, is a striking evidence of the poet's predilection for this form.

The method is, to penetrate by sympathy rather than to portray by intelligence. The most authoritative insight is not the poet's or the spectator's, aroused and enlightened by the spectacle, but the various heroes' own, in their moment of intensest passion. We therefore miss the tragic relief and exaltation, and come away instead with the uncomfortable feeling that an obstinate folly is apparently the most glorious and choiceworthy thing in the world. This is evidently the poet's own illusion, and those who do not happen to share it must feel that if life were really as irrational as he thinks it, it would be not only profoundly discouraging, which it often is, but profoundly disgusting, which it surely is not; for at least it reveals the ideal which it fails to attain.

This ideal Browning never disentangles. For him the crude experience is the only end, the endless struggle the only ideal, and the perturbed *Soul* the only organon of truth. The arrest of his intelligence at this point, before it has envisaged any rational object, explains the arrest of his dramatic art at soliloquy. His immersion in the forms of self-consciousness prevents him from dramatizing the real relations of men and their thinkings to one another, to Nature, and to destiny. For in order to do so he would have had to view his characters from above (as Cervantes did, for instance), and to see them not merely as they appeared to themselves, but as they appear to reason. This higher attitude, however, was not only beyond Browning's scope, it was positively contrary to his inspiration. Had he reached it, he would no longer have seen the universe through the *Soul,* but through the intellect, and he would not have been able to cry, "How the world is made for each one of us!" On the contrary, the *Soul* would have figured only in its true conditions, in all its ignorance and dependence, and also in its essential teachableness, a point against which Browning's barbaric wilfulness particularly rebelled. Rooted in his persuasion that the soul is essentially omnipotent and that to live hard can never be to live wrong, he remained fascinated by the march and method of self-consciousness, and never allowed himself to be weaned from that romantic fatuity by the energy of rational imagination, which prompts us not to regard our ideas as mere filling of a dream, but rather to build on them the conception of permanent objects and overruling principles, such as Nature, society, and the other ideals of reason. A full-grown imagination deals with these things, which do not obey the laws of psychological progression, and cannot be described by the methods of soliloquy.

We thus see that Browning's sphere, though more subtle and complex than Whitman's, was still elementary. It lay far below the spheres of social and historical reality in which Shakespeare moved; far below the comprehensive and cosmic sphere of every great epic poet. Browning did not even reach the intellectual plane of such contemporary poets as Tennyson and Matthew Arnold, who, whatever may be thought of their powers, did not study consciousness for itself, but for the sake of its meaning and of the objects which it revealed. The best things that come into a man's consciousness are the things that take him out of it—the rational things that are independent of his personal perception and of his personal existence. These he approaches with his reason, and they, in the same measure, endow him with their immortality. But precisely these things—the objects of science and of the constructive imagination—Browning always saw askance, in the outskirts of his field of vision, for his eye was fixed and riveted on the soliloquizing Soul. And this Soul being, to his apprehension, irrational, did not give itself over to those permanent objects which might otherwise have occupied it, but ruminated on its own accidental emotions, on its love-affairs, and on its hopes of going on so ruminating for ever.

The pathology of the human mind—for the normal, too, is pathological when it is not referred to the ideal—the pathology of the human mind is a very interesting subject, demanding great gifts and great ingenuity in its treatment. Browning ministers to this interest, and possesses this ingenuity and these gifts. More than any other poet he keeps a kind of speculation alive in the now large body of sentimental, eager-minded people, who no longer can find in a definite religion a form and language for their imaginative life. That this service is greatly appreciated speaks well for the ineradicable tendency in man to study himself and his destiny. We do not deny the achievement when we point out its nature and limitations. It does not cease to be something because it is taken to be more than it is.

—George Santayana, "The Poetry of Barbarism: III.
Robert Browning," *Interpretations
of Poetry and Religion*, 1900, pp. 188–221

G.K. CHESTERTON (1903)

Gilbert Keith Chesterton was an English polymath of the early twentieth century, a journalist, political philosopher, and author of fantasy and detective stories, Christian apologetics, and poetry. In this extract, Chesterton suggests that there are two "great theories" in Browning's poetry, what he calls "the hope which lies in the imperfection of man" and "the hope that lies in the imperfection of God." What Chesterton means by the first of these is that human imperfection suggests the very thing the individual lacks in the same manner in which a one-legged man's appearance indicates he should have another leg: People are incomplete, but it is that very imperfection that suggests the possibility that someday they will become perfect. The second of Browning's ideas is more striking: If our burden is sorrow and self-sacrifice, then God must be inferior to humans if God lacks the capacity to experience these things. Since this cannot logically be the case, the crucifixion of Christ became inevitable, since God, in order to be God, had to sacrifice himself. On both human imperfection and what Chesterton has called "the imperfection of God," Browning rests his optimistic philosophy of hope. In contrast to George Santayana's critique of Browning's verse in the extract before this one, Chesterton has presented us with a poet who justifies existence by showing it to be incomplete.

Chesterton addresses Santayana's essay directly. He believes that Santayana, unlike other critics, has discovered the virtue in Browning's verse but, unfortunately, has conceived this virtue to be its vice. Chesterton argues that all poetry is "barbarian," using Santayana's description, and must be so since it speaks to the irrational emotions in humanity. Since all emotions are primitive and deep-seated feelings, they cannot be rational: Poetry, Chesterton argues, speaks to human desire, and Browning's poetry is full of the happy optimism that cannot be rationalized by philosophy. With the fine turns of phrase that so often characterize his prose, Chesterton states that Browning looked on every face in the street and saw in each something quite distinct from all the others. It was this distinctive and optimistic love of people as individuals, rather than humanity as an indistinct mass, that marked Browning's thought and verse. The remainder of Chesterton's essay examines particular works by the poet in his own insightful way. At the conclusion, we are presented with the idea that even in the most vulgar of Browning's characters we can witness what elsewhere has been called "the spark of soul" and what Chesterton calls "the voice of God, uttering His everlasting soliloquy." No matter how rough and brutal the individual in the poem, no matter how coarse his behavior or vulgar his language, Chesterton sees behind them Browning's belief in the potential for people to allow the divine to speak through them. It is this voice that the poet seeks to deliver in his verses.

Chesterton is a unique writer and critic, his ideas typically coming from an unexpected perspective, his arguments often proving the opposite of what is commonly accepted to be true. In conjunction with Santayana's extract immediately preceding this one, the reader will be able to contrast two distinctive approaches to the spiritual component in Browning's poetry. Both critics are dealing with the same fundamental presumptions and make the same steps in their general argument, but the conclusions are as far apart as any could be. What is seen to be a flaw by Santayana is embraced by Chesterton as the reason for what is best in Browning's work. Language, form, emotion, reason, hope, love, and each and every individual from the poet's perspective mean something different in each critic's essay. Such contrasts are a fitting conclusion to a volume in which readers will have found Browning's entire artistic career marked by such extremes of devotion and vehement criticism that few other English poets have experienced.

The great fault of most of the appreciation of Browning lies in the fact that it conceives the moral and artistic value of his work to lie in what is called "the message of Browning," or "the teaching of Browning," or, in other words, in the mere opinions of Browning. Now Browning had opinions, just as he had a dress-suit or a vote for Parliament. He did not hesitate to express these opinions any more than he would have hesitated to fire off a gun, or open an umbrella, if he had possessed those articles, and realised their value. For example, he had, as his students and eulogists have constantly stated, certain definite opinions about the spiritual function of love, or the intellectual basis of Christianity. Those opinions were very striking and very solid, as everything was which came out of Browning's mind. His two great theories of the universe may be expressed in two comparatively parallel phrases. The first was what may be called the hope which lies in the imperfection of man. The characteristic poem of "Old Pictures in Florence" expresses very quaintly and beautifully the idea that some hope may always be based on deficiency itself; in other words, that in so far as man is a one-legged or a one-eyed creature, there is something about his appearance which indicates that he should have another leg and another eye. The poem suggests admirably that such a sense of incompleteness may easily be a great advance upon a sense of completeness, that the part may easily and obviously be greater than the whole. And from this Browning draws, as he is fully justified in drawing, a definite hope for immortality and the larger scale of life. For nothing is more certain than that though this world is the only world that we have known, or of which we could even dream, the fact does remain that we have named it "a strange world." In other words, we have certainly felt that this world did not explain itself, that something in its complete and patent picture has been omitted. And Browning was right in saying that in a cosmos where incompleteness implies completeness, life implies immortality. This then was the first of the doctrines or opinions of Browning: the hope that lies in the imperfection of man. The second of the great Browning doctrines requires some audacity to express. It can only be properly stated as the hope that lies in the imperfection of God. That is to say, that Browning held that sorrow and self-denial, if they were the burdens of man, were also his privileges. He held that these stubborn sorrows and obscure valours might, to use a yet more strange expression, have provoked the envy of the Almighty. If man has self-sacrifice and God has none, then man has in the Universe a secret and blasphemous superiority. And this tremendous story of a Divine jealousy Browning reads into the story of the Crucifixion. If the Creator had not been crucified He would not have been as great as thousands of wretched fanatics among His own creatures. It is needless to insist upon this point; any one who wishes to read it splendidly expressed need only be referred to "Saul." But these are emphatically the two main doctrines or opinions of Browning which I have ventured to characterise roughly as the hope in the imperfection of man, and more boldly as the hope in the imperfection of God. They are great thoughts, thoughts written by a great man, and they raise noble and beautiful doubts on behalf of faith which the human spirit will never answer or exhaust. But about them in connection with Browning there nevertheless remains something to be added. Browning was, as most of his upholders and all his opponents say, an optimist. His theory, that man's sense of his own imperfection implies a design of perfection, is a very good argument for optimism. His theory that man's knowledge of and desire for self-sacrifice implies God's knowledge of and desire for self-sacrifice is another very good argument for optimism. But any one will make the deepest and blackest and most incurable mistake about Browning who imagines that his optimism was founded on any arguments for optimism. Because he had a strong intellect, because he had a strong power of conviction, he conceived and developed and asserted these doctrines of the incompleteness of Man and the sacrifice of Omnipotence. But these doctrines were the symptoms of his optimism, they were not its origin. It is surely obvious that no one can be argued into optimism since no one can be argued into happiness. Browning's optimism was not founded on opinions which were the work of Browning, but on life which was the work of God. One of Browning's most celebrated biographers has said that something of Browning's theology must be put down to his possession of a good digestion. The remark was, of course, like all remarks touching the tragic subject of digestion, intended to be funny and to convey some kind of doubt or diminution touching the value of Browning's faith. But if we examine the matter with somewhat greater care we shall see that it is indeed a thorough compliment to that faith. Nobody, strictly speaking, is happier on account of his digestion. He is happy because he is so constituted as to forget all about it. Nobody really is convulsed with delight at the thought of the ingenious machinery which he possesses inside him; the thing which delights him is simply the full possession of his own human body. I cannot in the least understand why a good digestion—that is, a good body—should not be held to be as mystic a benefit as a sunset or the first flower of spring. But there is about digestion this peculiarity throwing a great light on human pessimism, that it is one of the many things which we never speak of as existing until they go wrong. We should think it ridiculous to speak of a man as suffering from his boots if we meant that he had really no boots. But we do speak of a man suffering from digestion when we mean that he suffers from a lack of digestion. In the same way we speak of a man suffering from nerves when we mean that his nerves are more inefficient than any one else's nerves. If any one wishes to see how grossly language can degenerate, he need only compare the old optimistic use of the word nervous, which we employ in speaking of a nervous grip, with the new pessimistic use of the word, which we employ in speaking of a nervous manner. And as digestion is a good thing which sometimes goes wrong, as nerves are good things which sometimes go wrong, so existence itself in the eyes of Browning and all the great optimists is a good thing which sometimes goes wrong. He held himself as free to draw his inspiration from the gift of good health as from the gift of learning or the gift of fellowship. But he held that such gifts were in life innumerable and varied, and that every man, or at least almost every man, possessed some window looking out on this essential excellence of things.

Browning's optimism then, since we must continue to use this somewhat inadequate word, was a result of experience—experience which is for some mysterious reason generally understood in the sense of sad or disillusioning experience. An old gentleman rebuking a little boy for eating apples in a tree is in the common conception the type of experience. If he really wished to be a type of experience he would climb up the tree himself and proceed to experience the apples. Browning's faith was founded upon joyful experience, not in the sense that he selected his joyful experiences and ignored his painful ones, but in the sense that his joyful experiences selected themselves and stood out in his memory by virtue of their own extraordinary intensity of colour. He did not use experience in that mean and pompous sense in which it is used by the worldling advanced in years. He rather used it in that healthier and more joyful sense in which it is used at revivalist meetings. In the Salvation Army a man's experiences mean his experiences of the mercy of God, and to Browning the meaning was much the same. But the revivalists' confessions deal mostly with experiences of prayer and praise; Browning's dealt pre-eminently with what may be called his own subject, the experiences of love.

And this quality of Browning's optimism, the quality of detail, is also a very typical quality. Browning's optimism is of that ultimate and unshakeable order that is founded upon the absolute sight, and sound, and smell, and handling of things. If a man had gone up to Browning and asked him with all the solemnity of the eccentric, "Do you think life is worth living?" it is interesting to conjecture what his answer might have been. If he had been for the moment under the influence of the orthodox rationalistic deism of the theologian he would have said, "Existence is justified by its manifest design, its manifest adaptation of means to ends," or, in other words, "Existence is justified by its completeness." If, on the other hand, he had been influenced by his own serious intellectual theories he would have said, "Existence is justified by its air of growth and doubtfulness," or, in other words, "Existence is justified by its incompleteness." But if he had not been influenced in his answer either by the accepted opinions, or by his own opinions, but had simply answered the question "Is life worth living?" with the real, vital answer that awaited it in his own soul, he would have said as likely as not, "Crimson toadstools in Hampshire." Some plain, glowing picture of this sort left on his mind would be his real verdict on what the universe had meant to him. To his traditions hope was traced to order, to his speculations hope was traced to disorder. But to Browning himself hope was traced to something like red toadstools. His mysticism was not of that idle and wordy type which believes that a flower is symbolical of life; it was rather of that deep and eternal type which believes that life, a mere abstraction, is symbolical of a flower. With him the great concrete experiences which God made always come first; his own deductions and speculations about them always second. And in this point we find the real peculiar inspiration of his very original poems.

One of the very few critics who seem to have got near to the actual secret of Browning's optimism is Mr. Santayana in his most interesting book *Interpretations of Poetry and Religion*. He, in contradistinction to the vast mass of Browning's admirers, had discovered what was the real root virtue of Browning's poetry; and the curious thing is, that having discovered that root virtue, he thinks it is a vice. He describes the poetry of Browning most truly as the poetry of barbarism, by which he means the poetry which utters the primeval and indivisible emotions. "For the barbarian is the man who regards his passions as their own excuse for being, who does not domesticate them either by understanding their cause, or by conceiving their ideal goal." Whether this be or be not a good definition of the barbarian, it is an excellent and perfect definition of the poet. It might, perhaps, be suggested that barbarians, as a matter of fact, are generally highly traditional and respectable persons who would not put a feather wrong in their head-gear, and who generally have very few feelings and think very little about those they have. It is when we have grown to a greater and more civilised stature that we begin to realise and put to ourselves intellectually the great feelings that sleep in the depths of us. Thus it is that the literature of our day has steadily advanced towards a passionate simplicity, and we become more primeval as the world grows older, until Whitman writes huge and chaotic psalms to express the sensations of a schoolboy out fishing, and Maeterlinck embodies in symbolic dramas the feelings of a child in the dark.

Thus, Mr. Santayana is, perhaps, the most valuable of all the Browning critics. He has gone out of his way to endeavour to realise what it is that repels him in Browning, and he has discovered the fault which none of Browning's opponents have discovered. And in this he has discovered the merit which none of Browning's admirers have discovered. Whether the quality be a good or a bad quality, Mr. Santayana is perfectly right. The whole of Browning's poetry does rest upon primitive feeling; and the only comment to be added is that so does the whole of every one else's poetry. Poetry deals entirely with those great eternal and mainly forgotten wishes which are the ultimate despots of existence. Poetry presents things as they are to our emotions, not as they are to any theory, however plausible, or any argument, however conclusive. If love is in truth a glorious vision, poetry will say that it is a glorious vision, and no philosophers will persuade poetry to say that it is the exaggeration of the instinct of sex. If bereavement is a bitter and continually aching thing, poetry will say that it is so, and no philosophers will persuade poetry to say that it is an evolutionary stage of great biological value. And here comes in the whole value and object of poetry, that it is perpetually challenging all systems with the test of a terrible sincerity. The practical value of poetry is that it is realistic upon a point upon which nothing else can be realistic, the point of the actual desires of man. Ethics is the science of actions, but poetry is the science of motives. Some actions are ugly, and therefore some parts of ethics are ugly. But all motives are beautiful, or present themselves for the moment as beautiful, and therefore all poetry is beautiful. If poetry deals with the basest matter, with the shedding of blood for gold, it ought to suggest the gold as well as the blood. Only poetry can realise motives, because motives are all pictures of happiness. And the supreme and most practical value of poetry is this, that in poetry, as in music, a note is struck which expresses beyond the power of rational statement a condition of mind, and all actions arise from a condition of mind. Prose can only use a large and clumsy notation; it can only say that a man is miserable, or that a man is happy; it is forced to ignore that there are a million diverse kinds of misery and a million diverse kinds of happiness. Poetry alone, with the first throb of its metre, can tell us whether the depression is the kind of depression that drives a man to suicide, or the kind of depression that drives him to the Tivoli. Poetry can tell us whether the happiness is the happiness that sends a man to a restaurant, or the much richer and fuller happiness that sends him to church.

Now the supreme value of Browning as an optimist lies in this that we have been examining, that beyond all his conclusions, and deeper than all his arguments, he was passionately interested in and in love with existence. If the heavens had fallen, and all the waters of the earth run with blood, he would still have been interested in existence, if possible a little more so. He is a great poet of human joy for precisely the reason of which Mr. Santayana complains: that his happiness is primal, and beyond the reach of philosophy. He is something far more convincing, far more comforting, far more religiously significant than an optimist: he is a happy man.

This happiness he finds, as every man must find happiness, in his own way. He does not find the great part of his joy in those matters in which most poets find felicity. He finds much of it in those matters in which most poets find ugliness and vulgarity. He is to a considerable extent the poet of towns. "Do you care for nature much?" a friend of his asked him. "Yes, a great deal," he said, "but for human beings a great deal more." Nature, with its splendid and soothing sanity, has the power of convincing most poets of the essential worthiness of things. There are few poets who, if they escaped from the rowdiest waggonette of trippers, could not be quieted again and exalted by dropping into a small wayside field. The speciality of Browning is rather that he would have been quieted and exalted by the waggonette.

To Browning, probably the beginning and end of all optimism was to be found in the faces in the street. To him they were all the masks of a deity, the heads of a hundred-headed Indian god of nature. Each one of them looked towards some quarter of the heavens, not looked upon by any other eyes. Each one of them wore some expression, some blend of eternal joy and eternal sorrow, not to be found in any other countenance. The sense of the absolute sanctity of human difference was the deepest of all his senses. He was hungrily interested in all human things, but it would have been quite impossible to have said of him that he loved humanity. He did not love humanity but men. His sense of the difference between one man and another would have made the thought of melting them into a lump called humanity simply loathsome and prosaic. It would have been to him like playing four hundred beautiful airs at once. The mixture would not combine all, it would lose all. Browning believed that to every man that ever lived upon this earth had been given a definite and peculiar confidence of God. Each one of us was engaged on secret service; each one of us had a peculiar message; each one of us was the founder of a religion. Of that religion our thoughts, our faces, our bodies, our hats, our boots, our tastes, our virtues, and even our vices, were more or less fragmentary and inadequate expressions.

In the delightful memoirs of that very remarkable man Sir Charles Gavan Duffy, there is an extremely significant and interesting anecdote about Browning, the point of which appears to have attracted very little attention. Duffy was dining with Browning and John Forster, and happened to make some chance allusion to his own adherence to the Roman Catholic faith, when Forster remarked, half jestingly, that he did not suppose that Browning would like him any the better for that. Browning would seem to have opened his eyes with some astonishment. He immediately asked why Forster should suppose him hostile to the Roman Church. Forster and Duffy replied almost simultaneously, by referring to *Bishop Blougram's Apology,* which had just appeared, and asking whether the portrait of the sophistical and self-indulgent priest had not been intended for a satire on Cardinal Wiseman. "Certainly," replied Browning cheerfully, "I intended it for Cardinal Wiseman, but I don't consider it a satire, there is nothing hostile about it." This is the real truth which lies at the heart of what may be called the great sophistical monologues which Browning wrote in later years. They are not satires or attacks upon their subjects, they are not even harsh and unfeeling exposures of them. They are defences; they say or are intended to say the best that can be said for the persons with whom they deal. But very few people in this world would care to listen to the real defence of their own characters. The real defence, the defence which belongs to the Day of Judgment, would make such damaging admissions, would clear away so many artificial virtues, would tell such tragedies of weakness and failure, that a man would sooner be misunderstood and censured by the world than exposed to that awful and merciless eulogy. One of the most practically difficult matters which arise from the code of manners and the conventions of life, is that we cannot properly justify a human being, because that justification would involve the admission of things which may not conventionally be admitted. We might explain and make human and respectable, for example, the conduct of some old fighting politician, who, for the good of his party and his country, acceded to measures of which he disapproved; but we cannot, because we are not allowed to admit that he ever acceded to measures of which he disapproved. We might touch the life of many dissolute public men with pathos, and a kind of defeated courage, by telling the truth about the history of their sins. But we should throw the world into an uproar if we hinted that they had any. Thus the decencies of civilisation do not merely make it impossible to revile a man, they make it impossible to praise him.

Browning, in such poems as *Bishop Blougram's Apology,* breaks this first mask of goodness in order to break the second mask of evil, and gets to the real goodness at last; he dethrones a saint in order to humanise a scoundrel. This is one typical side of the real optimism of Browning. And there is indeed little danger that such optimism will become weak and sentimental and popular, the refuge of every idler, the excuse of every ne'er-do-weel. There is little danger that men will desire to excuse their souls before God by presenting themselves before men as such snobs as Bishop Blougram, or such dastards as Sludge the Medium. There is no pessimism, however stern, that is so stern as this optimism, it is as merciless as the mercy of God.

It is true that in this, as in almost everything else connected with Browning's character, the matter cannot be altogether exhausted by such a generalisation as the above. Browning's was a simple character, and therefore very difficult to understand, since it was impulsive, unconscious, and kept no reckoning of its moods. Probably in a great many cases, the original impulse which led Browning to plan a soliloquy was a kind of anger mixed with curiosity; possibly the first charcoal sketch of Blougram was a caricature of a priest. Browning, as we have said, had prejudices, and had a capacity for anger, and two of his angriest prejudices were against a certain kind of worldly clericalism, and against almost every kind of spiritualism. But as he worked upon the portraits at least, a new spirit began to possess him, and he enjoyed every spirited and just defence the men could make of themselves, like triumphant blows in a battle, and towards the end would come the full revelation, and Browning would stand up in the man's skin and testify to the man's ideals. However this may be, it is worth while to notice one very curious error that has arisen in connection with one of the most famous of these monologues.

When Robert Browning was engaged in that somewhat obscure quarrel with the spiritualist Home, it is generally and correctly stated that he gained a great number of the impressions which he afterwards embodied in *Mr. Sludge the Medium*. The statement so often made, particularly in the spiritualist accounts of the matter, that Browning himself is the original of the interlocutor and exposer of Sludge, is of course merely an example of that reckless reading from which no one has suffered more than Browning despite his students and societies. The man to whom Sludge addresses his confession is a Mr. Hiram H. Horsfall, an American, a patron of spiritualists, and, as it is more than once suggested, something of a fool. Nor is there the smallest reason to suppose that Sludge considered as an individual bears any particular resemblance to Home considered as an individual. But without doubt *Mr. Sludge the Medium* is a general statement of the view of spiritualism at which Browning had arrived from his acquaintance with Home and Home's circle. And about that view of spiritualism there is something rather peculiar to notice. The poem, appearing as it did at the time when the intellectual public had just become conscious of the existence of spiritualism, attracted a great deal of attention, and aroused a great deal of controversy. The spiritualists called down thunder upon the head of the poet, whom they depicted as a vulgar and ribald lampooner who had not only committed the profanity of sneering at the mysteries of a higher state of life, but the more unpardonable profanity of sneering at the convictions of his own wife. The sceptics, on the other hand, hailed the poem with delight as a blasting exposure of spiritualism, and congratulated the poet on making himself the champion of the sane and scientific view of magic. Which of these two parties was right about the question of attacking the reality of spiritualism it is neither easy nor necessary to discuss. For the simple truth, which neither of the two parties and none of the students of Browning seem to have noticed, is that *Mr. Sludge the Medium* is not an attack upon spiritualism. It would be a great deal nearer the truth, though not entirely the truth, to call it a justification of spiritualism. The whole essence of Browning's method is involved in this matter, and the whole essence of Browning's method is so vitally misunderstood that to say that *Mr. Sludge the Medium* is something like a defence of spiritualism will bear on the face of it the appearance of the most empty and perverse of paradoxes. But so, when we have comprehended Browning's spirit, the fact will be found to be. The general idea is that Browning must have intended *Sludge* for an attack on spiritual phenomena, because the medium in that poem is made a vulgar and contemptible mountebank, because his cheats are quite openly confessed, and he himself put into every ignominious situation, detected, exposed, throttled, horsewhipped, and forgiven. To regard this deduction as sound is to misunderstand Browning at the very start of every poem that he ever wrote. There is nothing that the man loved more, nothing that deserves more emphatically to be called a speciality of Browning, than the utterance of large and noble truths by the lips of mean and grotesque human beings. In his poetry praise and wisdom were perfected not only out of the mouths of babes and sucklings, but out of the mouths of swindlers and snobs. Now what, as a matter of fact, is the outline and development of the poem of *Sludge?* The climax of the poem, considered as a work of art, is so fine that it is quite extraordinary that any one should have missed the point of it, since it is the whole point of the monologue. Sludge the Medium has been caught out in a piece of unquestionable trickery, a piece of trickery for which there is no conceivable explanation or palliation which will leave his moral character intact. He is therefore seized with a sudden resolution, partly angry, partly frightened, and partly humorous, to become absolutely frank, and to tell the whole truth about himself for the first time not only to his dupe, but to himself. He excuses himself for the earlier stages of the trickster's life by a survey of the border-land between truth and fiction, not by any means a piece of sophistry or cynicism, but a perfectly fair statement of an ethical difficulty which does exist. There are some people who think that it must be immoral to admit that there are any doubtful cases of morality, as if a man should refrain from discussing the precise boundary at the upper end of the Isthmus of Panama, for fear the inquiry should shake his belief in the existence of North America. People of this kind quite consistently think Sludge to be merely a scoundrel talking nonsense. It may be remembered that they thought the same thing of Newman. It is actually supposed, apparently in the current use of words, that casuistry is the name of a crime; it does not appear to occur to people that casuistry is a science, and about as much a crime as botany. This tendency to casuistry in Browning's monologues has done much towards establishing for him that reputation for pure intellectualism which has done him so much harm. But casuistry in this sense is not a cold and analytical thing, but a very warm and sympathetic thing. To know what combinations of excuse might justify a man in manslaughter or bigamy, is not to have a callous indifference to virtue; it is rather to have so ardent an admiration for virtue as to seek it in the remotest desert and the darkest incognito.

This is emphatically the case with the question of truth and falsehood raised in *Sludge the Medium.* To say that it is sometimes difficult to tell at what point the romancer turns into the liar is not to state a cynicism, but a perfectly honest piece of human observation. To think that such a view involves the negation of honesty is like thinking that red is green, because the two fade into each other in the colours of the rainbow. It is really difficult to decide when we come to the extreme edge of veracity, when and when not it is permissible to create an illusion. A standing example, for instance, is the case of the fairy-tales. We think a father entirely pure and benevolent when he tells his children that a beanstalk grew up into heaven, and a pumpkin turned into a coach. We should consider that he lapsed from purity and benevolence if he told his children that in walking home that evening he had seen a beanstalk grow halfway up the church, or a pumpkin grow as large as a wheelbarrow. Again, few people would object to that general privilege whereby it is permitted to a person in narrating even a true anecdote to work up the climax by any exaggerative touches which really tend to bring it out. The reason of this is that the telling of the anecdote has become, like the telling of the fairy-tale, almost a distinct artistic creation; to offer to tell a story is in ordinary society like offering to recite or play the violin. No one denies that a fixed and genuine moral rule could be drawn up for these cases, but no one surely need be ashamed to admit that such a rule is not entirely easy to draw up. And when a man like Sludge traces much of his moral downfall to the indistinctness of the boundary and the possibility of beginning with a natural extravagance and ending with a gross abuse, it certainly is not possible to deny his right to be heard.

We must recur, however, to the question of the main development of the Sludge self-analysis. He begins, as we have said, by urging a general excuse by the fact that in the heat of social life, in the course of telling tales in the intoxicating presence of sympathisers and believers, he has slid into falsehood almost before he is aware of it. So far as this goes, there is truth in his plea. Sludge might indeed find himself unexpectedly justified if we had only an exact record of how true were the tales told about Conservatives in an exclusive circle of Radicals, or the stories told about Radicals in a circle of indignant Conservatives. But after this general excuse, Sludge goes on to a perfectly cheerful and unfeeling admission of fraud: this principal feeling towards his victims is by his own confession a certain unfathomable contempt for people who are so easily taken in. He professes to know how to lay the foundations for every species of personal acquaintanceship, and how to remedy the slight and trivial slips of making Plato write Greek in naughts and crosses.

> As I fear, sir, he sometimes used to do Before I found the useful book that knows.

It would be difficult to imagine any figure more indecently confessional, more entirely devoid of not only any of the restraints of conscience, but of any of the restraints even of a wholesome personal conceit, than Sludge the

Medium. He confesses not only fraud, but things which are to the natural man more difficult to confess even than fraud—effeminacy, futility, physical cowardice. And then, when the last of his loathsome secrets has been told, when he has nothing left either to gain or to conceal, then he rises up into a perfect bankrupt sublimity and makes the great avowal which is the whole pivot and meaning of the poem. He says in effect: "Now that my interest in deceit is utterly gone, now that I have admitted, to my own final infamy, the frauds that I have practised, now that I stand before you in a patent and open villainy which has something of the disinterestedness and independence of the innocent, now I tell you with the full and impartial authority of a lost soul that I believe that there is something in spiritualism. In the course of a thousand conspiracies, by the labour of a thousand lies, I have discovered that there is really something in this matter that neither I nor any other man understands. I am a thief, an adventurer, a deceiver of mankind, but I am not a disbeliever in spiritualism. I have seen too much for that." This is the confession of faith of Mr. Sludge the Medium. It would be difficult to imagine a confession of faith framed and presented in a more impressive manner. Sludge is a witness to his faith as the old martyrs were witnesses to their faith, but even more impressively. They testified to their religion even after they had lost their liberty, and their eyesight, and their right hands. Sludge testifies to his religion even after he has lost his dignity and his honour.

It may be repeated that it is truly extraordinary that any one should have failed to notice that this avowal on behalf of spiritualism is the pivot of the poem. The avowal itself is not only expressed clearly, but prepared and delivered with admirable rhetorical force:—

Now for it, then! Will you believe me, though?
You've heard what I confess. I don't unsay
A single word: I cheated when I could,
Rapped with my toe-joints, set sham hands at work,
Wrote down names weak in sympathetic ink.
Rubbed odic lights with ends of phosphor-match,
And all the rest; believe that: believe this,
By the same token, though it seem to set
The crooked straight again, unsay the said,
Stick up what I've knocked down; I can't help that,
It's truth! I somehow vomit truth to-day.
This trade of mine—I don't know, can't be sure
But there was something in it, tricks and all!

It is strange to call a poem with so clear and fine a climax an attack on spiritualism. To miss that climax is like missing the last sentence in a good anecdote, or putting the last act of *Othello* into the middle of the play. Either the whole poem of *Sludge the Medium* means nothing at all, and is only a lampoon upon a cad, of which the matter is almost as contemptible as the subject, or it means this—that some real experiences of the unseen lie even at the heart of hypocrisy, and that even the spiritualist is at root spiritual.

One curious theory which is common to most Browning critics is that Sludge must be intended for a pure and conscious impostor, because after his confession, and on the personal withdrawal of Mr. Horsfall, he bursts out into horrible curses against that gentleman and cynical boasts of his future triumphs in a similar line of business. Surely this is to have a very feeble notion either of nature or art. A man driven absolutely into a corner might humiliate himself, and gain a certain sensation almost of luxury in that humiliation, in pouring out all his imprisoned thoughts and obscure victories. For let it never be forgotten that a hypocrite is a very unhappy man; he is a man who has devoted himself to a most delicate and arduous intellectual art in which he may achieve masterpieces which he must keep secret, fight thrilling battles, and win hair's-breadth victories for which he cannot have a whisper of praise. A really accomplished impostor is the most wretched of geniuses; he is a Napoleon on a desert island. A man might surely, therefore, when he was certain that his credit was gone, take a certain pleasure in revealing the tricks of his unique trade, and gaining not indeed credit, but at least a kind of glory. And in the course of this self-revelation he would come at last upon that part of himself which exists in every man—that part which does believe in, and value, and worship something. This he would fling in his hearer's face with even greater pride, and take a delight in giving a kind of testimony to his religion which no man had ever given before—the testimony of a martyr who could not hope to be a saint. But surely all this sudden tempest of candour in the man would not mean that he would burst into tears and become an exemplary ratepayer, like a villain in the worst parts of Dickens. The moment the danger was withdrawn, the sense of having given himself away, of having betrayed the secret of his infamous freemasonry, would add an indescribable violence and foulness to his reaction of rage. A man in such a case would do exactly as Sludge does. He would declare his own shame, declare the truth of his creed, and then, when he realised what he had done, say something like this:—

R-r-r, you brute-beast and blackguard!
Cowardly scamp!
I only wish I dared burn down the house
And spoil your sniggering!

and so on, and so on.

He would react like this; it is one of the most artistic strokes in Browning. But it does not prove that he was a hypocrite about spiritualism, or that he was speaking more truthfully in the second outburst than in the first. Whence came this extraordinary theory that a man is always speaking most truly when he is speaking most coarsely? The truth about oneself is a very difficult thing to express, and coarse speaking will seldom do it.

When we have grasped this point about *Sludge the Medium,* we have grasped the key to the whole series of Browning's casuistical monologues— *Bishop Blougram's Apology, Prince Hohenstiel-Schwangau, Fra Lippo Lippi, Fifine at the Fair, Aristophanes' Apology,* and several of the monologues in *The Ring and the Book.* They are all, without exception, dominated by this one conception of a certain reality tangled almost inextricably with unrealities in a man's mind, and the peculiar fascination which resides in the thought that the greatest lies about a man, and the greatest truths about him, may be found side by side in the same eloquent and sustained utterance.

For Blougram, he believed, say, half he spoke.

Or, to put the matter in another way, the general idea of these poems is, that a man cannot help telling some truth even when he sets out to tell lies. If a man comes to tell us that he has discovered perpetual motion, or been swallowed by the sea-serpent, there will yet be some point in the story where he will tell us about himself almost all that we require to know.

If any one wishes to test the truth, or to see the best examples of this general idea in Browning's monologues, he may be recommended to notice one peculiarity of these poems which is rather striking. As a whole, these apologies are written in a particularly burly and even brutal English. Browning's love of what is called the ugly is nowhere else so fully and extravagantly indulged. This, like a great many other things for which Browning as an artist is blamed, is perfectly appropriate to the theme. A vain, ill-mannered, and untrustworthy egotist, defending his own sordid doings with his own cheap and weather-beaten philosophy, is very likely to express himself best in a language flexible and pungent, but indelicate and without dignity. But the peculiarity of these loose and almost slangy soliloquies is that every now and then in them there occur bursts of pure poetry which are like a burst of birds singing. Browning does not hesitate to put some of the most perfect lines that he or anyone else have ever written in the English language into the mouths of such slaves as Sludge and Guido Franceschini. Take, for the sake of example, *Bishop Blougram's Apology*. The poem is one of the most grotesque in the poet's works. It is intentionally redolent of the solemn materialism and patrician grossness of a grand dinner-party *a deux*. It has many touches of an almost wild bathos, such as the young man who bears the impossible name of Gigadibs. The Bishop, in pursuing his worldly argument for conformity, points out with truth that a condition of doubt is a condition that cuts both ways, and that if we cannot be sure of the religious theory of life, neither can we be sure of the material theory of life, and that in turn is capable of becoming an uncertainty continually shaken by a tormenting suggestion. We cannot establish ourselves on rationalism, and make it bear fruit to us. Faith itself is capable of becoming the darkest and most revolutionary of doubts. Then comes the passage:—

> Just when we are safest, there's a sunset-touch,
> A fancy from a flower-bell, some one's death,
> A chorus ending from Euripides,—
> And that's enough for fifty hopes and fears
> As old and new at once as Nature's self,
> To rap and knock and enter in our soul,
> Take hands and dance there, a fantastic ring,
> Round the ancient idol, on his base again,—
> The grand Perhaps!

Nobler diction and a nobler meaning could not have been put into the mouth of Pompilia, or Rabbi Ben Ezra. It is in reality put into the mouth of a vulgar, fashionable priest, justifying his own cowardice over the comfortable wine and the cigars. Along with this tendency to poetry among Browning's knaves, must be reckoned another characteristic, their uniform tendency to theism. These loose and mean characters speak of many things feverishly and vaguely; of one thing they always speak with confidence and composure, their relation to God. It may seem strange at first sight that those who have outlived the indulgence, and not only of every law, but of every reasonable anarchy, should still rely so simply upon the indulgence of divine perfection. Thus Sludge is certain that his life of lies and conjuring tricks has been conducted in a deep and subtle obedience to the message really conveyed by the conditions created by God. Thus Bishop Blougram is certain that his life of panic-stricken and tottering compromise has been really justified as the only method that could unite him with God. Thus Prince Hohenstiel-Schwangau is certain that every dodge in his thin string of political dodges has been the true means of realising what he believes to be the will of God. Every one of these meagre swindlers, while admitting a failure in all things relative, claims an awful alliance with the Absolute. To many it will at first sight appear a dangerous doctrine indeed. But, in truth, it is a most solid and noble and salutary doctrine, far less dangerous than its opposite. Every one on this earth should believe, amid whatever madness or moral failure, that his life and temperament have some object on the earth. Every one on the earth should believe that he has something to give to the world which cannot otherwise be given. Every one should, for the good of men and the saving of his own soul, believe that it is possible, even if we are the enemies of the human race, to be the friends of God. The evil wrought by this mystical pride, great as it often is, is like a straw to the evil wrought by a materialistic self-abandonment. The crimes of the devil who thinks himself of immeasurable value are as nothing to the crimes of the devil who thinks himself of no value. With Browning's knaves we have always this eternal interest, that they are real somewhere, and may at any moment begin to speak poetry. We are talking to a peevish and garrulous sneak; we are watching the play of his paltry features, his evasive eyes, and babbling lips. And suddenly the face begins to change and harden, the eyes glare like the eyes of a mask, the whole face of clay becomes a common mouthpiece, and the voice that comes forth is the voice of God, uttering His everlasting soliloquy.

—G.K. Chesterton, *Robert Browning,*
1903, pp. 177–202

Chronology

1812	Robert Browning born May 7 in Camberwell, near London, to Robert Browning and Sarah Anna Wiedemann Browning.
1820–26	Educated at a boarding school near his home.
1826	Reads Shelley's poetry avidly.
1828	Studies at the new University of London but leaves the school after a short time there.
1833	Anonymous publication of his Shelleyan poem *Pauline*.
1834	Travels to Russia.
1835	*Paracelsus* is published.
1837	His play, *Strafford*, is produced.
1838	First trip to Italy.
1840	*Sordello* is published to poor critical reception.
1841	*Pippa Passes* is published.
1842	*Dramatic Lyrics* is published.
1844	Second trip to Italy.
1845	*Dramatic Romances and Lyrics* is published.
1845–46	Romance and elopement with the well-known poet Elizabeth Barrett.
1847	After living in various Italian locations, the Brownings settle permanently at Casa Guidi in Florence.
1849	First collected edition of Browning's work is published. Birth of a son and the death of Browning's mother.
1855	Browning's first masterpiece, *Men and Women*, is published.
1861	Death of Elizabeth Barrett Browning on June 29.
1862	Returns to live in London.
1864	Publishes *Dramatic Personae*, his second masterwork, to considerable acclaim.

1866   Death of Browning's father.

1868–69   Publication of *The Ring and the Book*, his third great achievement.

1879   *Dramatic Idyls* is published.

1881   Founding of the Browning Society in London.

1888–89   Publication of the sixteen-volume *Poetical Works*.

1889   On December 12, *Asolando* is published in London; that evening the poet dies at his son's house in Venice. He is buried on December 31 in Westminster Abbey.

Index